DOC

A MEMOIR

DOC

A MEMOIR

Dwight Gooden
and Ellis Henican

New Harvest
Houghton Mifflin Harcourt
BOSTON • NEW YORK
2013

This edition published by special arrangement with Amazon Publishing

For information about permission to reproduce selections from this book,
write to Permissions, Houghton Mifflin Harcourt Publishing Company,
215 Park Avenue South, New York, New York 10003.

www.hmhbooks.com

Library of Congress Cataloging-in-Publication Data is available.
ISBN 978-0-544-02702-2

Printed in the United States of America
DOC 10 9 8 7 6 5 4 3 2 1

"Never Would Have Made It"
Writer Credits: Marvin L. Sapp/Matthew Richard Brownie
Copyright: © 2010 Songs Of Universal, Inc. (BMI)/Marvin L. Sapp Music (BMI).
All rights for the world on behalf of Marvin L. Sapp Music administered by Songs Of
Universal, Inc./Unknown Publisher. All rights reserved. Used by permission.

Contents

Parade Rest

GROWN MEN AND WOMEN were clapping and waving. Little children were yelling themselves hoarse. Secretaries leaned out of upper-floor windows, tossing shredded computer paper to the street. A throbbing mob of blue and orange, people as far you could see, jammed together on the sidewalks, shouting out our names.

"Mookie, Mookie, Mookie!"

"Ray, Ray, Ray!"

Three men in shirts and loosened ties were dancing on a narrow ledge six stories up, doing a high kick they must have stolen from the Radio City Rockettes. One false step — they'd never kick again.

They didn't look too worried though. They were too stoked to care.

Big-bellied construction workers hugged total strangers, as rolls of toilet paper flew through the air. Wall Street office drones wept tears of joy. If I had to take a guess, I'd say zero New York children made it into school that day. Even some Yankees fans couldn't help but cheer. Anyone who beat the Red Sox was okay with them.

For only the second time in history, and for the first time in seventeen years, the New York Mets had won the World Series. We'd finished off the hated team from Boston, and now the official victory parade was rolling up Broadway. The crowds were so huge and so pumped, the wooden police barricades were no more than a suggestion. Every time an open convertible passed, another wave of fans would burst forward. Then the cops would run into the street and shoo them back.

So this is what two million people looks like?

The Canyon of Heroes, this stretch of Lower Manhattan is called, for all the great achievers who have been celebrated here. Not just sports champions, but people who really changed the world: Charles Lindbergh, Douglas MacArthur, Albert Einstein, the Apollo 11 astronauts, the American hostages released from Iran — all of them have taken that slow ride up Broadway to City Hall. And now it was our turn, this bad-boy mob of talent and heart, some of the greatest guys you could ever play ball with, as loud and rambunctious as the city we'd just won it all for.

Davey in the lead car followed by two sanitation trucks with snowplows, sent to clear the knee-deep confetti.

Keith and Gary, Howard and Jesse, pumping their firsts in the air. Lenny, Wally, and Tim, looking thrilled in their open cars. Darryl waving from a bright-red Cadillac. Ray Knight, the series MVP, was positively beaming. Pitcher Ron Darling's smile was so bright, he could have subbed for the lights at Shea Stadium.

Every time a politician tried to speak — Ed Koch or Alfonse D'Amato or Mario Cuomo — boos swelled up from the crowd. No one had come to hear *them*. The fans were there to cheer their champions — and themselves. "Thank you all for making a dream come true," our catcher Gary Carter said, and the people roared.

Of course they did. It was their dream too.

"This is so much fun," our manager, Davey Johnson, told the people on the sidewalk and the many, many others watching on TV. "I think we ought to try to do it again next year."

Mookie Wilson, our switch-hitting center fielder, was thinking even bigger. "Nineteen eighty-six," he thundered, "the year of the Mets. Nineteen eighty-seven, year of the Mets. Nineteen eighty-eight, year of the Mets." Our victory was barely twelve hours old, and Mookie was already talking dynasty.

It was a glorious celebration. And right at the front of the crowd, a small boy was standing with a hand-lettered sign.

WE LOVE YOU, DOC, it said.

Too bad I couldn't thank him or even wave.

I really wish I could have. But as everyone gathered in Lower Manhattan, I was twenty-five miles away.

As my teammates rode through the Canyon of Heroes, I was alone in my bed in Roslyn, Long Island, with the curtains closed and the TV on, missing what should have been the greatest morning of my life.

I'd spent all night in a sketchy housing project apartment near the Roosevelt Field mall, getting wasted with a bunch of people I hardly even knew. I was drinking shots of vodka. I was snorting lines of cocaine. And more lines of cocaine — and more lines of cocaine. I didn't leave the drug party until after the sun came up. As my teammates toasted our triumph, I was nursing a head-splitting coke-and-booze hangover, too spent, too paranoid, and too mad at myself to drag my sorry butt to my own victory parade.

I had never felt so lonely before.

I hope I never feel that way again.

You'd have to look hard to find another young athlete in any sport who had risen so high so quickly and then fallen so hard. Too much, too fast, too young, my life was spinning wildly, and I was the one who didn't have a clue.

I'd been the National League Rookie of the Year. I was the youngest player ever to appear in an All-Star Game, and when I stepped on the mound — one, two, three — I retired the side. Three days before my twenty-first birthday, I won the Cy Young Award as the league's best pitcher. That year, I also won the pitching Triple Crown, leading in wins, strikeouts, and earned runs. No pitcher had done that in thirteen years, and it would take another dozen before anyone did it again. For most of that breathless run, there was truly no stopping me. *Sports Illustrated* called me "Dwight the Great." I was featured on the cover of *Time.* Nike hung a 105-foot mural of me on Manhattan's West Forty-Second Street. I was facing west, coming out of my wind-up, looking like I just might hurl that ball across the Hudson River to New Jersey and beyond.

Heads up, LA!

And why not? With all that I'd accomplished as the Mets' young pitching ace, who could rule anything out?

New York's combative sportswriters could hardly agree on anything, but all of them seemed to agree on this: in a very short time at a very early age, I had become one of the most dominant pitchers in baseball, well on my way to greatest-ever territory. The Hall of Fame talk had already started. And now, to cap it all off, my team had just won the World Series in a come-from-behind seventh-game victory in front of the home crowd at Shea Stadium.

If I had died that minute, I would have died a happy man. In hindsight, that might have saved a lot of people a lot of grief — me at the top of the list.

I was still only twenty-one.

After Jesse Orosco threw his final game seven strikeout and the Red Sox were put away at last, I ran out of the bullpen, where I'd been warming up for a late-game relief call, and out to the pitcher's mound, dry-diving onto a twisted pile of my teammates. In an instant, it seemed like the whole team was there. Hugging, slapping each other's backs, rolling around together in the infield dirt. Fans were bursting past police officers in riot gear, including some cops on horseback, and jumping onto our pile. As quickly as possible, team security hustled the players off the field and into the safety of the locker room.

The party revved up fast. Champagne corks were flying as the TV crews grabbed their postgame sound bites. The players were shouting each other's names. People started pouring champagne over other people's heads. All of us agreed how great we were.

But in the early craziness of the locker room, two thoughts were crowding all the others out of my head: *I gotta call my dealer. And I gotta call my dad.*

My father was watching at home with my mom in Tampa. I called him from the clubhouse phone, getting it out of the way as soon as I'd had my second gulp of champagne. I always called my dad after a game. He deserved this victory as much as I did. "Yeah, it feels great, Dad — thanks," I told him before hanging up the phone. "I love you."

I traded a few more handshakes and hugs.

By then, the beer and the hard booze were coming out — the vodka and the Rémy Martin. That stuff was always kept out of view of the reporters, tucked away in the back of the players' lockers or in the equipment room. But it magically appeared that night. After what we'd just accomplished, who was going to complain? I had a couple of rounds, Absolut and grapefruit.

Then I grabbed my chance.

I didn't think anyone would notice in the excitement of the moment, and no one did. I slipped into the trainer's office, where I knew I could make my other call without being disturbed. I had the number memorized. I tried to appear casual, like maybe I was ordering a pizza.

"Hey, I'll be coming by later tonight," I said to my dealer.

"Congratulations, man!" he said.

"Yeah, thanks," I said. "Just make sure you're available, okay? It's gonna be a big party."

"I got whatever you need," he told me.

The drinks were still flowing. People were still hugging and calling each other's names. Guys who'd had little squabbles during the season were making up, shaking champagne bottles, and spraying each other.

I bumped into Bob Ojeda, who was shouting, "I love you, man!" I told Ron Darling how awesome he'd pitched in the series. Lenny Dykstra, as bouncy and wide-eyed as ever, looked as though he could hardly believe he was there — or that he'd whacked that clutch game three home run.

"The parade's gonna be awesome," Lenny said to me.

"Awesome," I agreed.

We had to get up early the next morning. I knew that. We were due at the stadium in Queens between eight and nine. Then we'd all pile onto buses and ride into Manhattan for the start of the parade. But no one looked ready to call it a night. I certainly wasn't. Word went around that the party was moving to Finn MacCool's, a bar on Main Street in Port Washington, close to where many of the players lived.

I was already too drunk to be driving. I'd had three or four glasses of champagne and at least as many vodka-and-grapefruits. But I didn't give drunk driving a second thought. Back then, I never did. I walked out to the players' parking lot and climbed into my car, a gray 1986 Mercedes 300SE. I turned on the ignition and, bleary but still fairly steady, I headed in the general direction of the bar.

But I never got there.

Instead, I jumped off the Long Island Expressway at the Meadowbrook Parkway and headed south, straight for the projects.

My whole plan was to meet my dealer, buy some coke, and do a little bit — then depending on how I was feeling and how late it was, maybe circle back to Finn MacCool's and have a few last rounds with the boys.

On my way to the dealer's apartment, I stopped and picked up my friend Bobby, who lived in the same projects. Bobby wasn't a close friend, just someone I'd partied with in Tampa who lived part-time in New York. He had introduced me to the dealer a few months earlier. When I first started buying, I would give the money to Bobby, and he'd make the transaction for me. But as I'd grown bolder, I was usually buying for myself.

We stopped at the dealer's apartment. I gave him the money for the drugs. Then Bobby and I headed back to his place to get high. The dealer followed us there.

Bobby's apartment was on the second floor. It was tiny, and people were already there. Bobby's sister was one of them, and there were others I didn't recognize, five or six women and seven or eight men. The music was loud — Run-DMC, Whodini, Public Enemy, old-school hip-hop. The TV was on, playing game highlights with the sound off. It was the last week in October. Even though the windows were open, it was hot and stuffy in there.

Everyone congratulated me.

"Oh, man," one guy said, hugging me so hard I could feel the heavy gold chain around his neck.

"Oh, man," I said back to him.

"You're a world champion," said a woman in a shiny gold top.

Right away, the drugs came out.

I laid two lines on a mirror Bobby handed me. I slid a rolled-up dollar bill into my nose and sniffed hard. Ah, that felt good.

I did it again on the other side.

A nice, warm feeling was already sweeping through me. This, I thought, is what I had been waiting for.

The first time I remember checking the clock, it said twelve thirty. Then, what seemed like twenty minutes later, it said a little after two o'clock.

I could hear fans partying in other apartments. People were yelling outside and lighting off fireworks. If they'd only known where one of the Mets was! It was crazy, even being there. Somewhere in my mind, I must have realized that. There was no security. At any moment, the cops could have burst in, and I would have been busted. Or someone could have robbed me. My $50,000 Mercedes was sitting outside.

But I didn't care. This was where the coke was, so this was where I wanted to be.

That's pretty much how the evening went.

Do a shot.

Do a line.

Talk nonsense.

Look at the clock.

Notice how late it was.

See the coke.

Do another line.

Forget about the clock.

Hear how great I am.

Do a shot.

Watch some highlights.

Bullshit with strangers.

Look at the clock.

Do another line.

And that clock was moving like you wouldn't believe. I knew I had to get up early, but I had a plan.

"I'm gonna stay here till four o'clock," I said to myself. "That'll give me time to go home, get an hour or two of sleep, grab a shower, and be at Shea in time."

The next thing I noticed, the clock said four thirty. "A couple of more lines, and I'm out of here at five," I told myself. "No matter what."

But the drugs kept coming. The shots too. People kept laughing. I was having too much fun to leave.

A girl came over and climbed onto my lap. She was pushing her breasts against me and wiggling around. We were doing everything but having sex. I'm sure if I wanted to, I could have taken her into the bedroom. But sex wasn't my top priority at that moment. I was far more interested in the drugs.

"Okay, I'll stay another thirty minutes," I thought, still managing to bargain the worry away. "Then I'll get out of here."

I looked out the window at one point and felt my first wave of fear. The purple-black sky was turning ever so slightly gray. Dawn was coming soon.

"I gotta get out of here pretty soon," I decided.

But I was still bargaining. Drug addicts are always bargaining with themselves.

Deciding to stay another fifteen minutes seemed totally logical to me. And then another. I was dripping with sweat. My eyes were totally bloodshot. My clothes stank. But I kept recalculating. I could still rush home, take a shower, get to the stadium, and make the parade. I was resigned to the fact that I wouldn't get any sleep. But I'd gone without sleep before. How often would my team win the World Series?

The coke was keeping me up. The booze had been keeping me mellow, though not so much anymore. Both of them had clearly wrecked my judgment.

The sun through the window slammed me hard.

"Uh-oh," I finally realized. "That's not good."

It was after six thirty by then.

Everybody was talking. But suddenly, the voices all sounded like noise. I didn't want to talk to anybody anymore, and I didn't want anybody talking to me.

The TV was shifting to the morning shows. The game highlights were still on the screen. I was on the couch where I'd been laughing and talking for hours. Now I was staring straight ahead. This wasn't fun anymore.

"I'm in no condition to drive," I thought. "Maybe if I do a line, it'll pick me up and I can get out of here."

I did another line, and things got worse.

"This is stupid," I said to myself. "You shouldn't even be here."

One guy looked at me and smiled. "You're a real dude," he said. A real dude? I was a real mess. That's all.

When I first walked in with Bobby, everyone was saying, "There's a hero." What were they thinking now? It was more like, "Look at that fuckin' guy."

As sunshine filled the small apartment, my high was evaporating fast. You can't say I was sober. After all I'd put into my body, that made no sense at all. I was just feeling numb and disgusted.

I still had some coke left. But without saying good-bye to anyone, I put the drugs in my pocket and quietly skulked out of there. I was praying no one would see me in the project parking lot.

I looked like crap. I smelled like crap. I can't vouch for my driving. As I drove toward home with the sun streaming in the passenger window, I was still sweating out of control.

And then I totally lost it.

I started crying, sobbing loudly, literally blubbering in the car.

This was pathetic.

I couldn't go to the parade this way. I knew that. But how could I not go? Everyone would know what I'd been doing all night. Or at least they would suspect.

My mind was racing nowhere. Everything was pouring down at once.

I walked into my empty apartment and started taking off my clothes. I was thinking I could get a quick shower and maybe still make the parade.

I had messages on my answering machine. The first three were from the Mets' PR man, Jay Horwitz.

"Hey, Doc, just calling to make sure you're up for the parade."

"Doc, you up?"

"Doc, let me know if you need a ride. No problem. We can send a car."

Just then, I heard a knock on the door. A loud bang, really. I didn't look outside, but I was pretty sure it was Darryl Strawberry. Darryl lived in the next complex over. A lot of times, we'd ride to the park together. Either he would drive or I would drive. I couldn't remember what plans we'd made the night before.

But I didn't answer. I was too dejected and too scared. After a few more bangs, the knocking stopped.

I finally got the courage to get into the shower. When I came out, I looked in the mirror and hated what I saw. I looked horrible.

In my insanity, I thought if I did one more line, maybe I would get the boost I needed. So I did another line.

The phone kept ringing. I heard my mother's voice on the machine. "Honey, are you on your way to the parade?" The Mets must have called her in Florida. My girlfriend, Carlene, called too. And Jay called again. "Hey, Doc. We're worried. Wherever you are, we'll send a car."

I started putting my clothes on. I wasn't sure what I should do. But who was I kidding? I was in no condition to go anywhere, much less to ride in front of two million people at the victory parade.

"Oh my God," I thought. "What am I going to do?"

If I did one more line, I thought, maybe my heart would explode and I would die. Or maybe I could buy an airplane ticket and go somewhere far and hide. I could stay away long enough that people would forget I wasn't there.

No answer seemed any good. What could I say when people started asking? Major League Baseball had called me in during the season. There were already rumors about me and drugs. This would prove everything. Who would believe me now?

I took off the clothes I'd just put on. I pulled on some shorts and a T-shirt. I climbed into bed and turned on the news, thinking, "I'd better watch this. I know they're gonna say something about me."

But as soon as my head hit the pillow, it seemed like the live parade coverage began. It couldn't have started that quickly, but that's how it seemed to me.

I stared at the TV through narrow, squinting eyes. And that's how I watched my own victory parade.

I saw Mookie and Darryl, Keith and Ray, and all the Mets I had played with.

I heard Davey talk and politicians get booed. I saw a kid with a hand-lettered sign.

PART I

Dreaming

1

Whose Dream

FROM FATHER TO SON AND father to son, that's how base-ball dreams have always been handed down. In one of my very earliest memories — maybe I am four years old — my mom is out in the kitchen of our little house in Tampa. My much-older sisters, Mercedes and Betty, are off somewhere. My dad is sitting in the den in his special chair, a huge black La-Z-Boy recliner, like he's commanding the whole room. The Cincinnati Reds are on the new color television, and my father has a beige wire poking out of his ear. He's following a second game on his transistor radio — the Atlanta Braves or the Chicago Cubs or the St. Louis Cardinals. Really, it could be anyone. He isn't yelling at the TV the way some sports fans like to. He is reaching into a bag of Doritos, sipping from a can of Budweiser with salt around the rim — I still don't know where that came from — and coolly analyzing everything that's happening on the field.

"I like that rookie catcher," my dad is saying. "Good field vision."

I'm on the floor, cross-legged with cookies and a plastic bottle of juice. There is no one in the den but Dad and me. So he's delivering his running commentary to a four-year-old who clearly has no idea what field vision is. But kids that age have minds like sponges. And somehow I am able to grasp that Johnny Bench, the Reds' cocky new catcher, is out on the mound with veteran pitcher Jim Maloney, and the two men are arguing about what Maloney ought to throw next.

"They clocked his fastball at ninety-nine miles an hour," my dad marvels. "What do you think he'll throw now?"

On the TV, I can see the catcher shaking his head like he isn't too happy. Then I stare blankly up at my dad.

"That's right," my father says. "Another fastball."

And that's exactly what Maloney throws — smack into Bench's waiting glove.

Thump!

"Told you," my dad says with a sharp nod and the tiniest hint of a smile.

When it came to the skills and strategies of baseball, Dan Gooden was seldom wrong.

Long before baseball became my dream, it was the dream of my father. He got it from the same place I did — from his dad. The Gooden baseball dream wasn't hatched on the thriving Gulf Coast of Florida. It was born three hundred miles away in the fading cotton fields of southwest Georgia, where my father's family had lived for generations. That part of the South was known as the Black Belt. It got its name from the rich, dark soil that spread out for miles from there — not the thousands of men and women, slave and free, who had tilled that land. When the slaves won their freedom after the Civil War, some of them set off for Chicago or Detroit or other points north. But many stuck around, living in the same wooden shacks and working the same plots of land they always had. Only now, many were sharecroppers or hourly employees.

Segregated southwest Georgia wasn't a place of much opportunity. But it was the only home they had ever known. They worked hard to provide for their families and found what enjoyment they could.

"Your grandfather wasn't just a good baseball pitcher," my father told me one Saturday morning as we sat in the den. "He might have been the best ever."

Dad wasn't joking.

My father's father was born just after the turn of the century. His name was Uclesee Gooden. I never met him. He died when my dad was eight. From what people said, he was six-foot-four or -five, nearly a giant for his day, with tree-trunk legs and gangly arms. He played for the Albany Red Sox, a local Negro sandlot team.

"He used to carry me in his arms to the park where he played," my father recalled. "People came from miles. His fastball was smokin'. He was the most powerful pitcher anyone had ever seen."

Years later, when I would meet my father's older relatives, they would look at me and say, "You're good, but you should have seen your grandfather pitch."

I wish I'd had the chance.

When Dad came along in 1927, it was only natural that he would find his way onto a baseball field. He wasn't the physical specimen that his father was. But he was lean and quick, and he was constantly practicing. My dad dropped out of school in the third grade and went to work in the fields and processing plants, as many of his relatives did. But Saturday and Sunday afternoons, he was always playing baseball, doggedly developing his own talent at his father's beloved game.

There was no organized Little League for colored boys in rural Georgia. Dad went from pitch-and-catch in the yard to pickup games in Albany and nearby Americus, showing raw, early promise. "I played all the positions at the beginning, but first base was the one I took to," he told me. "I hit right-handed, and you had to be quick to play first base."

As he grew older, the pickup games gave way to a traveling team that played around the area and sometimes out of town, the entry level of what today we might call semipro ball. And my dad began to wonder: would his bat and glove be his ticket out of Georgia? For a poor kid like my father, becoming a professional baseball player was a bold dream. But it wasn't a crazy one. There were the Negro Leagues, where competition was famously fierce. And in 1947, when my dad was nineteen, he got some even bigger inspiration. Jackie Robinson, who was born to a family of sharecroppers in Cairo, Georgia, debuted with the Brooklyn Dodgers at Ebbets Field, breaking the modern color barrier in major-league baseball. Jackie helped to usher in the whole civil rights era — and not just in sports. But he was playing in New York City — not Albany, Georgia. When Jackie was one, the Robinsons had moved to Pasadena, California. Progress was still a little slower in the South.

Dad was a good baseball player for country Georgia. But he never got the chance to measure how good. Did race sidetrack my father's baseball dream? Or did he just not quite have the ability? The truth is, he never knew. And that question hung over his life — and hung over our family — always.

Dad eventually got a job at the local Cargill plant, working as a belt operator on the production line. And though he still enjoyed playing, he began devoting more and more of his baseball time to coaching local teams. Pretty soon, he had three sons — James, Charles, and Danny. He moved to Chicago long enough to become a huge Cubs and Ernie Banks fan. Then he returned to Georgia, where he met a young woman from nearby Cordele, "the watermelon capital of the world," named Ella Mae Jones.

She was tall and sturdy. She had a sister and three brothers, including one, Willie Lee, who went by the name Red Boy and had some baseball talent. By the time my dad showed up, my mom was married with a baby daughter, Mercedes, called Merc by almost everyone. Mom and Dad fell in love. My mom divorced her first husband and married my father. Then, my sister Betty came along.

Ella Mae Gooden had an air of calm self-confidence and a clear sense of right and wrong. She went to church on Sundays and kept a tidy home. She was definitely more talkative than my dad, and she wasn't quick to get angry. But when she had cause to — Lord, you'd better watch out! She was known for keeping a .38 Special in her purse. Buried beneath a sweet and loving exterior was a woman who feared no one.

In 1956, when Cargill offered my dad a transfer to Tampa, my mom wasn't too excited about moving. But she had some family in the area, and my dad would be getting a nice raise. And for him, the move had another attraction: baseball was everywhere in Florida. The Cincinnati Reds had a spring training facility in Tampa, Al Lopez Field, and an A-ball team too. The New York Mets trained in nearby St. Petersburg. The Detroit Tigers were in Lakeland. There were AAA and AA and A teams wherever you looked. Imagine the coaching he could do there. To him, the idea of leaving sleepy Georgia for the sunny Gulf Coast sounded ideal for him and his family.

They moved into a Tampa neighborhood called Belmont Heights, not a fancy section but solidly working-class. My mom got a job at a nursing home and, later, a night job at a pool hall. Most of the neighbors were like the Goodens, hard-working, growing black families with at least a couple of kids. Fifteen years after Mercedes was born, thirteen years after Betty, my parents got a little surprise.

Me.

I was born on November 16, 1964, a Monday, not quite a year after President John Kennedy was assassinated and less than two weeks after Lyndon Johnson was elected to a full term. With the big age difference between me and my sisters, I was the younger brother who almost seemed like an only child.

"I thought I was finished having babies, then up popped Poodney!" my mother liked to say, using the nickname I got long before "Doc" or "Dr. K." Thank God baseball fans never picked up on that one.

My mom loved having a son, but my dad was like a shipwrecked sailor who'd finally been rescued. He wasn't the only male in a house full of women anymore. From the minute I was big enough to hold a baseball, he was rolling one to me.

As my mother often said to me: "Once you came along, it was always him and you, him and you. And all we'd ever hear from the two of you was baseball, baseball, baseball." I was still an "arm baby," she said, when my dad started carrying me to the ballpark, like his own father had carried him. Soon enough, my father was letting me put my tiny fingers inside his giant glove.

If Dan Gooden had been a power forward instead of a power-hitting first baseman, I'm sure I would have spent my childhood dribbling a basketball right beside him. I never would have made it to the NBA. Physically, I wasn't built for that. But I learned very young that baseball was the route to my father's attention and his heart.

When I was three or four, we were tossing balls in the yard. When I was five or six, I was hanging out at the ballpark on Sunday afternoons with his semipro Tampa Dodgers. When the action on the field slowed down, some of the team members would play catch with me. Dad got a kick out of that and started working closely with me.

We quickly got in a pattern. On weekdays, he would come home from work, have something to eat, and say to me, "You ready to go?"

"Where are you guys going?" my mother would ask.

"To Robles Park to practice," he'd say.

At the beginning, especially when it wasn't baseball season, my mom thought all this baseball practicing might be a bit much. She told my father, "Let the boy be a kid."

She had a right to be concerned, but I didn't feel like Dad was pressuring me. He always asked, "Do you want to go to the park?" And I almost always did. Maybe once or twice I told him I wanted to ride bikes with my friends, and he acted like that was okay. But practicing usually seemed like more fun. Spending time with my father. Learning the game he loved. I didn't even mind doing the drills he started dreaming up for me. And when we were finished for the day, my dad would ask me, "Tomorrow, you want to come back here and work out some more?" I almost always answered, "Yeah."

Eventually, my mother came around. One day, I told her directly. "This is what I want to do. This is what I'm going to be. You'll see, I'll be playing on TV. And when I get big and famous, I'll buy you a house."

By that point, there was no stopping me. I was happy practicing on my own. On weekends and in summers, I was the neighborhood alarm clock. I'd be out in the driveway early, throwing a ball against the garage or swinging a bat at a crumpled aluminum can. I didn't have to chase the can like I would a ball. I'm sure I drove the neighbors crazy.

Pretty soon, I was starting to show some actual talent on the field. When I was eight and nine, Dad's players would put me in some of their softball games. I was competing against adults, even though it was only softball. Then when I'd play with kids my age, I wasn't afraid of the biggest boy on the team or the home run hitter. Why should I be? I'd just competed against a field full of twenty-five-year-olds. I don't know if my dad did that intentionally or if it just happened because I was always around. But the experience definitely improved my skills.

Around that time, my nephew Gary Sheffield moved in with us, along with his parents, my sister Betty and her husband, Harold. Gary was four years younger than I was. But now I had a twenty-four-hour teammate in the house, someone else to share the family dream with. Gary and I slept in the same bedroom. Soon after the sun would come up, I'd pull him away from his favorite cartoon, *Scooby-Doo,* and drag him out to the yard. I hung a floor mat from the family car on the back fence, creating an uncontestable strike zone. Gary and I would play a game called Strike Out. I'd pitch a tennis ball and little Gary would strike out repeatedly. When it was my turn to bat, I'd hit home runs. But he was a quick study. And the same way I benefited from playing with older guys, he was benefiting from playing with me.

"How much do you like baseball?" my father asked me one day.

"I like it," I told him. "I love it."

"You ever think you might want to play professional?"

"Yeah," I answered. "That would be my dream." I told him what I had already told Mom, that one day I was planning to play on television and buy a house for her.

My father got very serious. "If you want to do that," he said, "it's a lot of work that goes into it. It ain't about just goin' up there and playin'."

"I know," I said. That was all Dad needed to hear.

All of a sudden, our training sessions at the park kicked up a notch. My father began working more and more on my pitching. I liked hitting and playing different positions. But Dad seemed to think that pitching was my strongest talent. And I was noticing real improvement there.

My father had some unusual training techniques for me. He was big on long tossing, having me throw the ball as far as I could. We did a lot of distance running and a lot of abdominal exercises. Then legs. "The legs and the abs, they're a pitcher's foundation," he told me constantly. "They bring all the balance and power to the arm."

I didn't understand a lot of what we were doing, but I didn't question him. Some days, we were out there for an hour or two without picking up a ball. Dad would put a board on top of a brick and have me balance there. He'd take me down to home plate and have me just stare back up at the mound. We talked about hitters who swing too early or swing too late. He laid it all out slowly. It wasn't like he was filling me up with too much too fast. I absorbed a lot of it.

"As a pitcher," my dad said, "you want to build the smaller muscles.

The small muscles are where you get your speed. If you get bulky, everything's tight and the extension's going to be shorter. You may look good on the beach, but it won't help your pitching." Dad never said anything specifically about steroids. They weren't even being talked about back in the 1970s. But knowing how they build up the body, I'm sure he would have warned me to steer clear. And when steroids were being described as the number one substance abuse problem in baseball, my dad's early lessons were still in my head. Steroids were one drug I was never tempted to play around with.

Dad used different techniques in the park with Gary, helping him develop his hitting and fielding. But for me it was always "Pitchers have to train like pitchers."

Today, training like this is common, up to the highest levels of baseball. But back in the 1970s it was unheard of. I don't know where my father learned it. I don't remember him studying anatomy manuals or reading many baseball books. He wasn't getting it from TV analysts. They were not talking baseball mechanics the way they do today. I never asked my dad how he knew so much.

All I know is, with me at least, his teaching was starting to work.

2

Dark Side

I GOT A HUGE SENSE of security growing up in such a tight family. Never once did I doubt that both my parents loved me and wanted what was best for me. I worshiped my dad, who seemed to worship me back. And my mom was the family glue, running the house, encouraging her kids to do well, and making sure we all felt special in individual ways. I've always felt sympathy for children growing up without that kind of support. It's a terrible burden to overcome.

That said, just beneath the surface — and sometimes bursting right into the open — the Goodens had some crazy stuff going on. Drinking, fighting, philandering, gunplay — you name it. It didn't strike me as all that unusual at the time or all that threatening. But looking back, I can see that we had some major issues swirling around our loving home on our solid block in respectable Belmont Heights. My father was far from faithful to my mother, and he didn't make much effort to hide it from me. More than once, my mom threatened to divorce him.

One wild day, she confronted my father directly outside his girlfriend's house. And I was partly the cause.

On Saturday mornings, before NBC's *Game of the Week* with Joe Garagiola and Tony Kubek, my father and I had one of our little rituals. We'd be in the living room out of my mother's earshot, and Dad would ask me: "Before the game starts, you gonna need a snack?"

He knew exactly what I'd say. "Yeah!" I loved candy and chips and those twelve-ounce cans of Tahitian Treat fruit punch.

He'd wander into the kitchen and say with a sigh to my mom: "Dwight says he's gotta have some chips. We're gonna run to the store. Need anything?"

Usually, she didn't, and Dad and I would head out to the car. But we didn't go straight to the market. Dad liked to make a stop on the way. "Got to drop something off for a friend," he'd say, pulling into the driveway of a house a few blocks from ours. "Be right back."

As a five-year-old, I was too young to understand exactly what was happening, and I never questioned him about it. But he'd go in the house, and a girl, twelve or thirteen years old, would come out to the car and sit with me. Dad would be inside the house for twenty minutes or half an hour.

The girl was always nice to me. "How are you doing?" she'd ask, trying to strike up a conversation. "What did you do today?"

We'd make uncomfortable small talk. Sometimes, she'd bring out a coloring book and some crayons. On other days, she was quiet and withdrawn. I don't know if she knew what was happening inside that house any more than I did. She probably did. A couple of times, I noticed a woman coming to the door with my father, giving him a little hug before he left.

I don't remember feeling particularly bothered by Dad's pit stops. But looking back, they must have planted something in my head. One afternoon when Dad was at work, I was riding my little bike in front of our house, singing a song I'd made up.

"Daddy has a girlfriend. Daddy has a girlfriend. . . ."

I wasn't trying to get my dad in trouble. Not consciously. But when my mom finished her vacuuming and stepped outside, she heard my new song.

"Dwight," she said sharply, screwing up her face like she'd just bitten into a lemon and grabbing the handlebars of my bike, "what in Sam Hell are you singing about?"

"Daddy's got a girlfriend!" I said, smiling cluelessly.

"Well, what does that mean, exactly?" she asked. She planted her hands on her hips, waiting for me to say more.

"Daddy's got a girlfriend," I said. "That's what it means. He hugs and kisses her when we go to the store."

Before Mom stomped away, I mentioned the lady on the porch and the nice girl with the coloring book. Mom was waiting at the kitchen table when my dad got home.

"The boy doesn't know what he's talking about," I heard my father protest. "It's just a song, for Christ's sake! I was just running an errand."

Mom didn't press the point. Not right away. But things weren't back to normal either. One afternoon a few weeks later, when Dad left for his "errands" without me, Mom grabbed her .38 Special and followed behind in her car. This upstanding Christian lady parked outside the girlfriend's house, lying in wait for Dad to come outside. When Mom saw the screen door open and the familiar feet hit the porch, she leaped from the car and started firing.

The first bullet grazed my father's left bicep. The second bullet whizzed past his girlfriend's head, lodging in the door frame. Dad went scampering off the porch and down the sidewalk.

He did not go to the hospital. He waited a few minutes for my mother to clear out. Then he drove himself back home. He dressed the wound in the bathroom. I don't know if he yelled at my mother or if she yelled at him. I never heard either one of them apologize. I do know the cops didn't come. No one was arrested. My mom had made her point her way.

That didn't end my father's straying. I don't think anything could have. Certainly not a little graze wound. Dad just found a middleman, spending more time with his good buddy Boo. While my mom was off at work, Dad would go to Boo's house to play cards and drink. If the weather was nice, they'd pull an extra card table into the yard for the bottles, the mixers, and the ice.

Sometimes, when I got bored, I'd ride to Boo's on my bike and ask Dad if he could spare any money. Almost always, he'd smile and hand me a few bucks, before shooing me away.

"Going to the movies?" he'd ask. "Have fun."

"Playing ball today? Good idea. See you tonight."

He did whatever it took to get me out of there.

When I told my sister Betty how generous Dad always was at Boo's house, she laughed and told me I was thinking way too small.

"You can get a lot more than five dollars," she said. "Ask him for twenty."

"Twenty?"

"Just go try it," she said.

Sure enough, when I rode up and asked for a twenty, Dad handed me a twenty. Then, I got even bolder, returning half an hour later for another ten. He forked over the ten. He didn't even ask why.

Eventually, I got some extra insight about my dad's generosity. One day, when he didn't get me out of there swiftly enough, a carload of women in party dresses pulled up.

"Boo's friends," my father explained hurriedly, before heading into the house with Boo, the ladies, and a couple of other guys.

Clearly, my parents didn't have a perfect marriage. When I was twelve, Mom and Dad announced they were splitting up. I raced up to my room and started crying. I loved my mother a lot. But I concluded

I'd have to live with my father if I was going to get any better at base-ball. Thankfully, I never had to make the choice because the bust-up never happened. Mom and Dad stayed together, and life just went on.

I'm not blaming Mom and Dad's troubles for my own later on. I stumbled into plenty completely on my own. But when it came to drinking and screwing around, I didn't lack for strong role models, that's for sure. And the whole idea of good, loving people sometimes doing reckless, self-destructive things — that was business as usual for the Goodens.

On my mom's side, feuding and fighting were damn near official sports. Mom had several nephews and cousins who put each other in the hospital after angry, drawn-out brawls. Then, no hard feelings on either side — they'd stop by during family-visiting hours and make sure everyone was doing okay. Dad's three older sons were constantly finding trouble and messing up their lives. They were all heavy drink-ers who wandered into harder stuff. None of them could seem to hold a job.

I was eight or nine years old before I realized that James, Charles, and Danny were my half brothers. I never met their mom. Sometimes they would visit in the summer. They were all wild guys, staying out late and going to bars where fights broke out. James, the oldest, finally went into the army. When he came home on leave, he was as polite and clean-cut as you can imagine. It was quite a shock. For the first time I felt like I had a real big brother. He took me out to Burger King on Friday nights when he got paid and to the Tuesday night wrestling matches at the Fort Homer Hesterly Armory. I loved Dusty Rhodes, André the Giant, and Haystack Calhoun. I'd get in fights with kids at my school about who was the greatest wrestler ever and whether the whole thing was a fake. I wanted so badly to believe.

The fun outings with James ended abruptly. One visit, he was cool and fun. But the next time, he'd done a total 180. Something in the army must have messed him up. He spent his next couple of visits drunk and acting crazy. He thought nothing of walking past Gary or me and grabbing a sandwich right out of our hands. We knew better than to ask for it back. One day, James stormed past both of us and into the backyard, picking every single orange off half a dozen orange trees. He carried them back in the house in a laundry basket and slammed the door. As he passed by us, he looked down at the oranges and said, "If you touch any of these, I will kick your ass." He definitely wasn't joking. Then he went upstairs to his room.

Gary and I said nothing. We just stared at the TV in silence, hoping not to antagonize him anymore.

I still don't know what that was about. But James never mellowed much as far as I could tell. I heard he was in and out of prison for drugs and robbery, and we didn't see him for long stretches of time.

But compared to psycho Uncle G. W., half brother James was a pussycat. G. W. was married to my older sister, Mercedes. When I was five years old and she was twenty, she and G. W. lived two houses away from us with Derrick, their eighteen-month-old son.

One afternoon, Merc was watching me and Derrick while my parents were off at work. She was sitting at the kitchen table. Derrick and I were goofing off on the floor. It was a day like many others until her badass husband came roaring through the door. He had a gun in his hand, and he was seething about something.

I don't know what set him off this time. With G. W., it could have been anything. The sound of kids laughing could make him furious. He could fly into a rage at the mailman for delivering a court order or unexpected bill. He got physical with my father once. Another time, my mom pulled a gun on him. He even took a knife to himself after my sister threatened to divorce him. When I was visiting Merc and Derrick, I always tiptoed around G. W.

Looking back, someone might have asked, "How could your parents leave you at Mercedes's house with G. W. around?" But they were family, and I don't think anyone ever gave it a second thought.

What I know for certain — what I saw with my own five-year-old eyes — was G. W. marching into the kitchen that day, raging at Merc, and opening fire with a handgun.

Bang.

Bang.

Bang.

Bang.

Bang.

It was five quick shots from a distance of two or three feet, all of them raining down on my sister. I'd heard fireworks before. I'd played cops and robbers. I'd faked dying. This was nothing like any of that. That gunfire was the loudest sound I'd ever heard.

Mercedes didn't scream. She didn't say much of anything. She just let out a tiny whimper and slumped to the kitchen floor. Purplish, red blood was pouring from her head and shoulders. The blood settled in a pool beneath her on the linoleum floor.

I didn't have time to think. I looked at Merc. I looked at her crazy husband. I scooped up little Derrick. I sprinted for the bathroom and locked the door.

My heart was pounding like a bongo. I crouched beside the tub, shivering and crying with Derrick in my arms.

I didn't say anything. I didn't know what to expect. Would G. W. come flying through the bathroom door? Were Derrick and I next?

G. W., bully-coward that he was, must have split immediately, leaving his son and nephew huddled in mortal fear and his helpless wife dying on the kitchen floor. Soon I heard sirens. Then cops and paramedics came rushing into the house, clearly uncertain about what they'd find.

"Show yourself," I heard one cop shout. "Put down your weapon and come out." No one answered, and soon the cops were busting open the bathroom door.

"Holy Christ!" one officer said when he saw Derrick and me on the floor. "You guys okay? Did you see anything?"

I was too scared to answer. One of the cops, a heavyset, middle-age guy with a red, round face, crouched gently down beside us. He kept himself at a safe distance. He removed his hat as if to say, "I'm one of the good guys here."

He just stayed quiet for a minute.

"I want my mommy," I whimpered, clutching Derrick tighter. That was the best I could do. "I want my mommy. I wanna see my mommy."

I'm not sure if the cop realized that the woman bleeding on the kitchen floor was Derrick's mom, not mine. "Okay, kid," he said. "Okay. Let me see what I can do."

I didn't want to leave the bathroom. It was too scary out there.

By then, the neighbors must have been gathering on the front lawn, sorting out for the cops exactly who was who in our family. A few minutes later, my mom rushed past everyone and into the house. She saw all the blood and could only watch as her daughter was wheeled away on a gurney. "G. W.," she said, almost spitting the letters out. She pulled Derrick and me out of there and walked us home.

No one had to explain anything to Mom or tell her how she should respond. She just acted. She grabbed her pistol and got in her car. She drove around Tampa, looking for her evil son-in-law. She didn't find him, which I guess is good. But I have no doubt at all in my mind: If she had, she wouldn't have suggested an anger-management course. G. W. would have been lying in the next pool of blood.

He was arrested a few days later and taken off to prison for a long, long time. Miraculously, Merc didn't die from her wounds, although she would never be the same again. She still suffers from seizures and carries a bullet in her head.

How could these things happen in the same family that was so supportive and made me feel so secure? That's not an easy question. For a long time, I buried most of these dark family memories. I took comfort from all the love I got at home, which truly was the vast majority of my experience, and I shrugged off the rest. I never wanted to dwell on the bad parts. But they must have affected me somehow. Did they plant silent seeds that grew into adult demons? Did I absorb unhealthy patterns that played out later on? Being related to all these people, did I have some genetic tendency to take reckless risks in my own life? Or is the majority of the responsibility my own? I've spent a lot of years trying to untangle all that. And the answer to all those questions, I am convinced, is yes. Yes, my upbringing had a huge affect on me. Yes, my family helped to shape the person I became. And yes, the choices I made — the good and the bad ones — had a giant affect as well.

Certainly, my family, like a lot of families, was a whole lot more complicated than I realized when I was growing up. But here's the strange part that gives me hope today: Whatever else was happening inside my family, I always felt loved, supported, and appreciated. I loved them, and they loved me. My family background might have set some traps for me. But it also laid a foundation for all I have been able to achieve in my life. I'm convinced that kids have a much higher tolerance than we give them credit for, as long as they feel that love.

I sure hope so, given some of my own failings as a dad.

3

Young Phenom

MY DAD TAUGHT ME how to throw a curveball when I was seven years old. I wouldn't recommend it. Before the age of twelve or thirteen, the weird, twisting motion can do real damage to a child's undeveloped arm. There's also the tendency for the kid — or the parent or the coach — to see the curve working and get all excited. Suddenly, the precocious young pitcher is throwing curveballs all day long. Better to stick with fastballs and changeups for a while.

But one day in the park, my dad showed me how to grip the ball with my middle finger on one of the long seams and my thumb just beside the seam on the other side of the ball. "Your hand should form a little C," he told me. "Pretend you're holding a cup of juice."

And right before I released the ball, he said, I should snap my wrist just so, letting the ball tumble off my index finger and fly toward the plate with a forward topspin.

"See it dive?" he asked.

I did. The ball started high then dropped suddenly as it approached home plate.

"Not bad," he said.

There was no denying it. I had a pretty good curveball for a seven-year-old, and I threw a lot of them.

Learning to throw a curve so young would turn out to be a key factor in my baseball and personal development, for bad and good reasons. Years later, people would ask whether I had been pushed too hard too early, and that's a legitimate question to raise. But those early curveballs also did something very positive for me. They gave me some of my earliest hints that I might have real talent on a pitcher's mound.

No other seven-year-olds I knew could throw curveballs. And I got a little thrill every time I saw one of those babies sail toward home plate then make its little dive at the end.

"See that one?" I'd called out to my dad behind the plate.

"Very nice," he'd call back. "Very nice."

I wouldn't say I was brimming with baseball confidence. Far from it. That would take years to build up, far more slowly than my skills did. At seven, I was still too shy to sign up for Belmont Heights Little League. I was happy just to practice with Dad and play with my neighborhood friends. Then a boy from a team called the Larkin Giants quit and my dad told the coach, Grover Stevens, I might be interested. I played third base and did some pitching and was immediately one of the better players on a very lousy team. After we lost eight or nine games in a row, I was so frustrated, I decided to quit.

"None of these kids are any good," I said, "except for me and one other guy." I'm not sure what I was expecting from a team of seven- and eight-year-olds.

Dad tried to talk me out of quitting. "If you're going to play baseball, you can't just quit," he said. "It's not fair to your team." But I was adamant, and he didn't press the point.

I kept playing pickup games with my friends. Dad and I kept going to the park. I knew he wanted me to keep at it. He didn't push me too hard, which could have driven me away from baseball forever. And when the next season rolled around, I told my father I'd been thinking about giving Little League another try. I think he knew I'd come around, but he wanted to make sure I'd learned a lesson from the experience.

"If you quit again," he warned me, "you're done. Forever. You gotta go out and do your best, no matter what the other guys are doing. Maybe they will learn from you."

I was still a terrible loser. I could get absurdly upset at defeat of any kind. If I was pitching and a player got a hit off me, I'd get furious. If, God forbid, someone hit a home run, I'd start crying on the mound. We could be winning 5–1, and I'd still burst into tears.

When I glanced over at the stands, I could see my father, looking like he wanted to die right there. He did not want to be *that* boy's dad. "Knock it off," he'd hiss in my direction. After the game, he wouldn't yell. But he'd try to calm me down with a stop at Baskin-Robbins, which took at least a double cone.

I noticed slow improvement on the field, even if my confidence was lagging. All that mat-ball Strike Out I'd been playing with Gary was paying dividends. Dad's drills in the park really helped. My fastballs and my curveballs were definitely getting me noticed among the seven- and eight-year-olds.

When I was nine, one of the players from my dad's semipro team was coaching a group of Little League ten-to-fourteen-year-olds. He'd been watching me play with the younger kids and said he thought he could use my arm. I was totally opposed to making the leap into the big-boy division. Those kids looked like giants to me. Playing with adults was one thing. I wasn't expected to be as good as they were. But older kids — I feared they'd show me up. I begged my dad, my coach, and the league director to keep me with the little ones. But everyone seemed to recognize I was playing far beyond my age. They wanted me to keep pushing myself, and I reluctantly agreed.

No one was more intimidating than Albert Everett, the very first pitcher I faced when I moved up. He was eleven or twelve, but he was built like a sixteen-year-old. Once I saw him hit a kid in the face with a fastball hard enough to break a cheekbone. Someday soon, I figured, he'd probably be drafted by the Reds or the Braves. The coach caught my eye in the dugout at the top of the third inning of that first game and said, "You're gonna pinch hit."

What?

"I have a headache," I told him. Then I wobbled in front of the team bench and gave the coach a pained, bug-eyed look. "It even hurts to put the helmet on."

"Then find a bigger one," the coach said.

"I gotta sit down," I moaned.

The coach shook his head. "Need you in there," he said. "Go get a hit." He gave me a spank on the butt and a little shove toward the on-deck circle. The kids on my team began to cheer, and I had no choice but to bat.

My knees were knocking. I could feel the sweat beading on my forehead. I didn't want any part of this. I kept thinking how this monster's fastball would feel, slapping me in the face.

All that fear got the better of me. I bailed out of the batter's box on every pitch. Albert whiffed me on three called strikes.

Ouch!

But I learned. Later that season, the tables were turned, and I had to pitch to Albert for the first time. A kid on my team offered a brief scouting report. "Just throw him curves," my teammate told me. "He can't hit 'em."

I threw two curveballs and jumped out to an 0-and-2 count. Then I got cocky and threw a fastball. Albert whacked it over the right-field fence, and I was sniffling again on the mound. I still had a ways to go, but even I could see I was making progress with my arm and my head. I was getting better every week. At nine, I was becoming one of the stronger pitchers among the ten- to-fourteen-year-olds.

It was that season my dad's friend Dennis from the Cargill plant started coming out to watch me pitch. He considered himself a good spotter of young talent, and he told my father he saw something in me. He had a unique way of being encouraging. He'd lean on the fence along the third base line and chatter constantly at players on the field. He liked to dream up little nicknames that only he understood.

When I was on the mound, he would wait until I reached 0 and 2 on a batter. Then, he'd start to yell.

"Operate on him, Doc! Time to operate, Doc!"

He told my father I performed like a surgeon out there. Steady and smooth. Getting the job done.

After I struck out the first kid and the next batter stepped up to the plate, Dennis would go at it again: "You got another patient, Doc!"

Pretty soon, everyone was calling me Doc.

Over time, "Doc" would morph into "Doctor D" and eventually "Doctor K." I didn't mind. I liked Doc from the beginning. As far as I was concerned, it was cooler than Goody, the other nickname that occasionally popped up, and a million miles cooler than Poodney, my mom's dumb name for me.

I kept playing Little League and pitching well. When I was ten, our team made it to the Little League World Series in Williamsport, Pennsylvania, which was very exciting except that as a ten-year-old, I had to sit in the stands and watch. I was too young to play. But I kept at it. Working with my dad in the park, practicing with Gary and the neighborhood kids — but still not as sure of myself as I should have been. I knew I was good. Everyone told me so. But I never really felt like one of the cool kids. I guess you'd say I was socially awkward. I'd spent so much time with my dad and older players, that inevitably meant less time hanging out with kids my own age. My talent was always a step or two ahead of my comfort and my confidence. When I was fourteen, I finally made it to another youth-baseball World Series, in Gary, Indiana. I moved us into the title game by throwing nine strikeouts against the East Coast champions from Auburn, Maine, then scoring the final run by stealing home. What I remember most was having my first plane ride and being away from home for two weeks.

All the while, a little tug-of-war was playing out at home. As Dad was working on my baseball, drilling me, quizzing me, Mom was making sure I got my homework done. "I know you want to do baseball," she said. "But there's no guarantees. You've gotta be able to do other things. You've got to get a job. You have to be accountable."

By the time I got to Tampa's Hillsborough High School, some of my slow-growing confidence on the diamond was actually carrying over to the classroom. I loved math and English. History not so much. But with Mom's nudging, I was getting my work done and earning pretty good grades. And Mom was constantly coming home with job applications for me. Wendy's, McDonald's, Busch Gardens, you name it. "Between schoolwork and baseball," I complained, "I don't have any time for this, Mom."

"Weekends," she said. "You can make time."

I handed the applications to my dad, who made them disappear. And even Mom eventually came around. As I kept practicing and kept getting better, she told me one day: "You need money, you ask for it. Don't steal. But you got no time for a job. You got to play ball."

Dad bought me a 1974 Plymouth Duster. I put spoke hubcaps on it. My friend tinted the windows — badly, but he tried — and I got an extra-long AM antenna to pull in WTMP 1150, "Today's R&B and Classic Soul." Thinking about that clunker makes me cringe today, but that car was my high school idea of an excellent ride.

Even with the car, I didn't have much luck with girls. My best friend, Troy Davis, and I once picked up two young ladies at a school dance and drove them to a park to make out. When WTMP powered down for the night, I couldn't pick up any other music on the dial. The Duster got uncomfortably silent. It didn't take long for the girls to climb out and join the two dudes parked next to us. They had an in-dash eight-track player. How could we compete with that? Troy and I sat there, dumbfounded, then went back to the dance and completely struck out.

I had no idea how to act around the opposite sex. One night, I took a girl to eat at Burger King. While we were standing in line, I started talking with another girl, the one working behind the counter. Her name was Carlene Pearson. As she was taking our order, I asked her what time she got off. That was my idea of smooth at the time.

Hillsborough High, a big public school on North Central Avenue in Tampa's Seminole Heights neighborhood, had a powerhouse baseball team. The coach, Billy Reed, was considered one of the best in Florida, one of two supercompetitive black baseball coaches in the Tampa area. The school's baseball stadium is now called Billy Reed Field. *Go Terriers!* But I didn't go out for the team until my junior year. Again, I was dragging my feet on my way up, and I kept resisting my dad's idea that I should pitch. I liked pitching. But I also enjoyed getting my uniform dirty, diving for balls in the infield. I liked first base, shortstop — even the outfield. Sometimes, I'd tell Coach Reed that my pitching arm was sore so he'd put me in a different position. He seemed okay with that. We had a lot of talent on the mound. At the start of the season, I was his number five pitcher. When major-league scouts came to check out the Terriers, they weren't coming to see me.

But Coach Reed started to notice that every time he'd put me in to pitch, no one seemed to hit the ball. And one afternoon, the coach pulled me aside. "You may have something, kid," he said.

That made me feel pretty good.

It was a lucky break that I got noticed at all. Early in my first season, several scouts came to see my friend Vance Lovelace, who was a senior and had also been on a nice pitching run. But Vance had a couple of rocky innings that day, and Coach Reed pulled him out.

"Get in there," the coach said to me.

As the pro scouts were walking out of the stadium, they must have heard my heat popping in the catcher's mitt. My dad might have mentioned something too. Whatever first got me noticed, they started paying attention to me. I was winning games, and the local media caught on. By the middle of my junior year season, reporters were writing me up in the papers. Scouts were showing up regularly at my starts. They were even standing behind home plate with radar guns and video cameras. Pretty soon, scouts were calling my house and stopping by the high school, taking me out of class to have me work out for them.

"Let me see you run a sixty-yard dash," they'd say.

"Throw one as hard as you can."

"Give me a curve."

I felt like I was back in Robles Park, doing sprints and board balances with my dad. And frankly, these scouts didn't seem to know any more than he did.

The whole idea of going pro became more real to me when Vance got picked up by the Chicago Cubs in the first round of the 1981 draft. That left me and my pal Floyd Youmans as the star pitchers on the Hillsborough team. But not for long. Coach Reed caught Floyd playing pickup basketball when he was supposed to be at baseball practice and kicked him off the team. Floyd moved to California to live with his dad for senior year and played ball out there.

That left me. Senior year, I was our best weapon on the mound — pretty much our only weapon. I'd outlasted everyone else. Many weeks, I took the mound three days. One solid start for sure. If we got a lead in that game, I'd stay in at least seven innings. Often, I'd do some mop-up work in the second game of the week. If we were playing another tough team that week, Coach would often have me start a third game, going six or seven innings if I could. That was a crazy lot of pitching for a high school kid, and it wouldn't be allowed today. But it got me in front of a lot of pro scouts. Our team did well that year. We made it to the state tournament. And I was becoming a high school baseball star. I was big man on campus. I got a lot of attention, and I was finally enjoying it. I got my gold tooth that year. And my pitching kept getting better. The University of Miami offered me a baseball scholarship and a free apartment if I wanted to go there after graduation. Mom thought that sounded like a fine idea. I felt like I was on a roll now, and my pitching was getting me there.

Late on a Monday afternoon, June 7, 1982, my dad tossed me his car keys. Dad drove a 1974 Plymouth Duster, just like I did. But his Duster wasn't all tricked out like mine. "Go have fun," he said with a smile. The major-league baseball draft was finally here. My friend Eddie Ganzi and I were heading downtown to the offices of the *Tampa Tribune* to watch my future unfold in real time.

Yes, I was big news at Hillsborough High School. But this was professional baseball across the whole United States and beyond. Weren't there guys like me everywhere? My dad didn't seem worried. "You've figured it out so far," he said. "Just trust all the pieces to fall in place. And tell ol' Tom I said hello."

Tom McEwen was a legendary sportswriter. He knew famous athletes and coaches everywhere. But he was also a true booster for local sports. His column, The Morning After, ran in the *Trib* six days a week. When people didn't think that was enough, he added a Sunday version, Hey, Tom, where he gave snappy responses to reader mail. No one did more than Tom McEwen to build Tampa into a first-rate sports town. He was one of the few white guys who dared to venture into the 'hood for games — even Little League games. "Bring your sleeping bags," he'd write, making a pint-size playoff game sound like the World Series.

This time, he invited me and a couple of prospects from Tampa Catholic — Richard Monteleone and Lance McCullers — to the newspaper office to watch the major-league draft. Back then, we didn't have wall-to-wall coverage on ESPN. The *Trib* was the one place in town that had a live feed of the draft. In the middle of the newsroom was a TV screen that looked like it might be announcing arrivals and departures at the airport. They laid out some donuts and oranges for us to eat.

There were rumors about my prospects.

Coach Reed had been gathering intelligence from his scout friends. "You might go as early as the fifth round," Coach said.

Others were making what sounded like crazy predictions. Scouts for the Reds and the Cubs had even called my house, saying if they picked a high schooler in the first round, it might be me. And the Cubs had the first pick overall.

As Eddie and I stared up at the screen, the first pick of the draft came and went. The Cubs picked a high schooler all right — but it wasn't me. They chose Shawon Dunston, a shortstop from Thomas Jefferson High School in Brooklyn.

McEwen was sitting next to me, and I leaned over and told him about the phone call from the Cubs scout. "Shake it off," he said with a laugh. "Everything changes on the fly, Doc. It's gonna be a long night, but good things are gonna happen."

As the next couple of picks went by without any mention of Dwight Gooden, Coach Reed's theory was starting to sound about right. I wouldn't get drafted early, but I was formulating a plan. I'd work hard and show everyone what a later-round steal I was.

Now it was the Mets' turn. They had the fifth pick of the first round. But I was daydreaming, busy convincing myself that ultimately the draft order didn't mean much.

Then I glanced at the board and saw something strange:

5TH PICK. NY METS. DWIGHT GOODEN. HILLSBOROUGH HIGH. TAMPA, FL.

Eddie's eyes popped open, but nothing came out of his mouth. Frantically, he was pointing at the board.

"Doc!" McEwen shouted. "You just went to the Mets!"

Monteleone and McCullers, both forecast to go well ahead of me, looked as shocked as I was.

"I don't think that's right, Mr. McEwen," I said, shaking my head.

"Whaddaya mean?" he asked me.

"I can't be the fifth pick," I told him. "Coach Reed didn't expect me to go until the fifth round. He talked to a lot of scouts."

"Things change," McEwen said. "I doubt there's any mistake."

"Well, why don't you call them?"

"Call the Mets?" McEwen asked. Clearly he thought I was crazy. But he picked up the phone.

"No mistake," he said when he hung up. "Dwight Gooden. First Round. New York Mets."

He shot me a huge smile.

"Great job, Doc," the dean of Tampa sportswriting said, shaking my hand.

I couldn't believe it. I knew I had ability. I didn't feel like I was undeserving. But there were some very talented players who were drafted after me that year: Barry Bonds, Randy Johnson, Will Clark, David Wells, Roger McDowell, Jimmy Key, Bo Jackson, Mitch Williams, Terry Pendleton, Rafael Palmeiro, Todd Worrell, Barry Larkin, and my high school teammate, Floyd Youmans. The list went on and on.

I was too excited to drive the Duster home. I gave Eddie the keys. I couldn't wait to see the look on my dad's face.

"We did it!" I yelled as Eddie parked the car and we ran up the sidewalk, as my dad was stepping onto the porch. "Fifth pick! First round. I was the Mets' first player."

The look on my dad's face, right then and there, might have been the happiest I had ever seen on him. That was it. All our time on the diamond. All those Saturdays in the den. The promise I had made to my mother. His dream and my dream, finally mushed into one.

Normally, Dad didn't show much emotion. Once or twice in my entire life, he said he loved me. But standing out on the porch that evening, he gave me a giant hug. He laughed long and loud. Then he went inside and got on the phone, calling what seemed like everyone he knew, making sure they understood how big this was.

Within a few minutes, news trucks from Channel 8 and Channel 13 were pulling up on our block. Other reporters were calling on the phone. Neighbors came out to see what all the excitement was. Soon, moms in housecoats and dads in Bermuda shorts were giving interviews about what a nice, decent kid I was. My mom was happy too. But she remained pragmatic.

"Will the Mets let you go to college first?" she asked.

Dad and I both laughed. "No, Ella," Dad said, "It doesn't work like that. The deal is for now."

Joe McIlvaine was a tall, geeky-looking fellow who had a short minor-league career as a pitcher in the early 1970s. By 1982, he was director of scouting for the Mets. Even though I'd been the team's first pick, the fifth in the entire draft, and Joe was the team's top scout, he confessed to me that he'd never seen me pitch. Every time he'd been in Tampa, he said, I was playing third base or outfield. He'd relied on scouting reports that local guys sent in.

But now his job was to sign me.

The night I was drafted, he called my house to congratulate me. He said he'd be flying down to Tampa, contract in hand.

Throughout the spring, quite a few agents had called the house, offering to represent me. Dad had met with several, but we didn't hire any of them. He got on the phone and told Joe: "I look forward to meeting with you." Then he looked at me and said, "I'll handle this."

Joe showed up in Tampa a couple of days later. Dad banished Mom and me from the living room. Through my closed bedroom door, I could hear Dad and Joe murmuring for what seemed like hours. But I couldn't make out anything they were saying. Finally, Dad called me in.

"Son," he said soberly, "we've still got some work to do on this contract. We're a long way apart." Looking at the Mets' top scout, he added, "Forty thousand is not right for a fifth pick."

"It's okay," Joe said, smiling weakly. His words were optimistic, but he looked worn-out.

Here was my dad, driving a relentless bargain with the head of scouting for the New York Mets. He was either making me rich or blowing the deal for me. I wasn't sure which. But he was definitely putting the screws to Joe.

"I'll go back to New York and see what I can do," Joe said. "Then we'll take it from there."

"Good," Dad told him. "We appreciate it."

That was that. After the Mets man was gone, Dad motioned Mom and me into the kitchen. We all sat at the table. "Their offer is nowhere near where it needs to be," Dad said.

"Everything else in the contract is fine," he continued, suddenly sounding like a lawyer or an agent. "Except the money."

I was confused. How did my father, who had a third-grade education and had worked his whole life at a chemical plant, know what should be in a major-league baseball contract? It was the same as the way I wondered how he learned all those pitching drills he put me through. Dad just knew stuff. I had my concerns, but I didn't say anything.

My mother spoke up. "Dan," she said, sounding slightly panicked, "did Dwight just lose his chance?"

"Oh, it's all a game," Dad said, not seeming at all concerned. "It's just a game they play with everybody."

A few days later, Joe was back in town. He took my mom, my dad, my sister Betty, and her husband, Harold, out for a three-hour dinner. Dad made me stay at home. I'm sure he thought I'd reach across the table and sign whatever paper the scout pulled out of his briefcase.

Joe raised the offer, but Dad still wouldn't budge. "Not enough," he told the scout. Joe left town again without a deal.

For a couple of weeks, the phone didn't ring. I know because I sat by it for hours every day. "Relax," Dad said. "They're not going to drop the ball on the fifth pick in the draft."

I wasn't sure. I started thinking seriously about the University of Miami and their baseball team. "I'll be the only guy ever drafted fifth who couldn't make a deal," I thought.

Joe kept returning. The offer inched up. But the standoff continued. "Good luck to you, Dwight," he said finally, shaking my hand after talks with Dad had stalled yet again. "I'm sure you've got a bright future ahead of you."

As I stood at the doorway and watched Joe walk to his car, I was ready to run after him, yelling, "I'll sign it! I'll sign it!" — if Dad didn't tackle me in the yard first. I was losing faith in my father's judgment.

My mom caught the look on my face.

"Dan, you need to go stop him and get this done," she said firmly. Again, Dad refused.

In the end, Joe came back with one more offer. An $85,000 signing bonus on top of the $40,000 that was then the standard first-year major-league salary, which sounded like a huge pile of money to me. But really, I just wanted to play baseball.

4

Getting There

HELD IT TOGETHER at Tampa International Airport as I told Mom, Dad, and Betty good-bye. But even before the plane pushed back from the gate, I was bawling in my economy seat. I don't know what the other passengers thought, seeing this tall, skinny seventeen-year-old wiping tears from his eyes. But I cried until the flight attendant brought me a Coke and some pretzels. I had never been away from my family for more than two weeks. Now I was flying off to start a full season of New York Mets rookie ball in Kingsport, Tennessee. I was excited. My dream was coming true. But I couldn't have been any more homesick if I was moving to China.

The Kingsport Mets played in a converted high school stadium with a falling-down left-field fence. I moved into the owner's basement. Slowly, I figured out that the Dominican players really didn't speak English. They weren't just messing with me. Dad told me I couldn't spend the bonus money right away. I survived on the $2.50 dinner specials at Kentucky Fried Chicken. The guys on the team were friendly enough. My old pal Floyd Youmans was there from Belmont Heights Little League and Hillsborough High. He'd been drafted right behind me, in round two.

The night of the draft, Floyd had called me to say he'd been drafted. "By who?" I asked. When he told me "the Mets," I figured he'd heard that I'd been drafted by New York and he was pulling my leg. "Yeah? That's great," I said, playing along. "What round?" He told me the Mets had picked him in the second round and I quickly countered that I'd gone in the first. Since Floyd hadn't been watching a live feed and I'd left the *Trib* office right after my name came on the screen, it took us a few days to figure out that both stories were real. And now we were teammates again. Together we didn't exactly burn up the Appalachian League, finishing the 1982 season at 28–40, good enough for last place. Compared with my teammates, I played really well. I made the Appalachian League All-Star Game. But I was still so shy and homesick, even with Floyd around, most nights I couldn't wait to call my family.

"Son, you gotta stop calling so often," my dad finally said. "The phone bills are sky-high."

Then Mom got on the phone and whispered, "Call as much as you need. Don't worry about that old fool." For once, Dad was the hard-ass and Mom was the softie.

Kingsport was where I first met Davey Johnson, then a roving instructor for the Mets organization. I think I impressed him with my knowledge of the game. Davey saw me in the bullpen one day positioning the catcher outside, then inside, then down the middle, so I could hit my chosen spots with my curveball.

"How the hell do you know all that?" he asked me.

"My dad taught me," I said. Then I proceeded to show Davey the different grips I used to make the ball dance and dive. I think that stuck with him.

There wasn't much glamour in rookie ball, but I could tell the Mets higher-ups were keeping an eye on their first-round draft pick. When I begged our manager, Ed Olsen, to let me pinch-hit in extra innings one day, Ed said sure. I didn't come close to getting on base. And when the game report landed in New York, word bounced back immediately from the team's front office: "What the hell are you guys doing down there?"

They didn't want their top pitching prospect facing some fastballing teenager with no control. I had a total of one at bat that year.

There was no fighting it anymore. I was a pitcher for good.

At the end of that rookie ball season, my father finally let me dip into the bonus money. I replaced my ratty '74 Duster with a silver 1983 Chevrolet Camaro Z28 with a four-speed automatic transmission and Crossfire 305 V8, detailed to my precise specifications. That car had tinted windows, fancy rims, Playboy Bunny decals, and "Mr. Dwight" painted on the doors. I went all out. I drove to Lynchburg, Virginia, home of the high-A Lynchburg Mets of the Carolina League, to start the 1983 season. I didn't have major-league swagger. I was still a couple of A's away from the bigs. Bringing home $245 every two weeks, I could barely afford to buy gas. But a young black man cruising around drowsy Lynchburg in a car like that — let's just say I didn't go unnoticed. I was beginning — *beginning* — to look the part of a professional athlete.

Too bad I didn't pitch like one.

The Camaro-driving first-rounder got off to a miserable 0–3 start. I wasn't getting *anybody* out. Soon enough, there was talk of bouncing me back to the single-A Mets farm team in Little Falls, New York. My career had barely started, and I already seemed to have hit a wall.

Luckily, our pitching coach was John Cumberland, a real gruff talker who'd had a short throwing career with the Yankees and the Giants. He ranted. I threw.

"Blowing your fastball by chumps in high school and rookie ball isn't working here," Cumberland announced during our first morning session.

"Okay," I answered. Cumberland barely took a breath.

"Guys here have faster bats, and your only location is right down the middle. They're sitting back, drooling, waiting to crush the hell out of the ball."

"I—"

"You've got a shitload of talent that's gonna go right into the sewer," Cumberland said. "So you know what you gotta do now, don't ya, Doc?"

"What?"

"The only thing you *can* do," he said, looking at me like I was in the back of the slow class. "You gotta put the fear of God into these sons-of-bitches! Christ, kid, you're throwing in the mid-90s. Scare 'em!"

I just nodded.

"From now on, anytime a guy gets a base hit off of you, the next guy up to bat, you knock his ass down. If a guy hits a home run off you, the next guy up gets drilled. Hit him."

I'd never pitched that way before. Frankly, it made me a little uncomfortable. Was he saying "Hit batters on purpose?" I guess he kinda was. But prior to that, I had no strategy of intimidation. Growing up, I relied on straight heat and controlling my curveball. Those were the two pitches I had, and that was enough.

I felt a little guilty the first few times I placed the fear of Jesus into a couple of opposing batters and nailed a couple more. I was not a naturally aggressive person. If anything, I'd always been a little shy. But Nice Guy Dwight really was becoming a different person on the pitching mound. I was playing on a whole new level. I knew I had to do something. I told myself, "Maybe this is just how it's done around here."

The Cumberland School of Batter Intimidation changed everything. "A little chin music goes a long way," the pitching coach said. The other teams got the message: "Don't mess with Doc."

After a few super-aggressive outings, Cumberland had me dial back. Pitching hard and inside opened up my game a lot, and I kept doing it throughout the summer. The results were hard to miss. All the hitters were more cautious with me.

In May, we drove up to the big town for an exhibition game at Shea Stadium against the Salem Redbirds, the San Diego Padres A-ball team in the Carolina League. And I was going to pitch. We were the opening act before a regular Mets-Padres game. I'd seen major leaguers play at spring training in Florida, but I'd never set foot in a real major-league stadium before.

Shea seemed amazing to me. Just the size of it was staggering. I was in total awe. TV did not do it justice. I know some people ragged on Shea, saying it lacked grandeur, that it wasn't as impressive as some big-league parks. Well, to me, this was a cathedral of baseball. The field was nicer than anything I'd ever seen before, perfectly manicured and perfectly level. There were maybe four thousand people in the stands when we first took the field.

But as I was taking a measure of the scene around me, New York was also measuring me. The Mets' first-round draft choice had brought his stuff to New York, and all the sportswriters wanted to see. Was he really worth the hype? I had nothing on my mind but total domination.

I pitched well. I struck out fourteen batters. I had a one-hitter going, but I blew the game in the ninth. I gave up a couple of hits and then a home run, and then I nailed a batter with a ball in the neck. By the time the trainer came to look at the stunned batter, our manager, Sam Perlozzo, was on the mound, pulling me from the game. I felt horrible as I walked back to the showers. Joe McIlvaine, the Mets scouting director who had signed me, came into the locker room with a big smile on his face. "No reason to be down," he said. "You impressed a lot of people today."

"I should have won," I told him. "I won't lose another game this season. Why couldn't I win here?"

"Don't worry about it," Joe said.

I wasn't worried. I was just mad at myself. This was my first shot at

Shea, and I felt like I'd blown it. Weren't we supposed to win? Wasn't I supposed to win? I went back to Lynchburg and won every game I pitched after that.

Some weekends, Carlene came up from Florida, and that was fun. I didn't consider us too serious, and neither did she. When Carlene wasn't around, my roommate Darryl Denby and I would stroll through the mall, wearing our Lynchburg Mets jackets and hats, hoping to meet girls. You'd have to call our success rate "very hit or miss." Something else happened in Lynchburg that didn't seem important at the time. Living on my own, I discovered the pleasures of alcohol, especially forty-ounce bottles of Schlitz Malt Liquor. Other guys on the team would go out and shoot pool at night or come home from a game, order a pizza, and smoke some weed. Some guys would even smoke pot on road trips, then hit those southern truck stop buffets and put away four thousand calories for five bucks.

I wasn't into pot. Getting high just made me sleepy. I didn't get the thrill. But I liked the way those forties loosened me up and made me more social. I'd been sneaking Budweisers from my dad's refrigerator since I was in my early teens. I wasn't a frequent drinker then, and I didn't drink that much when I drank. I don't think I'd ever tried malt liquor before. Now that I had, I liked it. It had a higher concentration of alcohol than regular beer, delivering some extra bang for our minor-league bucks. I can honestly say I kept my drinking mostly under control. I told myself that drinking was just a part of growing up, like meeting girls and making money. Weren't other kids my age off at college, going to parties, and exploring their independence? I'd skipped my chance to go to Miami, but these were my college days. Still, I knew enough not to let my mom and dad know I'd started drinking regularly — especially malt liquor. My dad, the Bud man, would definitely have frowned on me hitting the hard-core stuff.

One night before a road trip, three or four girls were at our apartment until three a.m., laughing and drinking. None of the ladies stayed over, but Darryl and I definitely lost track of the time. Across the street, our team bus was leaving at eight a.m. sharp for Maryland and a game with the Hagerstown Suns, a Baltimore Orioles affiliate. Darryl and I knew all along that we'd be tired. But we were having fun, and we figured we could get some rest on the bus. The malt liquor was flowing, and I guess you could say we were negotiating with ourselves.

Bad idea.

We didn't wake up until 8:40. I looked out the window at the stadium parking lot. The bus was gone. I jumped out of bed and started throwing pieces of my uniform into a duffel bag.

"Darryl!" I yelled down the hall. "We fucked up!"

From his room, all I heard was a groan. Then, "What the hell?" as his senses kicked in. "Why didn't the Dominicans wake us up?"

We jumped into the Camaro and raced to Hagerstown, getting lost in our panic on the way. Three hours later, we arrived at Municipal Stadium. The game was in the fourth inning. And there was no way to sneak in quietly. The only way to get to our team was to enter the field near third base and trot to the visitors' dugout on the first base side. We waited in the stands for just the right moment, a couple of sheepish guys in full Mets uniforms. At the break in the inning, hoping no one would notice, we jogged right across the field. I've done some embarrassing things since then, things worse than that. But at that point in my life, this took the cake. Even Sam, our even-keeled manager, blew up at that.

Joe McIlvaine called from New York. He was fairly calm under the circumstances. "We need to be sure that you know why you're there, okay?" Joe said when he got me on the phone.

"It won't happen again," I said, and I meant it. That was another one I never mentioned to my dad.

That was the first time I ever remember alcohol interfering with me doing my job. I was sure it was a onetime slip-up, and for a while it was.

Sam came up to me at least once a week and said, "One more start and you're going up to double-A." Then it wouldn't happen. Week after week, he said that, and I didn't get called up.

Lynchburg won the A-ball division with a record of 96–43, and we were headed to the playoffs. After my shaky start, I finished the 1983 season with a kick-butt record of 19–4. I had 300 strikeouts in 191 innings and 10 complete games. This was the pitcher the Mets believed in enough to draft me in round one. These numbers definitely got me noticed in New York. To celebrate, we had a team party at a pizza shop. Sam approached me again that night.

"You're going to — " he started to say. I cut him off.

"I know, Coach," I said. "I know."

"It's not what you think," he said, shaking his head. "You're going to Tidewater, triple-A." He didn't have to tell me that Davey Johnson was managing the Mets AAA club in Tidewater, Virginia. "Davey wants you for their playoffs."

All of a sudden, an old, familiar feeling swept over me. "I want to stay here," I said immediately.

I knew it was an honor, Davey Johnson wanting me to leap entirely over AA ball and help his AAA team. It was flattering too. But I was doing well in Lynchburg. I felt loyal to my teammates there. I was having fun. The Lynchburg team was on its way to winning the Carolina League. Didn't they need me?

"That's not how it works, kid," Sam said. "You'll be one step away from the majors. You should be excited."

I didn't feel excited at all. Partly, I guess, it was anxiety about what I might be facing in Tidewater. How well would I play there? And partly, it was — I wouldn't call it homesickness, but I was well aware that Lynchburg's season ended a couple weeks earlier than Tidewater's would, no matter how well we did. Part of me really wanted to go be with my family back in Tampa.

"When do I have to leave?" I asked Sam.

"They want you there tomorrow, Doc," he said.

I drove to Norfolk, where the AAA Tidewater Tides played at Metropolitan Memorial Park. At Tidewater, I pitched just as well as I did back in Lynchburg. We won the playoffs, then went out to Louisville to play in the AAA World Series, a round-robin event between the winner of the International League (us), the American Association (the Denver Bears), and the Pacific Coast League (Portland Beavers).

I dominated the final game against Denver, the White Sox farm team, and we won the AAA World Series. I flew back to Tidewater the next day, jumped in my car, and drove home to Tampa.

Meanwhile in New York, 1983 had been a flop of a season for the big-league Mets. They'd gone through two managers, George Bamberger and Frank Howard. Their 68–94 finish was only enough for sixth place in the National League East. Rumors were flying that Davey Johnson would be moving up to Shea from Norfolk for the 1984 season to manage the team. Throughout the playoffs with Tidewater, he'd been telling me, "If I get to manage the Mets, I'm taking you with me." He got the nod in November.

Just a few days later, I was back in the off-season instructional league in St. Petersburg, playing catch on the side of the field, when Davey walked by. "Davey." I flashed him a smile. "Remember what you said?"

"Oh yeah," he assured me as he kept strolling. "You're in."

During spring training, I didn't stay at the team hotel. Since my parents lived just twenty minutes away in Tampa, I drove home every night. And as the end of spring training approached, my dad started asking me if I thought I would make the team. Spring training was coming to a close, and I still didn't have an answer for him.

I woke up extra early the last day, after tossing and turning all night. I was on the road early and got to the ballpark before almost anyone. I was hoping Davey would notice and tell me one way or another right away, before everyone else came in. After the game that day, I knew, the team would be flying out to Cincinnati to begin the regular season. I hated the idea of bringing my luggage with me in the morning and then being told I hadn't made the team. That would be mortifying.

I told my dad to put my bags in his trunk before he drove over for the game. If I made the team, someone could run out to the parking lot, grab the bags, and load them onto the bus.

If I didn't, no one would have to know they were there.

During pitching drills and warm-ups, I heard nothing. In the dugout, I saw a chart listing who was pitching that day. My name wasn't on it. Mel Stottlemyre, the pitching coach, walked by and said, "We might use you today, Doc. I'm just not sure yet."

That made me think they were still undecided. Normally when a game started, the other pitchers hung out in the bullpen. But there was no way I was leaving the dugout.

The innings crawled by. I still had no clue. During spring training, the managers sometimes sat outside the dugout. Midway through the game, I saw the Mets' general manager, Frank Cashen, approach Davey. I couldn't hear what they were saying, but they whispered back and forth. Not long after that, Davey walked over to me. He had his hand out.

"Congratulations, Doc," he said, smiling. "Didn't I tell you? You made the team. Now get out to the bullpen. I'm gonna use you in the seventh."

Before I trotted to the bullpen, I asked one of the clubhouse kids to get my stuff out of my dad's car and put it on the bus to the airport. I went into the game and struck out four of the six batters I faced.

After the game, I told my dad I made the team.

He had the same look on his face he did the day I was drafted, like this dream of ours kept coming true. I was on my way to the majors — drafted, signed, and tested — a full-fledged member of the New York Mets. I was heading off to opening day in Cincinnati, ready to face the team my dad and I had watched on television in the family den.

Truly, everything after that was gravy.

PART II

Playing

5

Rookie Season

WHEN I WAS CALLED UP to the big team, I felt like a whole lot of people had been waiting around for me, and I thought I understood why. To the players, the fans, and the sportswriters who'd been following my progress in the minors, I was the bright, shiny hope for a baseball team that desperately needed some.

These were tough times all around in New York, and not just for the Mets. Crack was exploding. Crime was high. People felt jittery in their own neighborhoods. When the rest of life is difficult, sports can bring important relief. That was true in Georgia in my father's and grandfather's days. Maybe it would be true again in New York, a city with two professional baseball teams. But being a sports fan is a whole lot more fun when your team has a shot at winning. Given all the hype about me in the minors, Mets fans were thinking I could help turn some things around for them, maybe bring back some of the fun that had been sadly absent since the Mets' World Series season of 1969. Of course, I wasn't going to rescue the struggling franchise alone. That would take a team effort, literally. I was nineteen years old. But I could help. I knew I could. And I was about to learn something else: if I could do that for New York, there was almost nothing New York wouldn't do for me.

This was a city in search of a savior. Maybe it was wishful thinking. But coming into the 1984 season, a whole lot of Mets fans thought that savior might be me.

The Mets' idea was to let me get a taste of major-league life before I actually took the mound, especially in front of the home crowd in New York. Everyone knew what a pressure cooker Shea Stadium could be. Our first nine games that season — fourteen of our first seventeen — were away games. So I had some time to ease in.

We opened at Riverfront Stadium in Cincinnati on April 2. I'd grown up watching the Reds in spring training at Al Lopez Field. I'd played that one minor-league exhibition game at Shea, but this was my first time in a major-league park as a major-league player. I was totally in awe at how huge and perfect everything seemed. So that's what 46,000 people looked like? The center-field fence might have been in Cleveland or Chicago, it looked so far away. As I walked onto the turf, one of the first players I saw was Pete Rose. The legendary "Charlie Hustle" was walking from behind the batting cage directly over to me. When I was growing up in Tampa, Pete was like a god. I could still remember my father and his friends, grilling steaks in the backyard and laughing about how Pete terrified pitchers across the National League. Now he was reaching out to shake my hand, welcoming me to the majors.

"Hey, kid," he said. "You had a heck of a year, didn't you? Hope it continues. I look forward to facing you out there."

I told him I came from Tampa and had shaken his hand one day outside Lopez Field. He didn't remember that, of course. But he couldn't have been nicer. And I could hardly believe this wasn't a dream. I hadn't even played a game yet, and Pete Rose knew who I was.

"Good luck to you," Pete said.

"Thanks," was all I could think of to answer.

Clearly, I was a long way from Tidewater, Lynchburg, and Kingsport. I couldn't get over how the equipment managers and clubhouse kids made life so easy for us major-leaguers. Carrying our gear and our luggage. Straightening our lockers. Laundering our uniforms. After every game, a spread of chicken, steak, cold cuts, cheese, bread, vegetables, beer, and soda was waiting for us, even when we were the visiting team. If you wanted gum, it was right there. Sunflower seeds, right there. Chewing tobacco, right there.

Rookies had a few special chores to perform, our own little hazing ritual. Before we stepped onto the field, we were expected to fetch coffee for older stars like George Foster and Keith Hernandez. No one cared if I was a first-round pick. The rookie pitchers Ron Darling, Sid Fernandez, and I were responsible for lugging the balls out for batting practice.

After two games in Cincinnati — we won one, we lost one — we flew to Houston, where we won all three. I made my first major-league start on Saturday, April 7, in the Astrodome, four games into the season. The team flew my mom and dad to Houston to watch me pitch, laying on the full star treatment. The whole experience was exciting — for me and my folks. Someone gave Dad a hat and a satin Mets jacket, which I don't think he took off until he got back to Tampa — and maybe not even then.

I made it five innings and picked up the win. I pitched — not great but okay. I was nervous the whole time. But I guess I made an impression on the Astros' Ray Knight, who told reporters after the game: "His fastball explodes just like Nolan Ryan's." All in all, it was a fairly gentle initiation to major-league baseball.

"So what did you think?" my dad asked after the game. "Can you make it in the majors?"

"Without a doubt," I said confidently. "I should win a lot of games."

My second start, on Friday the thirteenth, was against the Chicago Cubs. Thirty-three thousand fans came out to Wrigley Field, wondering if all my advance billing was even close to true. I didn't make it past the fourth inning. We got stomped 11–2. This time, when I talked to my dad on the phone, all my old insecurities were back. I told him, "I don't know. I don't think I'm ready yet."

Chicago certainly didn't think I was. After the game, I told a local reporter I was a little irritated at the way the fans cheered so loudly as I jogged off the mound when I was yanked. I also said I didn't like the way the Cubs had run up the score. It was a dumb thing to say. The paper came out, quoting me calling the Cubs "hot dogs." The next day before the game, their shortstop, Larry Bowa, came over to me.

"Look," he said. "We weren't trying to show you up because you're a rookie or anything. It's just the way our fans are. They get excited when we start scoring runs." And he told me I should be more careful what I say to the writers. "Keep it boring and unemotional," he said. "Otherwise, you're just giving material to the other team."

Caution around the media wasn't a lesson I ever learned very well. Over the years, the reporters would get plenty of mileage out of me. But the experience in Chicago did make me want to shut down the Cubs every time I ever faced them again. I'm proud to say I almost did. My career record against the Cubs was 28–4. That was no accident.

When we finally got back to New York, I moved into the Marriott hotel across from LaGuardia Airport. Now planes were overheard during home games — and while I was trying to sleep. But not for long. A veteran pitcher, Ed Lynch, showed me around and helped me find a place to live. I landed in a quiet basement apartment in a small building in Port Washington, Long Island. It was about a twenty-minute drive to Shea Stadium, and lots of other players lived and partied nearby. Darryl Strawberry and his wife, Lisa, were a couple of blocks away.

On April 25 in Montreal, my fourth start of my rookie season, I felt I hit my stride. I was on the mound for seven innings against the Expos in a 2–1 pitching duel. My fastballs were smoking. My curveballs were dancing around. My control was solid. I got ten strikeouts and lots of bewildered looks. The game was tight and went extra innings. We didn't put the Expos away until Keith Hernandez doubled in the eleventh and sent in the winning run. But I really felt like a major-league pitcher that day.

In the locker room after the game, Davey Johnson and my teammates said over-the-top nice things about me. "He is way ahead of his years," I heard Davey telling the reporters. "He could have lost his composure today, but he didn't let adversity bother him."

"Once or twice in a lifetime, a pitcher comes along like Gooden," Keith said after the game. "Today was the best I've seen him throw. As the game progressed, he got better and better."

Wow! Some of this praise seemed a little overblown to me. But it definitely helped to build my confidence. We came back to New York, and I got my revenge on the hot-dogging Cubs, an 8–1 blowout. It was only May 1. I'd been in the majors just a month, and I already felt like I had found my groove. The fans just went crazy, and the sportswriters seemed to agree. That night, United Press International called me a "crowd-pleasing hero," comparing me with the Mets great Tom Seaver, who'd recently been scooped up by the White Sox: "While Seaver is still searching for his first victory with his new club, Gooden is rapidly growing into one of the top pitchers in the National League . . . Showing a 93-miles-per-hour fastball and a sharp-breaking curve, Gooden allowed only four hits over seven innings and struck out 10 for the second straight game."

Damn!

My only disappointment was that I didn't stay on the mound for all nine innings. After 120 pitches, Davey pulled me out. "I have to keep a close eye on your pitch count," he told me. "The same number of pitches here will take more of a toll than they did in the minors." Not all managers, I later learned, had Davey's understanding of that.

I just loved being out there. I'm not ashamed to admit that. The mound at Shea was starting to feel like a stage to me, a stage I was learning to command. As my rookie season revved up, the crowds grew larger, and I knew that a lot of people were coming out to see me. "Doc! Doc! Doc!" they would chant when I took the mound. And as my strikeout count rose, my old nickname morphed as well. Playing off the box score strikeout symbol, people started calling me "Dr. K." I thought it was funny when I heard that the first time. I had no idea it would stick. In late May or early June, I noticed a small group of fans had created a living scorecard in the front row of the upper deck in left field, right at the foul line. Whenever I pitched a strikeout, they would hang a big red "K" from the upper-deck railing where everyone could see it. "The K Korner," they called themselves, and the fans got a real kick out of that. It was the first place the TV cameras went when I struck out a batter.

My eyes went there too. I didn't want to be too obvious, but as the ball was being thrown around the infield after a strikeout, I often turned to left field, sneaking a peek and doing a quick tally of the Ks.

Strikeouts became almost an addiction for me — and for the fans. Once I'd get two strikes on a batter, the people would rise to their feet and begin clapping. The K Korner would start waving the next K in the air, taunting the batter and pulling me along. I figured the whole thing worked only to my advantage. It put extra pressure on the hitters. What self-respecting hitter would want to have his failure memorialized with yet another Shea Stadium K? If the pitch was even close and the hitter didn't swing, the umpire might be slightly more inclined to call a strike. A lot of times, unless I had two or three balls in a count, I would intentionally aim a hair out of the strike zone to make the hitter chase a pitch he was unlikely to reach.

The whole thing fed on itself. The more strikeouts I threw, the more the fans expected — and the more I expected from myself. Just as Davey predicted, my pitch counts tended high. But I didn't feel any soreness or discomfort in my arm. I only started icing it after games when I saw other pitchers doing that. I figured if the older guys were doing it, maybe a nineteen-year-old rookie should too. But the ice wasn't reducing any swelling or pain because, in my case, there wasn't any. Not yet.

As summer arrived, I was starting to feel almost like a rookie rock star, and the energy from the spectators only spurred me on. As I got to know the hitters better, I could tell when I had someone in the palm of my hand. Especially if I threw inside high and tight or knocked someone down early in the game, I could really see it in the hitters' eyes. Sometimes I'd notice a batter move his front foot out of the box just as I was releasing the ball. Once I saw a batter do that, I knew I could open up the outside part of the plate. I wanted the whole lineup to feel jumpy. Every few at bats, I'd throw something inside and hard. Even when the pitch was a mistake, I wouldn't let the batter know it. I didn't want anyone getting comfortable when they were trying to hit me.

It was exciting playing in front of the home crowds. But it was out on the road, spending time together, where I really got to know the other Mets players. The road is where we genuinely grew into a team. The closer we got, the more distinct the individual personalities became. Mookie Wilson, our switch-hitting center fielder, was always cheery and up for action. Left fielder George Foster, who'd been a hard-hitting part of the "Big Red Machine" in mid-1970s Cincinnati, brought a real slugger's swagger to our crew.

Second baseman Wally Backman would storm through the visiting team locker room like a growling dog, yelling that the guys we were playing were "horseshit" or "fucking pussies" who didn't have a chance against studs like us. Sometimes, he'd look at me and just shake his head.

"You know these fuckers are scared of you, don't ya?" he'd say about opposing batters. "Your fastball comes in at their belt and ends up near their face. Half the time they're swinging in self-defense. Use that to your advantage, Doc. Don't back down from anyone."

Ever since spring training, Darryl Strawberry had been working on my attitude. Two years older than I was, with way more life experience, Darryl specialized in attitude. "You're a professional now," he told me. "So carry yourself like one. Act like you belong here. Walk with your head held high."

Darryl and I often got compared with each other. But we were very different people. I was Tampa. He was LA. I'd grown up with a doting father. He'd barely known his. What I took as nice and friendly, he saw as naive and vulnerable. He could be a kind mentor one moment and a loose cannon the next, spewing random venom from the corner of the locker room or the back of the plane. Darryl had no problem communicating exactly what was on his mind, even if he wasn't always 100 percent certain what that might be. Frequently, he'd rip guys apart to reporters, then turn around the next day and quietly apologize. It took me a while to realize that if he was trash-talking other guys behind their backs, he might be doing the same to me.

Darryl and I had a lot in common. But I also had the sense that I might be complicating things for him as I staked out my own place on the team. A year before I'd shown up, he'd been the Mets' bright, shiny object of 1983, winning Rookie of the Year and crushing National League pitchers with twenty-six home runs. After I turned up, a lot of the talk wasn't just "Darryl" anymore. It was "Darryl and Doc." Once in a while it was even "Doc and Darryl" who were going to save the Mets. I don't think he really liked that.

Some of the older players could see that my confidence still didn't quite match up to my talent. They made genuine and generous efforts to help. During Mets at bats, first baseman Keith Hernandez would stand at the top of the dugout swearing at the opposing pitcher for some perceived injustice. Then when we were on the field, he was constantly advising me about what pitches to throw. Most of that season, I was throwing to a young catcher, Mike Fitzgerald, who didn't know the hitters much better than I did. Keith was a computer with a glove. He knew all the National League batters. He didn't need Ralph Kiner's TV stats. He had all the hitters' quirks obsessively cataloged in his head.

"Throw him fastballs down and away," Keith muttered into his glove as he strolled to the mound the first time I faced the Braves' six-foot-six power hitter Dale Murphy. "He gets caught chasing that shit. You make a mistake with that, he's only gonna hit a grounder anyway, if he even makes contact. Then throw him bad curveballs. Make him chase them."

Keith's intel was almost always right, as I learned when Dale sent my one breaking ball into the right-field seats.

When I wasn't pitching, Keith would hunt me down and point out little details I wouldn't notice on the mound. He demanded that I watch Mike Schmidt, the Phillies' Hall of Fame third baseman, "every fucking at bat, okay?"

"Take a look at his stance," Keith said. "When he spreads his legs, he gets extension with his arms. He's thinking fastball. When he stands more straight up? He's thinking curve." Keith's lessons never stopped.

Mike Torrez was the same way. A veteran player in his last year with the team, Mike had no hint of resentment at us younger guys coming up. "As long as I'm on the team, I'm gonna help you out," he told me. He was passionate about playing and teaching the game the right way. He often had me sit with him in the dugout. As the games progressed, there would be pop quizzes. He would stop and ask, "Okay, what would you throw in this situation?"

However I answered, Mike would ask, "Why would you do that?"

I felt like I was back in Tampa with my father, analyzing the game of the week. Mike's advice was ten times more useful than any scouting report. Keith and Mike were extraordinary resources, influencing how I pitched and, more important, how I thought about pitching.

Rusty Staub was just as generous, a real Mets great who still had a passion for baseball and always had time for me. Nearing retirement and mostly being used to pinch-hit, Rusty liked to get to the ballpark early, just like I did. We developed a ritual of going into the clubhouse and playing a card game called Casino. Once I started winning games and Rusty had a pinch-hitting streak, we had no choice but to keep playing. Both of us were too superstitious to stop.

Rusty tried to show me how to handle myself like a pro — on and off the field. His approach was exactly the opposite of Darryl's. In May, I got shelled by the Astros when they came to New York. Nolan Ryan, one of my real idols, pitched a complete game, and I was gone by the second inning. Before the game was over, I had already showered and dressed. I left the stadium without talking to any of the reporters.

The next day, Rusty pulled me into the trainer's room. He sat me down and gave me an earful. "You can't just leave like that," he said. "You're in front of your locker when you pitch well. When things don't go well, you still gotta be in front of your locker. Good, bad, or anything in between, you have to talk to the writers — even when you stink."

Like me, Rusty came up to the majors at nineteen and had to learn everything on the fly. He played 150 games his first year. It took him a while to become the great hitter he turned into. Truly, he pushed himself there. In me, I think he saw a young and naive ballplayer who could easily get eaten alive.

As a rookie, my salary was still $40,000, which wasn't bad for a single nineteen-year-old in 1984 who was being comped in all the New York restaurants. But Rusty was making seven or eight times that, and he didn't mind spending on elaborate meals. He took me to the legendary Chicago steakhouse Ron of Japan on Ontario Street. It was like Benihana, only better. It blew my mind when the chef came right out and started cooking at our table. Rusty ordered two or three dinners, then looked at me.

"Whatever we eat here, stays here," he said, winking. "It's nobody's business." I knew the team was on him to watch his weight. His secret was safe with me.

There were so many big-league rules to learn. It was Hubie Brooks who decided to share his grand-slam dating advice. Walking off the bus into the hotel in Montreal, Hubie tapped my shoulder and smiled.

"Lemme tell you a little somethin' about the road, Doc," he said. "You gotta learn this early, 'cause I don't want to hear about you getting tangled up in some bullshit."

"What do you mean?" I asked. We kept walking into the lobby, where a dozen young women seemed to be waiting for us. And it was still early in the day.

"Look around," he said, his eyes scanning the couches and chairs. "It's gonna be pretty easy to get laid out here, but it'll be a little bit tougher to stay out of trouble."

"Yeah?"

"You're gonna be going to a lot of cities," he explained. "You mess around with a gal, you can't let them think it means anything, right?"

"Sure," I said, "I hear you."

"So you pick one, then bang 'em and get 'em out of your room," he advised. "Politely. Don't lead them on. Don't give 'em any souvenirs. Don't cuddle excessively. God knows what can happen if some chick gets mad at you, hunting you down, claiming she's pregnant, or making up stories about you."

"Okay," I said. But this was all new to me. In the minors, there wasn't much of a groupie scene. Certainly not out on the road. There weren't too many women hoping to meet A-ball players from out of town. And we weren't staying in fancy hotels or unwinding in velvet-rope night-clubs. After games, we often got on the bus and drove to a truck stop for dinner or went straight to the next town.

I couldn't imagine I'd be needing Hubie's advice. As a rookie, I was much too shy to be trolling hotel bars for groupies. And I had a girl-friend. Carlene was coming up regularly. For me that first season, a big night of running around was a beer with Keith. But Hubie seemed eager to share.

"Some of the guys have an old reliable in a city," he went on. "You've been with her. She's cool. You can call her when you're in town and not expect a headache. Unless, of course, you replace her with a new old reliable, and she finds out."

Hubie just shook his head at that.

"Then you got fuckin' problems," he said.

I said thank you and left it at that.

Throughout April, May, and June, my fame was building in New York. But it was at the 1984 All-Star Game at Candlestick Park in San Fran-cisco where the national media got their first close look at me. For weeks, the New York reporters had been reminding me, "Kid, if you get in the game, you'll be the youngest ever to play in an All-Star Game."

I didn't want to start getting cocky. I'd been in New York just three months. But I got voted onto the team, and I was hoping I'd do some-thing more than warm the bench.

During an interview session with the players, one writer kept asking me: "Are you sure you're nineteen?"

"Yes," I said.

"You're the most mature nineteen-year-old I've ever seen. Are you really just nineteen?"

"Yes, sir. I'm sure."

I heard he called down to the Hillsborough County Health Depart-ment to get ahold of my birth certificate.

ABC had Howard Cosell interview me before the game. I was totally in awe of him and his long, complex questions like the ones he used to ask of Muhammad Ali.

"Excuse me, can you repeat that?" I had to ask the legendary broadcaster when he stopped for my answer. I was too busy staring. I hadn't paid attention to whatever he'd said.

With the All-Star Game, I really felt like I had arrived, arrived somewhere I hadn't even dared imagine I would be. There were Nolan Ryan and Mike Schmidt, Dave Winfield and Reggie Jackson, George Brett and all the others in the same ballpark. Some of them even complimented me, saying, "I hear you're tough to hit," or "You're off to a great career, keep it up."

I appreciated the kind words and the attention. But some of it made me feel strange. It wasn't that I had no faith in my pitching. I knew I could usually bring it on the mound. But people were starting to expect an awful lot from me, maybe even more than I could deliver yet.

I snapped at one sportswriter who called me great. "Don't use the word 'great' around me," I told him. "You can't be great until you've done it for ten years."

The National League manager Paul Owens sent me in to pitch the fifth inning of the game. Gary Carter, the sure-footed catcher for the Montreal Expos, caught me that day. With very little fuss, I struck out the side.

After the game was over, Gary came over and tapped my chest. "Man," he said, "wouldn't it be great to do this every fifth day?"

I didn't hesitate a second.

"Hell, yes, it would," I said.

6

Cy Season

FINISHED OUT MY ROOKIE year with a nice pile of numbers and a big boost in confidence. "I guess I can play at this level," I told my dad. At the end of the season, I was 17–9 with 276 strikeouts, the most ever by a rookie pitcher and the most I would ever record in my career. For my efforts, I was voted National League Rookie of the Year. Dad was impressed with the honor but not the trophy. "I thought for sure it would be a great, big, fancy thing," he told me with a shrug. "That doesn't look like much at all." The Mets hung with the Cubs as long as we could, but they won the East before losing in the playoffs to San Diego. Still, we gave the fans a genuine turnaround from 1983 and a reason to be hopeful about 1985.

I liked being in New York and spending time with my teammates. I really did feel like I was living the dream. But as soon as the season ended, I jumped on a plane to Tampa and moved back into the house with my mom and dad. That might sound weird, given the rush of what I'd just been through. But I missed them. Gary was around. Betty and Mercedes came over a lot. Forget all your stereotypes about professional athletes and their high-flying lifestyles. Many nights that fall and winter, the 1984 National League Rookie of the Year was sitting on the edge of his parents' double bed watching *The Cosby Show*, *The Jeffersons*, and *Good Times*.

I think my folks enjoyed having me around — except for the constant phone calls. Fans, reporters, agents checking my availability, high schools wanting me to talk to their students. That last one seemed strange to me. I was only two years older than the seniors. I didn't know anything about the world. A modeling agency even called, asking me to model some clothes. And girls were calling day and night, whether I was home or not. My dad got a kick out of that — before he got totally sick of it. "He sleeps this time of night, child!" I heard him say from the bedroom at three o'clock one morning. He offered to install a separate line in my bedroom. I convinced my parents to get an unlisted number.

One of those people calling the house was my new agent, Jim Neader, who was working with the Mets on a new contract for me. Jim told me the money was going to get a whole lot better. Just knowing that, I bought myself a new Mercedes 380 SE to drive in Florida and I sent my mom looking for the new house I'd been promising her since before I was throwing curveballs. She found a nice place on East Elm Street with four bedrooms — one for me — and a fenced-in backyard.

I'd go drinking sometimes with my friends from the neighborhood and Hillsborough High, but nothing remotely wild. I didn't have any need to prove I was still one of the guys. I hadn't been gone that long. Everything that was happening to me was so new and exciting, it was like it was happening to all of us. And I couldn't imagine risking what I hoped was coming next. I wanted to see if my rookie season was just a dream or not.

I was following the off-season news in the Tampa and St. Petersburg papers and talking on the phone with some of my teammates. Heading into the 1985 season, we traded Mike Fitzgerald, Herm Winningham, Hubie Brooks (gosh, who'd advise me about women now?), and Floyd Youmans to Montreal for Gary Carter. I was especially sorry to see Floyd slip away. He had still been on the Lynchburg farm team. But he and I had been playing together since Belmont Heights Little League, and he'd been drafted by the Mets right behind me. Still, after pitching to Gary in the All-Star Game, I knew what a phenomenal piece of the puzzle he could be. He seemed to like my throwing style, and I was certain he would draw the best out of me.

Just before spring training, Jim finalized my new deal, $275,000 plus $200,000 in bonus money. When I got back to New York, I bought an even fancier new Mercedes to drive up there, trading in my pimped-out Camaro Z28 for a silver 500 SEL with tinted windows and flashy rims. I moved into a larger, two-bedroom apartment in Roslyn, Long Island. I bought a nice new gold watch, and for my other wrist, a gold bracelet inlaid with diamonds.

For the first time in my life, I had real money, and I was learning to spend it.

Darryl, who'd been Rookie of the Year in 1983, and his wife, Lisa, came over a lot. When the Mets were at home, my girlfriend Carlene usually came up and stayed with me, although we did have a temporary roommate. It was Lenny Dykstra. Now came my turn to look after a rookie. I'd played with Lenny in Lynchburg and was with him at Mets spring training in 1984. This year, he got called up after the season started. I knew he was talented and completely nuts. I had no problem offering him my spare bedroom until he could land an apartment of his own. When we came back from an early road trip, he asked if his girlfriend, Terri, could stay for a few days.

"Knock yourself out," I said. I guess Lenny took that literally.

The night Terri arrived, the four of us went out for drinks together.

Then, we all headed home. As Carlene and I were settling into bed, we heard a giant racket in the other bedroom. It sounded like people screaming and maybe lamps being thrown.

"You should go check on them," Carlene said, nudging me out of bed. "It sounds like they're killing each other in there."

I could definitely hear some heavy stuff breaking. I didn't want the neighbors to call the police. I got up, put my clothes back on, and knocked. It took a minute. Then a sweaty but smiling Lenny opened the bedroom door a crack, looking like he'd just pulled up his jockey shorts.

"Everything okay in there?" I whispered.

"Sorry, dude," Lenny said. He called everyone dude. "I think I broke your bed. Actually, *we* broke your bed." Then he started laughing. "I hope you understand," he said. "Terri and I haven't seen each other for a while."

"Don't worry about it." I shrugged. Finally I understood why the fans called Lenny by the nickname "Nails." I knew he'd bring that same pounding passion onto the field.

Much has been written and said about my wins that season, my various records and awards. But it was the simple joy of playing well that I loved the most. I took the mound. I threw the ball. My fastball kept rising. My curveball got even filthier than it was. People had trouble hitting me. I struck a lot of them out. I had some good fielders behind me. And working the other half of the innings, our hitters put runs on the board. After a so-so 6–3 start, I won and I won and won.

And then I won some more.

In Gary Carter, I had the perfect partner to bring out the fire in me. I was quiet and focused on the pitcher's mound. He was the Energizer Bunny behind the plate. He was aggressive, and he never shut up. On the days I had my good stuff, he kept demanding more of it. On the days I struggled, he would pop his fist in his glove and yell at me:

"Come on, Doc! What the fuck are you doing? You're better than this!"

He had a single standard, and he always stuck to it. He wanted me to dominate. Every game, every batter, every pitch.

There is no stardom like New York stardom, and I was becoming a real New York star. After that 6–3 start, I began a breathless 18–1 run. It was a mad dash into the hearts of Mets fans, and it really wasn't even that hard. Even I could see what a hell of a year this was going to be. Fans were eager for my autograph. Kids kept asking for pictures with me. I was raised to be polite and accommodating. I always tried to oblige. Everywhere I went people shook my hand and knew my name.

"Hey, Doc," they'd say. "We're counting on you. We going to the playoffs this year?"

"I'll do my best," I told them.

The K Korner was becoming huge. Red Ks, black Ks, multicolored Ks — they were popping up all over the stadium, even some at away games. At Candlestick Park, it was black Ks on orange paper, Mets fans taunting the Giants in their own color scheme. The groupies weren't just lingering in hotel lobbies anymore. They were waiting for me outside the ballpark at Shea and away. One day, my sister Betty was walking out to the parking lot with me after a home game when a group of female fans rushed up. I think they were surprised I wasn't alone. "You're too old for him," one of them yelled disgustedly at Betty. "All you want's his money."

"I don't think they like me," she laughed as we got into the car and shut the doors.

The game crowds kept growing larger. The team noticed an attendance bump on the days that I pitched. Thirty, forty, sometimes fifty thousand people were coming to watch me work. It was all pretty head-turning for an awkward twenty-year-old.

Nineteen eighty-five was the year I learned I couldn't hide. The media knew me. The other teams knew me. The fans certainly did.

Almost everyone was being swept up in the story of the great young pitcher who brought it, the shy boy dominating the big leagues, the savior not just of a struggling baseball team but of the struggling city it symbolized.

I was tossed into a whirlwind of attention, endorsements, and fame. I signed a lot of contracts with big companies. Jim made deals for me with Polaroid, Kellogg's Corn Flakes, *Sports Illustrated*, Spalding, even Toys "R" Us. Major brands with major marketing budgets.

I shot a Diet Pepsi commercial with Catfish Hunter, the older pitcher showing the younger one how to throw an illegal pitch using moisture from the ice-cold can. Bruce Springsteen featured me in the video for "Glory Days." *Playboy* published my diary. I recorded a novelty rap song with the same guys who had written "The Super Bowl Shuffle" with the Chicago Bears. I told David Letterman no, even though I was a major *Late Night* fan. I was just too nervous to sit on Dave's couch. NBC asked me to host the season opener of *Saturday Night Live,* but I begged off on that, as well. They went with their fallback choice, Madonna. A gigantic photo of me went up at Pennsylvania Station. Underneath was my strikeout total, constantly kept up to date. This was getting ridiculous.

For sheer impact, nothing quite matched the mammoth Nike billboard that covered the whole side of a building just west of Times Square. To anyone standing on the Manhattan sidewalk, the ad looked shockingly huge. The question it asked was just as shocking:

"How does it feel to look down the barrel of a loaded gun?"

The first time my mom saw the billboard, she said the picture didn't look at all like me. I told her it came from my photo. But she held her ground. "I don't know," she said. "You look scary up there." The man on the side of the building, she explained, looked too fierce to be the nice boy she had raised.

I laughed and told her only my fastball was scary.

Everyone seemed to want a piece of me. My fame kept spreading, and not just to places that sports stars normally went. *Playgirl* magazine named me — *me!* — one of the "ten sexiest men" of 1985 along with *Miami Vice* star Don Johnson, ballet star Alexander Godunov, and actor Aiden Quinn. That made me feel pretty good — until I noticed who else was on the "sexiest" list: New York governor Mario Cuomo, *Nightline* anchor Ted Koppel, and fat-boy comedian John Candy.

Candy? Really?

I did my best to handle it all. That didn't come naturally to me. It was fun sometimes, having people telling me how great I was. But every time I heard that, I thought, "I know I have talent. But I don't think I'm as great as you think I am." Sometimes, I even said it out loud.

The praise kept pouring in. Jesse Orosco, my sometimes late-inning reliever, said I reminded him of Fernando Valenzuela. No, Gary Carter said. Think Bob Gibson. Mel Stottlemyre, the veteran pitching coach who'd worked with lots of major talent, said even Bob Feller wasn't this good at my age. Sandy Koufax said he'd trade his past for my future. Mickey Mantle said he wanted to be me. Davey Johnson pushed all the comparisons aside. My talent, he said, just was. "He has command of pitches and of himself," Davey told reporters one day. "He's a prodigy — that's all. Why try to define it? How can you define a prodigy?"

Some of this stuff got downright intellectual. George Will, the conservative essayist and brainy baseball fan, compared me with both the posse at the end of *Butch Cassidy and the Sundance Kid* ("Who are those guys — they're really good!") — and the fellow Washington brainiac Dr. Charles Krauthammer.

Will wrote, "We knew how baseball's lesser pitchers — which means all other pitchers — felt when they first glimpsed Dwight Gooden. They thought, He is unreasonably good, and it is unreasonable to doubt that he will get even better. . . . Like Gooden, Washington's Dr. K plays a game of inches — or precision."

Maybe someone who reads Will — or Krauthammer — can explain to me exactly what that means.

Even Richard Nixon weighed in.

"What's he going to be like when he's thirty?" asked the former political slugger who became a major Mets fan after leaving the White House and moving to New Jersey.

Was I the best pitcher in baseball — or the best pitcher who had ever touched his foot on the rubber and picked up a rosin bag? Was the Hall of Fame a lock already? Was there any stopping me? I didn't want to think about any of that. Couldn't I just play baseball?

Writer Peter Richmond managed to get it all into a single paragraph: "At the age of 20," he wrote, "Dwight Gooden is simply the best pitcher in baseball, and getting better. If all goes well for the next fifteen or twenty years, he'll be the best in the history of the game."

That was a big if. And frankly, I didn't know how to answer comments like that. I didn't want to seem unfriendly or unappreciative. I didn't want to brag either. Plenty of times, I just didn't know what to say, so I said as little as possible. "I hear comparisons with the great pitchers all the time," I told Richmond when he and I spoke in Cincinnati. "But I don't like to think about it. I just like to do the things I'm capable of doing. All I want to do is play baseball."

Often, when writers didn't get what they were looking for from me, they would go see my family, trooping one after another into my parents' living room. My dad would tell stories about me playing with the grown-ups when he managed the sandlot Tampa Dodgers. "Even as a boy," my father said, "he never lost his cool."

They'd ask Mom how she felt seeing me pitch now. "I'll be watching him and my stomach is turning," she told one writer. "But he's so calm. He's always been like that."

"You know," my sister Betty said in one interview. "He's so quiet, he'll say there's nothing wrong no matter what. The only way we know how good he's doing, if he's homesick or worried or whatever, is watching his face and how he pitches."

Despite it all, I was still just a twenty-year-old kid. I was old enough to be the best pitcher in baseball. But I still wasn't old enough to order a drink or even organize much of a social life.

That year, when we were on the road, Keith Hernandez would often find me and ask, "Doc, you pitching tomorrow?"

If the answer was no, that was all he needed to hear.

"Okay, you're coming out with us," he'd say.

We'd go out for dinner, then hit a couple of bars. At that time I was still basically just drinking beer. One night in Chicago, we were in a bar off of Rush Street and my Pepsi commercial came on the TV. The bartender looked at me, looked at the TV, then looked at me again.

"Hey, you're Doc Gooden!" he said.

I nodded. "Yeah."

"You know, you're not old enough to be in here," he said, turning suddenly serious.

I looked at him. Then I looked at Keith. Just as Keith was about to make a case for me, the bartender started laughing and said, "Go ahead. The drinks are on me. Get wasted. I hope the Cubs pound you."

They didn't of course. Not many teams did. I was aiming to win twenty-five games that season. By August 25, I was the youngest player ever to win twenty. That's what I cared about most.

By the time the season was over, I threw sixteen complete games, won twenty-four and lost four. It was the best pitching record in either the National or American Leagues. Attendance at Shea jumped by nearly one million from the previous year. It would keep on growing throughout the rest of the '80s, until we were the number one draw in the National League.

I won the Cy Young Award, declaring me the number one pitcher in the National League. I earned baseball's pitching Triple Crown, which is only given if a single player has the most wins and strikeouts and the lowest ERA. Maybe someone wins it every decade, if that.

I would never perform quite so well again.

But who was Dwight Gooden?

My mom and my sister put their fingers on something true, I believe. While my heat was terrorizing batters and making them jump back from the plate, I was still very much the shy boy from Tampa, awkward, lanky, sheltered, still unsure of myself. It just so happened I was burning up the National League. That didn't change who I was, who I had always been. It was almost like I was two people in one. That both those people could inhabit the same body was a conflict that wouldn't end quickly or well.

7

Party Time

W ANNA PARTY?" THE WOMAN in the black negligee asked me, the taller of the two.

She and her friend — I never learned either of their names — were lounging in my older cousin's bedroom on his mammoth king-size bed. The bedroom door was halfway open. I was sitting on a couch in the living room, peeking through the door. Bo, my cousin, had gone out to fetch me some pot.

My mother had always warned me about the "occasion of sin." My dad had a more colorful way of making the same point. "Lie down with dogs," he liked to say, "you might get fleas."

This was January 1986, between my second and third seasons with the Mets. I had plenty to feel good about. I was making excellent money. My $475,000 baseball package was about to jump to $1.3 million. The endorsement deals were still pouring in. After I won the Rookie of the Year and Cy Young Awards, and all the TV ads, people seemed to know me everywhere — not just in Tampa and New York, and not just sports fans. Mets fans were still talking about the dominant season I'd had. Even I felt like I'd pitched well. And the team was only getting stronger. In November, we'd traded with the Red Sox for lefty pitcher Bob Ojeda, a veteran starter who could bring new leadership to our rotation. We were slowly assembling a truly lethal lineup. It wasn't out of the question that we could go all the way.

So why was I feeling so bored?

My previous off-seasons, I'd been happy to sit around the house with my parents and have a few beers with my friends. Just waking up in the morning felt new and exciting to me. But now, for reasons I wasn't exactly sure of, I was having trouble getting used to the off-season pace. Had I finally begun to think of myself as a real big-leaguer? Had I been enjoying the faster New York lifestyle a little more than I thought? One hundred and sixty-two games a year, even if you're not an everyday player, is a frantic rhythm for anyone. During the season, I could work off my excess energy on the mound, then decompress on the off-days with my teammates. I had focus and purpose and regular demands on me. Now, not so much.

Tampa in the winter felt like a floating void. My high-school buddies weren't doing much of anything. Being around my parents' house just felt like more of the same. I was a big star now, a bigger star than I'd ever imagined I'd be. But that wasn't a job title with actual duties. It wasn't enough to fill all my days. I didn't have hobbies like a lot of ballplayers did. They'd play golf with business guys or fly around the world on hunting and fishing trips. None of that was part of my off-season routine. My dad would occasionally put together a team for a charity softball game. I played some neighborhood pickup ball. Other than that, my major form of distraction was drinking beers with my friends and driving around in cars, often with a six-pack in my lap.

Idle hands, idle minds: I can see now I was ripe for trouble. I had just turned twenty-one.

While I'd spent the spring, summer, and early fall playing and practicing baseball, my friends had been polishing their screwing-off skills.
They could turn doing nothing into a full-time job. Me, I needed a
schedule. I needed a focus. I still do today. When I was a kid I had my
dad filling hours with drills and practice. Then, I had Mel Stottlemyre
and Davey Johnson in my ear, reeling me in and pushing me along.
If not them, Keith Hernandez and Gary Carter. But sitting down in
Tampa, I was mostly on my own. I needed to be told I'd be pitching in
two days in San Diego. All I had back home was time and my aimless
friends. I hung out some with my dad. But mostly, I drove to the projects, picked up my friends, then cruised around. By January, even that
was tiresome. I couldn't wait for spring training to begin.

I had tried smoking weed before. It only made me hungry and sleepy.
But I thought I might give marijuana another chance. Maybe this time,
it would ease the restlessness I was feeling, or at least mellow me out. So
I drove to my cousin Bo's house. I knew that he would have some.

He was a cousin from my mom's side of the family. He traded in pot,
cocaine, and women. It was a little strange, my relative being a pimp
and drug dealer. But that's what Bo was. When I got to his house, he
said he was totally out of weed — but, no problem, he'd be right back.

"Yeah, great," I told him half distractedly.

Looking past Bo's shoulder, I could see two of his ladies fooling
around with each other on the bed.

From what I could tell, they were probably ten years older than me,
and they looked like they could be the backup dancers at a Prince con-
cert. The taller one was dark-skinned, trim, and small-breasted. The
other one was lighter and shorter, all tits and butt. Bo caught me staring into the bedroom.

"Don't pay any attention to them, Doc," he cautioned me. "You don't
want to get tangled up in that. Sit down on the couch. Watch some TV.
I'll be back before you know it."

I grabbed a beer and sat. I left the TV off.

In a minute, I could hear the ladies giggling in the bedroom. I looked up, and I could see them making out. The shorter one, I could see, had on purple-colored underpants, white boots, and nothing else. Through the door, I could see one of the women grab a handheld mirror and tap some white powder out of a little baggie. The tall girl used an ID card to push the powder into lines. I was mesmerized by their attention to detail — almost as much as I was mesmerized by them.

I'd heard people mention cocaine in Tampa. It sounded like a scary drug to me. I had the sense, without really knowing, that people sold it in the projects. No one on the team had ever offered me any, and the topic only came up a few times. When outfielder Jerry Martin joined the team from Kansas City my rookie season, everyone knew he'd been arrested the previous October for buying cocaine. Along with Willie Wilson, Vida Blue, and Willie Aikens, he'd served ninety days in a minimum-security prison. Commissioner Bowie Kuhn suspended Jerry for a year but then turned around and reduced his suspension. None of the other Mets seemed concerned about any of it.

It wasn't like drug use in sports was a shocking idea. In 1985, six Pittsburgh Pirates — Dave Parker, Lee Lacy, Dale Berra, Lee Mazzilli, John Milner, and Rod Scurry had been called before a Pittsburgh grand jury and questioned about drug use in professional baseball. Their testimony led to drug trials, which made headlines. UPI called baseball's drug problem the "number one sports story of 1985."

The team owners and the Major League Baseball Players Association began negotiating a drug policy, but those talks went nowhere. "These guys must think they're dealing with the sugar plum fairy," complained Yankees owner George Steinbrenner, who was pushing for mandatory drug tests. "We have players that need help and the union is trying to pretend that no one is using drugs." Union president Donald Fehr said the players felt insulted by the owners' "guilty until proven innocent" approach.

In December, while I was hanging around Tampa, the union did take one step: publishing a children's coloring book called *The Pros Say It's O.K. to Say No to Drugs*. It had messages from forty players—including me.

Given where I was heading, is that ironic—or what? The Dwight Gooden page said: "If anyone tries to give you drugs, say NO! and tell your mom or dad."

If only I'd followed my own advice!

But if I'd been scared of coke, all of a sudden the potent white powder seemed like something sexy women did. And these two seemed to have the mechanics down cold. Chopping up the powder. Lining it up just so. Taking long sniffs, first one nostril, then the other. Then they busted me.

"Come on in," Miss Negligee said with a laugh.

She had just finished snorting a line of powder. She looked up from the mirror and pushed one of her nostrils closed and gave an extra sniff. She smiled and offered me her straw.

She asked if I wanted to party.

"No thanks," I said.

I was still nervous about messing with cocaine. I wasn't even sure I knew how to use the drug. "I'm all right," I said.

There were two beautiful, half-naked women on a bed in front of me, and you couldn't call them inhospitable. I was shy, but I was also a guy. I was just hoping they'd transition away from the drugs toward something I knew a little more about.

"You're in the major leagues, right?" the shorter, lighter-skinned woman asked, smiling at me.

"Yeah," I said, taking another sip of my beer. "I pitch for the Mets."

"Ooooh," the other one said eagerly. "Come on over. We won't tell anyone."

Pretty soon, the three of us were all doing vodka shots, as I joined them on the bed. Then the coke came back out. They certainly seemed to be having fun with it. When they asked me again, I was in.

"I'll try a little bit," I said with a smile. I was nervous as hell. But I wasn't there for the coke. At the time, it felt like nothing more than a way to connect with these two sexy women. I dragged my finger along the credit card, picking up some coke dust, then put it on my tongue. My face got numb. It felt weird but also good. They saw this and smiled.

Then, I snorted some cocaine, and it was love at first sniff.

The shy-and-laid-back Dwight was a different person that night. Confident, relaxed, actually social. Alcohol had been my release from stress and pressure. But compared to cocaine, drinking was nothing. Cocaine was a jet, and beer was a rickety trolley. Coke gave me a feeling I'd always wanted but didn't know how to find. It convinced me immediately that nothing else mattered at all. No pressure. No worries. No need to stop. I had never heard that cocaine had calming properties. But that night it made me feel calm. The drug hit quickly, and I had no confusion. This is how I wanted to feel.

I fooled around with the girls. It was a lot of fun. We drank and did more coke. They really seemed to like me. I know I liked them. Between the snorting, they took turns making me feel good. Then about an hour after he'd left, my cousin came back. He took one look in the bedroom — I was sweating and talking a mile a minute — and he knew what was up. He started yelling at the girls. Then he looked disgustedly at me.

"I know you didn't do what I think you did," he said.

"I only did a little," I lied.

"Here," he said furiously, handing me the pot. "I got some weed for you. Take it and get the hell out of here. Get your act together."

"I don't need that anymore," I said to him, grinning now. "I want what they got."

He glanced at the girls and shook his head at them. "I can't believe you got him messed up on that stuff," my cousin said. "What the — ?"

"So can you give me what I want?" I interrupted. After the hour I'd just had, weed seemed pointless.

"Can't do that, cousin. You know better."

"If you don't give it to me," I said, "I'll go find it myself."

After more arguing and pleading and a quick good-bye to the girls, I left my cousin's house empty-handed and met up with one of my friends. Sure enough, he told me where I could score some cocaine.

I don't think it would be correct to say I got addicted to cocaine after just that one experience. That would come gradually, over time. All I know is I liked what it did for me that night, liked it more than I ever imagined I would. And I wanted more of it.

The next day, I didn't come down very hard at all. I just felt a little tired. When I saw my dad at home, I didn't want to look at him. I didn't want him knowing what I had done. I didn't like that feeling. But I didn't hate it as much as I liked the rush I got from cocaine.

Within a couple of weeks, I was a seasoned user. I didn't start using every minute or every day. Cocaine didn't fill my days like a job or a hobby would have. But cocaine was never entirely out of my mind again. It got me through to the second week of February.

When I reported for spring training, I took a look around, and I was pretty sure that a couple of my teammates were doing coke like I was. Maybe I was only wishing, but I don't think so. When we were out at night, I'd see them disappear at unexpected times and come back just looking different. No one came out and said anything. Not at that point. I figured they didn't want me to know they were doing it. I sure didn't want them to know that I was.

I couldn't always hide it, not if anyone was paying close attention. There were days when I was visibly messed up. Pitcher Ed Lynch, who was eight years older than I was and had been around a little more, stopped by my locker one afternoon. He sized me up and down and just shook his head.

"What?" I asked him.

"You know what, man," he said.

I didn't make eye contact with him for the rest of the day. I'd just signed a new contract for over a million dollars. I knew coke could be dangerous. I guess I still had my mother's voice bouncing around in my head. When I was a kid, every time there was a story in the paper about drugs, she made me read it. "Don't be messing around with drugs," she would say. "If I ever catch you, sure as I'm sitting here, I'm gonna let them put you in reform school."

By this point, there was far too much at stake for me. I'd been doing too well to risk blowing it. Everyone was certainly expecting a lot. The general sentiment around the organization seemed to be: "If Gooden wins twenty-plus games again, and Ron Darling and Sid Fernandez and our other starters can win twelve or thirteen games each, we should be okay."

Only twenty-plus? That was a lot of wins, I thought — and a lot of pressure. Could I really do that again?

I felt dominant. My arm felt strong. There was no reason I couldn't match last year and then some. But going into the season with those expectations did take some of the fun out of baseball in my mind. It certainly added to the pressure. It played to my old insecurities and made the game feel more like work. How come I didn't feel like that in '84 and '85? Maybe I hadn't set the bar so high yet. The sportswriters sure hadn't. But now they had.

On opening day of the 1986 season, we played the Pirates at Three Rivers Stadium in Pittsburgh. I pitched a complete game, struck out six batters, and we won 4–2. When the game was over, the first question from reporters was: "What happened today? You only had six strikeouts."

Damn, I thought! Didn't they notice I won the game?

All I could think of as I left the ballpark that afternoon was: "Man, I could use some cocaine.

8

Series Season

NINETEEN EIGHTY-SIX WAS THE year it all came together for the New York Mets and it all started to unravel for me. Nothing dramatic at first. Just some troubling hints.

The year got off to an awkward start. Frank Cashen, the Mets' general manager, blew up at me in January when he heard I was walking on crutches in Florida. I'd been tossing a ball with my nephew Gary, and I'd sprained my ankle. I didn't think anything of it. I iced the ankle and used the crutches as a precaution. But Frank's comment to the Mets beat reporters—"right away, you start to wonder about the severity"—raised some early questions about what I might be trying to hide.

Nothing. I sprained my ankle throwing with Gary.

In the first week of April, I missed a preseason game. A friend was driving me to the training facility in St. Petersburg when another car ran us off the road. We didn't crash. We didn't even make contact. I wasn't hurt. The police weren't called. But especially after the crutches questions, Davey thought I hadn't given him a proper heads-up. "Doc, you gotta tell me *everything*," Davey had said, before hitting me with a $500 fine.

Five games into the season, with the team 2–3, the Mets' front office woke up to my picture on the cover of the New York *Daily News.* "I AM NOT A VIOLENT PERSON," the headline said. The story described a loud disagreement at a Hertz rental car counter at John F. Kennedy International Airport, where I'd been returning a car with my sister Betty and my girlfriend, Carlene. I don't know why I got so angry at the Hertz clerk. But I did call her a stupid bitch when I thought she was giving Betty and Carlene an unnecessarily hard time. That was stupid of me. I lost my cool. Like it or not, I just had to realize I'd be under a whole new level of scrutiny now. At the level I was playing, my private life would never be private again.

The next day in the locker room, the reporters didn't have any baseball questions for me. I still hadn't come to grips with the new reality. "Everyone seems like they're waiting for the first thing you do," I complained. "Anything — and then, *boom!* It's a big issue." You can imagine how well that went over.

I didn't slide into a deep, dark hole and stay there. And the difficulties I had that year were more than matched by the triumphs my team and I had on the field, successes I still feel proud of. If you look at the statistics from that Series-bound season, you'd have to say that, overall, I pitched quite well, best on the team, among the best in baseball. In 1986, I won seventeen games and lost six. My two hundred strikeouts were fifth in the National League. At various points that season, I had an ERA lower than any other pitcher's. That summer, I became the youngest pitcher ever to start in an All-Star Game. I was twenty-one years, seven months, and thirty days old. All through the regular season, I was the Mets' ace, even if I was sometimes an unsteady one.

If it weren't for 1985, I'm convinced 1986 would have been nothing but bows and backslaps for me. It's just that, given where I'd set the bar — and where the fans and sportswriters were now setting it for me — my good that year never felt quite good enough. Not to me. Not to the celebrating Mets fans.

I won five of my first six starts, including a complete-game two-hitter against Houston on May 6. Then something happened I definitely wasn't used to. I slid into a slump. Not a deep one — but for me, it qualified. I wasn't used to having any. My next eight games, I went 3–3 with two no-decisions. After the shutout against the Astros, my ERA was 1.04. It crept up quickly to 2.58.

The loss I really hated was June 18 in Montreal, 7–4. I walked six batters in six innings, the most I'd walked since my rookie season in 1984. That night in Montreal, Tim Wallach became the first batter ever to hit two home runs in one game against me. To make the sting even worse, my childhood pal Floyd Youmans was pitching for the Expos. When Floyd and I met for dinner after the game, he shrugged and said: "So you're not Superman."

I didn't like to hear it. But he had a point. I was learning that I might not be. Two days later, the Associated Press asked, "What's wrong with Dwight Gooden?"

A pattern began to develop. No matter how well I was pitching, I was putting more pressure on myself. Was I as good as last year? I wondered. Was my Cy Young year a fluke, or was something really inside me, something repeatable? The K Korner was restless. The fans wanted strikeouts — more strikeouts. I found myself worrying more about strikeouts than who I was facing at the plate. I hated seeing sports page headlines that read: "METS WIN, BUT GOODEN ONLY FANS FIVE."

Even though my mom knew nothing about fastballs, I needed someone to talk to. I called her one day when I was feeling low. "Maybe I can't do it again," I said.

She knew me better than anyone. She'd seen me doubt myself many times before. She knew I needed a shot of confidence. "If you did it," she told me, "that means it can be done. And if it can be done, you can do it."

No one could do that for me like my mom.

To this day, I have tried to pinpoint how much my off-time drug use affected my on-field performance — and exactly when the damage began. And how much was I hurt by overusing my arm or other causes? I am haunted by those questions even now.

But give the coke credit: it helped me shove some of that pressure and anxiety aside. I didn't use every day or even every other day. But as the season rolled on, my use slowly began to escalate. A friend of mine from Tampa hooked me up with a connection in New York on Long Island. Whatever I needed, he could supply. I knew enough not to get high the day or two before a pitching start. But once in a while after I pitched, I'd go out that night and party, drinking and using cocaine. I was sliding predictably out of control.

In between starts, instead of calling home and catching up with my family, I began hanging out and going to parties and nightclubs with my new druggie friends. If Carlene wasn't around, I'd run around with women I had met in clubs on Long Island. These weren't the kinds of women I would date and bring home to meet my mom in Tampa. But they were happy to go out with me, get high, and fool around. Once in a while, I'd go into Manhattan to a club called Bentley's, where the women and the drugs were even looser. My life off the field was becoming booty calls and blow.

Tim Raines, the great base-stealing outfielder for the Expos, has said that his drug problem grew so severe in Montreal that he kept coke in his pocket and sometimes did lines during a game. That could be true. I don't know. I know there's been similar speculation about me, that I played while I was high on cocaine. But me? High on the field in '86 or ever? No way.

I would have been far too hyper and jittery out there. My precision would have been shot. All those people watching me. The paranoia setting in. I'd have made that second wild inning against Pittsburgh look like a model of ball control.

And then there would have been the issue of stopping. When I did coke, I could never do just a line or two and say, "Enough." I'd have been sneaking into the dugout, snorting lines every inning or two. I'd have been wrecked by the sixth, for sure.

People look back on the 1986 Mets and say, "Now that was one wild group of guys!" We were young. We were loaded with talent. We had a city that loved us and fans who were desperate to win. We were an in-your-face team for an in-your-face city, perfectly matched with the times. Brawling with opposing players. Tearing up the nighttime across the National League. Stomping around New York with attitude and bravado. Rioting inside our own team plane. Someone even told some crazy story about slicing off the head of a cat. That one never happened.

I hate to undermine our bad-boy image, but here's the truth: most of what we did that season really wasn't all that wild. Darryl, Lenny, Ron, and I — when we got together on an off-night or after a game, we weren't doing much more than drinking or playing poker. We weren't exactly known for being faithful to the women in our lives. Our wives and girlfriends had plenty of reason to be mad. When they were away, we did meet other women in bars. We did take some of them home with us, sometimes two and three at a time. We boasted about our conquests, the way idiot clueless guys have done as long as there have been idiot clueless guys. And sometimes, we got caught.

One time in St. Louis, there were these two girls — they were sisters. Darryl and I had met them before and we'd messed around. Carlene didn't make this particular trip but Darryl's wife, Lisa, did, so he couldn't hook up with the sisters. They were both mine. The next morning, I was in the hotel room with the girls. I heard a knock at the door. I was still half asleep. I thought it must be housekeeping. I didn't even look through the peephole. I just opened the door.

It was Carlene! In St. Louis! At my door!

"Oh, shit!" I thought. But she was already marching past me and into the hotel room. She saw the girls in the bed. She broke down in tears. There was no way to explain. She shot back out of the room and got a flight back home. The sisters totally flipped out.

"Should we leave?" one of them asked.

"Yeah," I said. "You probably should leave."

I knew Carlene and Darryl's wife, Lisa, were close friends. I knew there was only one way Carlene would've flown halfway across the country without telling me first. I asked Darryl if he told Lisa about me and the sisters.

"I didn't tell her to tell Carlene," he said. "I just told her, 'Doc's got these girls staying with him in his room.'" As tight as Lisa and Carlene were, he had to know that wouldn't stay secret for long. But wasn't Darryl my friend? As far as I was concerned, friends—let alone team-mates—don't do that to each other.

All I could think was, "Thanks, Darryl."

We were aggressive young men with money in our pockets and tes-tosterone to burn. But in a funny way, we were all still fairly young and innocent. I know I was. Drinking, carousing, staying out late—that was just our way of letting loose and having fun. That and a little drug use on the side.

We were much more a team of drinkers than of druggies. Through-out the season, I never saw cocaine on the team plane or shared in hotel rooms. People did drugs the way I did—alone or with friends from outside. We kept that stuff separate and quiet and to ourselves. I thought I was being discreet, the way most drug users do, I guess. But word was obviously trickling around the leagues: some players were doing more than getting drunk at night. And my name was one of the ones that kept coming up.

During the second half of the season, Gene Orza and Donald Fehr from the Major League Baseball Players Association called me in for a meeting. I went to their office in Manhattan.

"There are rumors out there that you're hanging out in the wrong places, doing illegal stuff," Gene said. At a charity dinner that summer, Commissioner Peter Ueberroth had told Ray Knight that he'd heard a black superstar on the Mets was doing illegal drugs. Ray had asked Darryl about it. Without hesitation, Darryl had said, "It's Doc."

The reality is it could have been either one of us. It could have been players of a different race, as well. Darryl was just savvy at deflecting it, then later denying he'd said anything. Naturally, when confronted by the union heads, I denied it. I didn't point a finger at Darryl or anyone else. I just said it wasn't me.

"Will you take a urine test?" Donald wanted to know.

I stalled. "I'll think about it," I said.

I asked Jim, my agent. He said I was under no obligation to do a urine test. Jim was a nice guy and had no power over how I conducted myself. He didn't pry into what was going on.

Afterward, the Mets never officially called me in for a talk or anything. Davey came up to me once before a game and asked if everything was okay, and I told him I was fine. Obviously, it wasn't. But that was as far as it went. I had fairly open relationships with Davey and pitching coach Mel Stottlemyre. I felt like I could tell them almost anything—except for the truth about this.

Even with all that swirling around, I could still get out there and really pitch. We clinched the National League East on September 17, a night game, with a 4–2 win over the Cubs in front of 49,989 crazed Mets fans at Shea. I pitched all nine innings. I was smokin', and I don't mean pot. That was one of my very best moments in baseball, ever. From the sixth inning on, the fans were on their feet. We'd laid the foundation over the past three seasons. They could hardly wait to taste the rewards.

The fact that I could deliver that is something I have never stopped feeling grateful for.

The Mets hadn't won anything since 1969. Hadn't been to the post-season since 1973. The dugout was full of Mets executives and their families. Cops with helmets were waiting off to the side of both dugouts and stationed all the way around the field. The last out was Chico Walker, a lefty. I got him to a 1–2 count. Keith Hernandez came over to the mound and shouted "fastball" emphatically. I ended up throwing Chico a curve, one of the few times I didn't take Keith's advice. Chico hit a ground ball to Wally Backman at second base. Wally fell to his knees to secure the ball, making absolutely sure he didn't bobble or lose it. Then he threw to first, easily getting Chico out. As Keith caught Wally's throw, one of the first fans on the field was already running past him. Even before Chico was officially called out, two dozen people jumped the wall and were out on the field. There were so many people out there, Keith joked to me later, he figured if Wally hadn't stopped the ball, one of the cheering fans would have.

In my excitement, I raised my arms and looked at Gary Carter, who was running toward me. By then, fans had already stolen his mask and helmet. But instead of waiting for Gary, I turned and tried to run off the field. Thousands of fans were rushing toward us. Darryl lost his glove. Many of the players instinctively grabbed the caps off their heads, hoping to save them. But that was mostly futile. The caps were snatched and gone. I was hugged, then tackled and nearly buried alive. I looked up and realized I was at the bottom of a growing human pile. I was happy. Then, all of a sudden I was on the ground and scared. I couldn't get up for what seemed like forever but was probably forty-five seconds at most. I didn't know who was on top of me. At one point, Keith jumped onto the pile. Davey sent police to the mound to rescue me. But it was Greg Pavlich, our bullpen coach, who managed to swat some of the fans away. He pulled me up from the pile, and we made a mad dash to the dugout, where anyone who dared to enter was assaulted with ice, water, talcum powder, beer, shaving cream, and green dye. "I don't think they know how to celebrate," Davey said, some mystery liquid dripping down his face. "It might be more dangerous in here than out there."

We went to Houston to face the Astros and their star pitcher Mike Scott in the playoffs. If they were going to beat us, it'd be on his shoulders. He had over three hundred strikeouts that year, pitched in the All-Star Game, and would go on to win the Cy Young Award — not to mention the MVP of this playoff series. He had a ninety-one-mile-an-hour fastball, but that wasn't as intimidating as the rumors that he scuffed the ball. All season long, people tried to catch him. But they never did. All I know is that whatever he was doing, the ball danced like a Wiffle ball. We had a lot of hard-charging characters on our team, but the idea that he scuffed the ball turned them into butter.

I pitched against Mike in game one and gave up a homer to Glen Davis in the second inning. I lasted eight innings without giving up another run. But we couldn't hit Mike and lost 1–0. Guys were frustrated, inspecting the balls, complaining to the ump, you name it. I used the same balls Mike did. I could see that some of them were scuffed. But Mike looked clear, and no one could prove otherwise.

We won the next two, then lost one — to Mike Scott again. The series was tied 2–2 when I went against Nolan Ryan in game five. For me, it was a dream come true. Nolan was a pitcher I'd watched on Saturday afternoons in complete awe with my dad ten years earlier. He was such a dominant pitcher that coming to the plate to face him made my knees turn to jelly. He wasn't even that big of a guy. He had big legs and a high kick, and that's where most of his power came from. It was a long game. Neither one of us, Nolan or I, was willing to go to the showers. I went ten innings, gave up two runs, and didn't get the decision.

Gary Carter saved us in the bottom of the twelfth with an RBI single, scoring Wally Backman and getting the win. Up 3–2.

We flew back to Houston to play game six the very next day. This was really our game seven. If we lost, we'd be going back up against Mike Scott, and he was deep inside our heads by then. We all had the same feeling. We weren't going to hit the guy. Talk about losing the game even before you get out there! Our only chance was to avoid playing the game. The Astros jumped out to an early 3–0 lead on us in one of the most nerve-racking playoff games of all time, and I wasn't even pitching. It took us sixteen innings to finally put the Astros away, 7–6. Jesse Orosco came in and somehow picked up his third win. We were going to the World Series at last.

The game had run so long, from 3:05 to 8:30, we had to rush from our lockers to William P. Hobby Airport. The only time we had to celebrate was on our chartered plane back to New York. Which we did. With gusto. Beers came out. Then little bottles of the hard stuff. Then people started throwing slices of cake. Then one of the players' wives threw up in a seat back, and Darryl thought it might be fun to see how far back an airline seat could really recline. The answer? All the way back to flat, if you pushed it hard enough and broke the back off. By the time we got off, the whole cabin was smeared with food and alcohol and worse. Two rows of seats were destroyed. It looked like someone had tipped over a dumpster in there on Mardi Gras Day.

United Airlines sent Frank Cashen a bill for $7,500, which under the circumstances was fairly moderate, I thought. Frank marched the bill down to the clubhouse. He presented the bill to Davey in front of everyone.

"This is disgraceful," Cashen said. "And I'm not paying for it. You guys are."

Davey allowed him to finish and let a moment of silence pass. "Is that all, Frank?" he said.

It was, and Frank left the room. Then Davey spoke to the team.

"Do you have any idea how much damage we caused on that plane?" he asked. "Any idea? Would anyone like to explain? Does anybody have anything to say?"

No one said anything.

I looked at Darryl. He looked stone-faced. I noticed Wally staring at his feet.

"What are we going to do about this?" Davey asked, sounding like a very angry fourth-grade teacher after the class had just pulled some totally boneheaded prank. "What should we tell Frank? What do you think?"

Still no one said anything.

"In that case," Davey continued, "you know what I think? I think in the next four games, you guys are gonna put a shitload of money in this team's pocket, more than enough to cover this bill. So fuck this bullshit."

He tore up the bill, and then he tossed it away. And the Mets front office didn't bring up the issue again. We had a World Series to play.

I wish I could say I had something left by the time we played the Red Sox. But the truth is I was done. Tired. Sore. At my limit. Totally out of gas.

That season, I had thrown over 250 innings. Against the Astros, I'd given up three runs across eighteen innings of ball with no room for error at all. By the time I got to the World Series, my arm and my body had hit a wall. I had never experienced anything like it before.

The Red Sox had the kind of lineup I usually liked to face. With the exception of lefties like Wade Boggs and Rich Gedman, they were heavy with right-handed power-hitters like Jim Rice, Don Baylor, Dwight Evans, and Dave Henderson. Guys like that normally feed into my high fastballs and breaking balls out of the zone.

But not now.

Had I been at the top of my game, I could have gone to town on them. Instead, I had nothing to show. Even when I got ahead in the count, I couldn't put them away.

We lost game one at Shea, 1–0, a real pitching duel between Bruce Hurst and Ron Darling. I opened game two against Roger Clemens. But my fastball wasn't the same. I had no bite on my curve. I started going for location, just trying to get outs. Nothing I tried was working. I wanted to pull my hair out. I was shelled for six runs on eight hits in five innings. This was the World Series, the biggest stage of all. Dr. K couldn't K that Sunday afternoon. The Red Sox were up on us, 2–0.

After we lost the first two games at home to the Red Sox, the whole World Series could have easily slipped away. We had to travel to Fenway Park in Boston for the next three straight. We were mentally and physically flat. People kept telling us — we kept telling ourselves — "It's the World Series. You should be up for it." But those six games against the Astros took a lot out of all of us, not just me.

After blowing those first two games, the second with me on the mound, we had a day off before game three. Davey looked at us sulking in the clubhouse before we left Shea. He could always read us.

"I don't want anyone coming in here tomorrow," he said sternly. "Just get the hell out of here. Forget about baseball."

His words took some of the pressure off. Then Lenny Dykstra opened game three with a home run, the first of four runs in the first inning, and got us going again. Bobby Ojeda outpitched Oil Can Boyd for a great 7–1 Mets turnaround. Then, in game four, Gary Carter's two home runs and Ron Darling's seven shut-out innings evened the series at two.

I came back in for game five, and I stunk just as much as I had in game two. I hated the way my arm felt. I tried pushing through on World Series stamina and adrenaline. None of it worked. I gave up four runs on nine hits in just four innings. Even Sid Fernandez's strong relief wasn't enough. That was the end of me in the series. A 4–2 loss sent us back to Shea trailing the series 3–2.

Luckily, my teammates did what they had to without me. They looked inside themselves. They pulled back from defeat again. They remembered what the Mets were made of. The moment everyone remembers is Mookie Wilson's grounder through Bill Buckner's legs in the bottom of the tenth in game six, forcing game seven. Everything that happened during that at bat, from Bob Stanley's wild pitch that scored Kevin Mitchell to Mookie's staying alive to hit that bouncing roller up the first base line, was magical. Shea Stadium erupted and shook so much, I bet they felt the rumble in Manhattan. Game seven was a heart-pounding, come-from-behind 8–5 win, but compared to that ball through Bill Buckner's legs, the play was almost anticlimactic.

Now it was time to celebrate.

The champagne came out in the locker room.

The party began.

A parade was set for the morning.

I wanted a sniff of cocaine.

9

Off-Season

WHEN I WENT HOME TO TAMPA after the World Series win, I didn't go *home* home like I had the past four years. I went wild celebrating. For two weeks, I hung out with friends, stayed late in clubs, bought drugs, and rented hotel rooms to do those drugs in with people I'd met at those clubs. Actually, it was more than two weeks. The whole off-season was one big blur — an aimless, messy, sometimes violent blur. Not all of it was my fault. Not everyone around me behaved well. But I was the one who put myself in that position, and I was a walking target for trouble.

In past off-seasons, I'd spent hours watching sports with my dad, going to my nephews' games, even catching the occasional wrestling match. Not this year. I barely took the time to drop my bags off at home before heading out on a weeklong bender. And then another. And another. I was dying to prove something to my friends back home: even though I'd won the World Series, even though I was earning big money and living in New York, I was still just a regular guy. I tried to prove that by being stupid and never going home.

Zero father-son time. A desire to prove myself to people still hanging around from high school. It was a bad combination. Dad didn't complain. That wasn't his way. But as November rolled on without much sign of me settling back in, Mom grew concerned. On one of the rare occasions that our paths crossed at home, she shot me a puzzled look. "Why don't you hang out more with your dad?" she asked.

I felt guilty hearing her say that. I told her we'd be spending more time together real soon, just as soon as I caught up with my friends and went to see Monica Harris, a girl in Tampa I'd just started dating after Carlene and I decided to break up at the end of the World Series. Or Debra. Debra Hamilton was a local girl I'd gotten involved with, briefly, in 1985. She was one of several. But Debra got pregnant, and Dwight Gooden Junior was born on March 8.

Even Harold, my sister Betty's husband, lobbied me. "Your mom mentioned to me that she and your dad are concerned about you," he whispered one day when I went to their house to catch an NFL game—or half of one, anyway. Harold was careful not to embarrass me or make a big deal in front Betty and Gary.

"I'm doing fine," I lied.

"Dwight, they never see you," he pleaded. He looked me up and down. "Is everything okay?"

"Yes, Harold," I said, smiling at him. "I'm twenty-two." I had him there.

"Slow down, Doc," he told me, glancing over my shoulder to make sure my sister wasn't listening in. "Spend more time with them. Do ya some good."

"I hear you," I told him. Then I looked at the clock on the stove. "Gotta go, Harold."

I got into my Mercedes. I picked up some friends. We stopped for a couple of six-packs, and we drove. We talked, laughed, looked for trouble. That was our daily routine. If we had a big group, we'd borrow my dad's conversion van, drive it to the park, and party there. At night, we'd drive somewhere, go to a club, look for women — I wasn't serious yet with Monica — find a drug dealer and snort cocaine.

The money in the glove compartment went to fund the parties. I never knew much about measuring coke. So I'd just ask a dealer for $300 worth or, if it was a big party, $3,000 worth. I took whatever the dealer gave me and accepted his honesty. I'm sure I got taken many, many times. Some of the money came from my salary and endorsements. But I earned a lot of it at autograph signings and appearances. In those days, I could earn $10,000 at a baseball card show, and we usually got paid in cash. A guy once paid me $2,000 to eat lunch with his son on Long Island, while another paid me $3,000 to have dinner with his clients for one hour. I could earn about the same giving a pitching lesson to a Little League kid, a Little League kid with a successful dad.

Rumors about me and drugs were all over Tampa. No one seemed to have proof of anything. But I didn't understand how the talk could have spread so fast. Some of the rumors were crazy. Someone said I'd been pitching on cocaine ever since high school. Some of the rumors were close to true. A friend of mine told me, "I heard you missed the parade because you were in a crack house." Well, it was powder cocaine, not rock, I thought. But I was only quibbling there.

I didn't know what to do. But I thought I had to do something. And that something wasn't to quit. It was to talk to the media and lie.

On November 11, I gave an interview from my parents' house, insisting I had no problem with drugs or alcohol. I was emphatic. I said I only drank beer and not that much of it. "Drugs? No. I never use them, and I never will." And I didn't stop there. I laid it on thick. I said that in my next contract, I would insist on a drug-testing clause. "It can be for a test every week, every two days, as often as they want, and it can be forever," I said.

This was a bold gamble — maybe a reckless one — for someone slipping into drug addiction. Taunting a suspicious media is usually not a great idea. I hoped my offer would end the rumors. It didn't, of course, but I still felt eager to show everyone that I was okay. A week later, I got the perfect opportunity — with President Ronald Reagan at the White House. It's a World Series tradition, the winning team being invited for a presidential handshake. Still feeling embarrassed that I'd missed the victory parade in New York, I wasn't about to pull a no-show in Washington. Not all the players seemed to feel that way. Of the twenty-four guys on the roster, only ten showed up for the Rose Garden ceremony. Gary Carter was there. So were Jesse Orosco, Bob Ojeda, Lee Mazzilli, and owner Jeff Wilpon. Keith, Darryl, and Mookie were not.

Even though he was a lifelong Chicago Cubs fans, President Reagan gave a very friendly speech, saying the Mets had shown America that "the other team from New York could win." Gary presented the president with a blue and orange warm-up jacket that said REAGAN across the back. He gave Vice President George Bush a Mets cap. Fred Wilpon made everyone laugh when he promised to come back next year with the rest of the uniform. Then the president walked down the line of players, stopping and shaking everyone's hand.

"Hi, I'm Ronald Reagan," said the leader of the free world, one of the most recognizable men on earth. "Hi, I'm Ronald Reagan."

When he got to me, I told him: "Mr. President, you don't have to do that. I know who you are."

He smiled and nodded and kept introducing himself. I don't know what he was thinking, but he seemed like a nice man.

If the off-season had been an exercise in irresponsibility and addiction, at least it had been playing out quietly. Mostly so. On December 13, that all changed. That day, I went to Town and Country Field in Tampa and played in two charity softball games for the local Kidney Foundation. My dad was on dialysis, and I had done a few events for them over the years. I was joined by my nephew Gary, Vance Lovelace, my childhood friend Troy, and some other local athletes and celebrities. After the games, a bunch of us took some teenagers who were waiting for kidney transplants to a University of South Florida basketball game at the Sun Dome. We dropped the kids off, then Gary, Troy, Vance, a couple of other guys, and I drove our own cars to Chili's Bar and Grill for some burgers, wings, and beers.

We had some drinks. We were laughing, telling jokes, reenacting our favorite plays from the day, and taunting each other about our softball prowess. I didn't think we were bothering anyone. But then I noticed that a couple of tables away, a sunburned, fortysomething Tampa police officer kept looking up from his hamburger. He was in his uniform. His radio was on the table.

He caught my eye and motioned to me to keep the noise down. I nodded back to him.

"Come on, guys," I said, addressing my friends. "Let's cool it."

"What are you talkin' about?" one of the guys asked.

I nodded toward the cop. "Him," I said.

The table erupted again in laughter. "We're not being that loud," my friend said. The table laughed even harder.

The cop said nothing else. He just got up and moved — not farther away from us, but closer, with his back to us. Maybe he was eavesdropping on our conversation. He was still sitting there when we finished up, paid the bill, and drove off toward a party at another friend's house — a convoy of young black males in luxury and sports cars.

We headed west on Fowler Avenue toward Nebraska Avenue, not a great area in Tampa. Gary was in the first car in a brand-new red Corvette I had given him that year. Then it was Troy and me in my silver Mercedes 380SE with a license plate that said DOC, followed by Phil's gold Datsun 280ZX and another Mercedes.

We came up to the intersection, hoping to turn left. Another car was ahead of us, waiting for the traffic to clear. On the far side of the light, a Tampa police cruiser was facing us, watching us approach the intersection. I don't know if it was just a coincidence or if the cop from Chili's had tipped someone off. But Gary nudged out into the intersection. The car ahead of him made the left turn but the light changed while Gary was still in the intersection. I think seeing the cop made him nervous about running the light. So instead of punching through, he backed up and waited for the light to change again. When it turned green again, we all made it through. That's when the cop threw on his lights and siren and pulled up behind Gary.

But Gary had giant speakers in his back window. They made it hard to see and even harder to hear. I don't think he knew the police car was there. Rather than keep pursuing Gary, the cop drifted back and pulled me over instead.

I'd had a couple of beers, but wasn't even close to drunk. I'm sure I wasn't over the legal limit. I didn't have any drugs in the car. "I can't believe this," I thought. I'd just spent a day doing some good at a charity outing, and now the cops are harassing me. Up ahead, I saw Gary pull his car over as well.

A burly young cop leaned down and rapped on my window with his flashlight. "License and registration," he said.

"You already know who I am," I sighed. "What did you pull me over for?"

"Be quiet and hand me your license and registration."

This was already getting off to a bad start.

"This is bullshit!" I fumed. As soon as the words left my mouth, I could see a half dozen cop cars swarming in. "Why are you guys always harassing me?" I said. "I'm tired of this."

"Listen," the cop said sharply. "Knock it off or you're going to jail."

"For what? You're harassing me."

"That's it," the cop said, reaching for my door handle. "Get out of the car!"

He was angry now. I got out and saw a handful of cops walking toward us. "You had no reason to stop me," I said. "Explain what the stop is about."

"Again," the cop warned. "Knock it off or you're going to jail."

Gary and all my other friends were on the sidewalk now, watching from a distance. The cop saw them and asked, "They're with you?"

"Yes," I said. "We're all together. What the hell does that have to do with anything?"

"Shut up!" he said.

He reached for his cuffs. As he did, I made the mistake of reaching for his hand. It was just a reflex. I wasn't trying to provoke him. But I shouldn't have done that. I was thinking, "Hey, come on. You don't need to lock me up."

To his credit, that cop wasn't the one to explode. But when the other officers saw that, he couldn't stop them from rushing me. They knocked me to the grass next to the boulevard. I took a beating on the ground — nightsticks, knees, and punches. One cop hit me in the head with an eighteen-inch flashlight. I tried to protect myself. I tried to fight back. But basically it was the Fourth of July going off on my face. The gold cap on my front tooth I got when I was a teenager? Gone. The tooth it covered? Gone.

In all, the report said later, twenty-two Tampa police officers were on the scene. Nine dove into the ruckus. When I tried to stand, I was pushed backward. Gary rushed up and was quickly cuffed and arrested. I was pushing and shoving to get the cops off me. By that point, there were so many of them, they were punching each other. One cop saw me pushing and yelled, "He's going for your piece!"

That led to another flurry of punches as another cop pulled his pistol out and pointed it under my chin.

"Say your prayers, motherfucker!" he shouted.

I thought for sure I was going to die. I immediately stopped moving.

One cop got my left arm behind my back. He twisted it so hard, I cried out in pain. "Good!" I heard one of them yell. "Break his fucking arm!" I guess he'd forgotten I was a rightie.

"Doc Gooden," one cop said, spitting out my name. "Local fuckin' hero. I'll never watch another Mets game again."

A middle-aged white couple out for an evening stroll happened on the scene. When they saw what was happening, they stopped and shouted at the cops.

"Why are you guys doing that to him?" the woman raged. "What's going on here?"

My blood was all over my shirt, not to mention the cops and the grass. The couple pleaded with the officers to let go of me.

"Get out of here, or you're going to jail," one of the cops responded. "Get lost!"

The arm twisting soon gave way to something worse, a chokehold around my neck. The more I resisted, the less I could breathe. For a second, I felt like giving up. I thought, "Okay, well, this is how I'm going to die." Then, I got the idea of pretending I'd passed out. Maybe then they'd leave me alone. I went completely limp.

"He's out!" I heard someone say. "He's out! Get off him!"

At that point, the cops seemed to panic. Other officers pulled the chokehold cop off me. I lay on the ground, perfectly still, hearing more sirens and cops barking orders.

A couple of them picked me up, shackled me, and threw me in the back of a police car. As we started to move, I looked out the window. I discovered we were headed nowhere near the police station. Instead, we pulled into the empty parking lot at the Tampa Greyhound Track on Nebraska Avenue. "They're going to kill me," I thought. "This is the perfect spot to get rid of me."

I had never been more frightened in my life.

They pulled me out of the car and sat me on the pavement. My bleeding head was resting against one of the back tires of the police car. They started discussing strategy. Radios and walkie-talkies were chirping with activity. More sirens were coming our way. A paramedic truck arrived. Two black cops showed up. They weren't going to kill me after all, I decided. They were just trying to make what happened look less black and white. The black cops rode with me to the hospital, where I got twenty stitches in my head, before they took me to jail. I was charged with disorderly conduct, resisting arrest, and battery on a police officer — I never served a day on any of them. A few hours later, I was released on my own recognizance.

When my parents came to pick me up, my mom took one look at me and started bawling. It had taken a little more than a month for me to go from World Champion to "black-male Gooden, violent perp," beaten by the police in my own hometown.

When we got home, news trucks were parked all over my neighborhood. It looked like draft day all over again. Only this time, the angle wasn't "local boy makes good." Family members started arriving right away, including some of my bad-ass cousins from my mother's side who like to settle their grievances with gunplay. Quickly, they hatched a plan.

"Let's get these motherfuckers," one of them said.

The idea was that we would get our revenge by driving around Tampa at a high rate of speed. Then, when a cop pulled us over — *any* cop — *bang*! We were going to blast him.

I am not normally an angry person. But I was so filled with rage, this actually made sense to me. We mentioned none of it to my mom and dad, of course. But five of us slipped out to my oldest cousin's pickup — three in the front, two in the back. I was in the cab. Two or three of my cousins had guns. All of us were cursing the police. We were going to right this wrong in one bloody flourish.

We made it a single block before I came to my senses. "I can't go through with this," I said.

"What do you mean?" my oldest cousin asked, patting his pistol. "This is real!"

"Nah," I said. "This is crazy. This isn't going to help. It's just gonna get me locked up for a long time."

I got out of the truck and walked back to my parents' house.

The local papers were all writing about what happened to me. The NAACP was calling the incident "racial." The Tampa police said their officers used reasonable force in trying to subdue me and defended the department's relationship with the local black community. But by Christmas, the US Department of Justice was investigating why the cops had pulled us over and whether they had used excessive force. Tampa mayor Sandra Freedman said the case showed an urgent need for more black police.

My lawyer, Joseph Ficarrotta, filed civil suits against the Tampa Police Department and General Hospital, which we won. He had a field day with the cop race switch and the testimony of the nice, white couple who'd been passing by. We gave the money to charity.

In January, I suggested to Gary that he and I take a trip to New York. We could get away from all the negativity in Tampa, I told him. We'd leave the cops and the news behind and spend some time together like we used to. I knew it would take me away from the partying too. Maybe, I thought, I could get my life under slightly better control. A memorabilia dealer I knew, Mead Chasky, agreed to pick us up at LaGuardia Airport. We'd hang at my apartment, hit the city, and forget about all the craziness since the World Series.

Good idea, in theory.

After the plane landed, Gary and I walked up the Jetway, and the first people to greet us were half a dozen officers from Port Authority Police, all dressed in nice dark suits.

"Are you Dwight Gooden?" one of them asked.

Gary was right beside me. I felt so terrible for him. The look on his face was priceless. Somewhere between disgust and disbelief. I imagine my face said, "Here we go again."

"You have to come this way," the officer said.

"What's this about?" I asked, trying to stay calmer this time.

"Do you know a woman named Carlene Pearson?"

"Yes?"

"She tried to bring a loaded handgun into the terminal."

"Hmmmm," I thought of saying, "maybe I don't know her." I didn't say that.

We went into a security office, and there sat my ex-girlfriend Carlene along with Mead and Lisa Strawberry, Darryl's wife. Talk about a dangerous pair!

I did what I could to help Carlene. "She carries the weapon for protection," I said. "I'm sure she meant no harm."

"I forgot it was in my purse," Carlene interrupted.

I knew about the gun. In early 1985, one of my cousins gave her a small .38 Derringer for safety. But please! I didn't think she'd be bringing it into airports — especially not in New York with its no-messing-around gun-control laws. Apparently, she'd been out with Lisa. They bumped into Mead. He mentioned he was picking me up at the airport. Carlene and Lisa thought it might be a great chance to catch up.

Just great.

Gary was beyond pissed when I drove to the courthouse to bail Carlene out, even more so when she showed up at the apartment and insisted on coming out to dinner with us in Great Neck at Peter Luger Steakhouse. He didn't say one word the entire meal. He just shook his head and mumbled, "I can't believe — ."

Back in Tampa, I partied right into spring training.

What started out being fun was quickly becoming a habit I couldn't realistically control. The important things in my life — my dad, Monica, Gary, little Dwight Junior, even baseball — were all being elbowed aside for cocaine. I didn't see it at the time. I thought I was just hanging out and having a normal young man's good time. But my real priority was to get high. And the results weren't pretty. Often, I felt crappy in the morning. I was hanging out with people I wouldn't normally hang out with. And I was hurting those closest to me. I didn't know when to stop. I was the guy from last night who was still wearing a party hat while the maid was vacuuming the living room rug. Everyone else had gone off to work, and I couldn't make it off the couch.

The 1986 World Series New York Mets were already beginning to change. Ray Knight had left in free agency. With his departure, a major stabilizing force was gone from the club. I told myself this wasn't affecting my pitching. But one morning in spring training when I didn't feel like practicing, I lied to Davey Johnson and told him a friend had been in a car wreck. Other days, I showed up with red eyes and a bad attitude. I snapped at ball boys and fellow players, which was out of character for me. And I wasn't pitching right. My first time on the mound in spring training, I gave up nine runs in the first inning.

Maybe I shouldn't have made that comment back in November about being drug-tested. One day early in spring training, my agent, Jim, mentioned to me on the phone, "The Mets want you to agree to some drug tests. It's part of reworking your contract."

"I've got it under control," I told him. "No problem."

"They could be coming very soon," Jim warned me.

"That's fine," I said. I had the bravado and delusion of a real coke addict. I thought I'd beaten the system all winter, when in truth the things I'd been doing had everyone suspicious about me and drugs. No one who's behaving himself is the subject of *that* many rumors or has *that* many mishaps.

When I walked into practice one morning in late March, the Mets' trainer, Steve Garland, came over to me.

"Hey, Doc," he said, sounding unusually serious. "I need to get some urine from you." He handed me a plastic cup.

A quick wave of fear rushed over me. I tried to think of how I could duck this. I couldn't think of anything. Cocaine, I had heard, stays in the system a good seventy-two hours. I had used less than twelve hours before. I peed in the cup and hoped for the best.

For the next few days, I heard nothing at all. I figured I had dodged that bullet. Then I arrived at camp one morning about a week later, and the man who drafted me, Joe McIlvaine, told me Frank Cashen wanted to see me in his office.

That couldn't be good.

Jim, my agent, was already sitting with Frank when I walked in. So was Steve, the trainer who had taken my pee.

"Dwight, sit down," Frank said solemnly. His expression was flat. He was as pale as I'd ever seen him. He seemed hurt more than mad. "We have some bad news here."

"Okay," I answered. My mind began to scramble for answers. Excuses. An alibi. Anything. I knew I would have to say something.

"You tested positive for cocaine," Frank said.

"They must have gotten my test mixed up," I blurted. "I can retake it. It's wrong!"

"No," Frank said quietly. "It's not wrong. We've been worried for quite some time."

"There's got to be a mistake!" I protested. "I've never done drugs. Never will."

But my lying didn't seem to be working with Frank.

"There's no mistake," he said.

Then he just sat there. His silence filled the room. Jim wasn't saying anything to help me get a retest. Steve Garland was examining his shoes. Joe McIlvaine just looked let down.

"You have a choice," Frank explained slowly and patiently. "We want you to get help. You can go to rehab and earn your salary. Or you can skip rehab, and face a yearlong suspension without pay."

I just wanted to leave the room. The walls felt like they were closing in. So I stalled. "Can I think about this and come back to you tomorrow?" I asked.

"Dwight," Frank said sternly. "We need to act on this ASAP. You've got five minutes to give me an answer. Here's a phone if you need to call someone." He slid his desk phone toward me. I didn't have anyone to call. I couldn't imagine discussing this with my parents. I didn't have the guts. It struck me immediately that no matter what I chose, I'd be starting the season far, far away from the Mets.

I started bawling.

But I cried more because I was caught, not because I'd come to any realization that I needed help. "I'll do the treatment," I said.

"That's good," Frank said.

"I think it's for the best," Jim said, nodding.

Dr. Allan Lans, a psychiatrist who had been hired by the Mets to work with troubled players, came into the room. He told me about the Smithers Addiction Treatment and Research Center on Manhattan's West Side. "I think it's the best place for you to go," he said. I'd be far away from Tampa, he explained, and in New York, the Mets could keep an eye on me. He said he'd fly up there with me that night.

The drive from the training facility in St. Petersburg to my parents' house in Tampa seemed to pass in about thirty seconds. It wasn't nearly enough time for me to think of the perfect way to break this news to them. Just seeing me walk through the door at eleven a.m. would be alarming, I knew. Wasn't I supposed to be at practice? From the looks on their faces, I didn't have to open my mouth for my mom and dad to know something was wrong. I just blurted it out.

"I'm afraid I have some bad news," I said, borrowing Frank's opening line with me. "I tested positive for cocaine." My mother's eyes widened and she gasped. Then she began to cry. "Oh, Baby," she said. My father stared straight ahead. He didn't say a word. He turned and walked to the sofa.

"I've agreed to get treatment," I told them. Still my dad said nothing. My mother hugged me. "I'll get the help I need, and I'll be as good as new." My mother nodded her head against my chest.

"I'm proud of you," she said. My dad still said nothing. He couldn't even look at me.

PART III

Hurting

10

Dusting Off

A S THE METS OPENED THE 1987 season at Shea Stadium against the Pittsburgh Pirates, I was across the East River in Manhattan, pretending to get rehabbed. Smithers was an upscale facility with about one hundred beds. The people who worked there seemed dedicated and well-meaning. I'm sure if I'd been committed to my own recovery, the program could have helped me a lot.

But I wasn't, and it didn't.

I had no knowledge of addiction — how it got started, what made it so stubborn, how treatment might help me get over it. I was clueless. Drugs and alcohol were sapping my talent. They were complicating my daily existence. They were fraying my personal relationships. But I wasn't at Smithers to wrestle with any of that. As far as I was concerned, I was there to knock twenty-eight days off the calendar, act like I'd been humbled, then take my throwing arm back to Shea.

I didn't drink or use drugs while I was in Smithers. But whatever other rules there were, the good people who ran the place were bending for me — or I was breaking them on my own. Unlike most of the other residents, I had a room to myself. They ate in a cafeteria. I had Chinese food smuggled in. TVs were strictly prohibited. I had a little portable. Newspapers were forbidden too. Most days, I read the *News,* the *Post,* and *New York Newsday.* I was supposed to be focused on getting clean now, not at all concerned with the outside world. But the outside world wasn't leaking into my room. It was gushing. And that allowed me to remain in complete denial that I had a problem. Take full responsibility for myself? Heck, I didn't even do my own laundry. I had no idea how to work the machines. Two older female patients volunteered to help me.

I attended two or three treatment sessions a day. Mostly, the group sessions convinced me that the other patients were far more screwed up than I was. Whatever they were describing, I didn't think it had much to do with me.

Some of the counselors knew who I was and were in awe of what I did. Some of them were fans. Some of the patients were too. But the ones who were there to truly change themselves took one look at me and could tell I wasn't committed to getting better. Generally, they kept their distance from me. No one challenged me, argued with me, or called me out on my bullshit. The counselors had enough experience to recognize an addict in denial. But what could they do? No one can cure an addict who won't cure himself.

Sunday was visiting day. Jay Horwitz came pretty much every week. My mom and my sisters visited a couple of times. Monica came once. But I called her constantly, and not just because I was bored. I was trying to convince her to marry me.

We were both very young. I was twenty-two. She was twenty-one. And I hadn't shown much interest in settling down for a committed relationship, not with the big-league dating opportunities even shy ballplayers had. But I was lonely. I liked Monica a lot. And I was nervous about how I'd be accepted when I got out of Smithers.

Many of my teammates were married. From where I was sitting, wedded bliss and major-league baseball didn't necessarily go hand in hand. But all spring, I'd been hearing from Frank Cashen and other Mets executives that it was time for me to settle down.

"You sure this is what you want to do?" Monica asked me more than once on the phone. "Are you sure?"

I called her twice a day. For a week, she put me off. "Let me think about it," she said.

After a week, she finally agreed.

I was elated, but I wasn't ready to tell my parents. They knew I wasn't mature enough to get married. I had shown no desire to settle down. Since I'd gotten home from the Series, I could hardly sit in the den with my dad and watch half a football game. What made me think I was ready for a real family of my own? But Monica ended up telling my sister Betty. Without my knowing it, Betty spilled the news to my mom and dad even before I got out of rehab.

When I returned to Tampa, my mom said how happy she was to see me. Then she folded her hands in her lap and calmly asked, "So is there anything you want to tell us?"

"No." I shook my head. "I'm doing great," I said.

"Son," my dad said quietly, "are you getting married?"

I didn't know that my sister had told them. I was caught off-guard. I squirmed, but I knew that I'd been busted. "Yes," I finally blurted out. "Monica and I are getting married." Then I started to cry.

"You're only twenty-two!" my dad thundered, pounding his fist onto the arm of his chair. "You just started dating! What's the rush?"

I had no response.

"Well, whatever you decide, you know we'll support you," my mom finally said, the closest thing to a blessing I was going to receive.

After a few weeks' warm-up with the Tidewater Tides AAA team, I went back to work on June 5, making my post-rehab debut at Shea against Pittsburgh. It was my opening day. Spending that time without drugs or alcohol was good for my body—for my mind, as well. And to help enforce my new sobriety—to keep me from screwing up so publicly again—I knew I'd be tested regularly for drugs. I'd agreed to the tests in my new contract, hadn't I?

Not everyone was thrilled I was coming back. The morning of my return, Dick Young, a writer the fans and the players loved to hate, wrote a rough back-page column for the *New York Post*. To him, drug addiction was a moral failing. "STAND UP AND BOO," the headline said. But more than 51,000 Mets fans did just the opposite when I walked out to the mound. They stood up and cheered. God, that made me feel good! They embraced me with a standing ovation. I hadn't been humbled by Smithers. But I was genuinely humbled by New York's support.

We beat the Pirates 5–1 and flew right out to Chicago to play the Cubs. On the plane, I started drinking again and didn't think twice about it. No one else seemed to. Straw and some of the pitchers even toasted me across the aisle.

Thanks to Major League Baseball's drug testing, I stayed away from the coke for a good long time. But from that flight forward, I didn't see any reason not to drink alcohol.

I pitched near the top of my game that entire post-Smithers season. Even Dick Young was impressed. Missing the first two months, I nonetheless chalked up fifteen victories and a 3.21 ERA. I could still thrill the fans and please myself. I was just on. My frustrating World Series, I discovered, wasn't a lifelong curse.

The Mets championship lineup was really beginning to change, for better and for worse. Ray Knight had been the first player to leave our World Series team. We got the spectacular David Cone from Kansas City. We also traded Kevins, Mitchell for McReynolds. But there was still enough of the old camaraderie that after my short rehab, I slid comfortably back onto the team. I stayed clean. My old friends didn't seem to hate me. I was piling up wins.

Pitchers Bob Ojeda and Rick Aguilera both got injured. With that and my absence for rehab, we had a rough first half of the season, falling as much as ten and a half games behind the first-place Cardinals. But after the All-Star Break, we'd closed the gap to one and a half games by the time the Cardinals came to Shea for an early September series. Some of us on the defending champion team began to believe the old magic might be coming back. But injury struck our pitching staff again. The Cards pulled away from us before losing in the World Series to the Minnesota Twins.

Monica and I got married on November 21 at her family's church in Tampa in front of six hundred guests. My brother-in-law Harold and my childhood friend Troy were my co–best men. Gary Carter, Dave Magadan, and several other Mets attended. We all danced to the sounds of Monica's cousin's R & B band. Once we returned from our Hawaiian honeymoon, we lived a relatively quiet existence at my parents' house until it was time to return to New York for the 1988 season. Frank Cashen must have been smiling. Married life was settling me down.

And I jumped into this new life with both feet. Four days after Monica and I got married, my lawyer filed custody papers for my son, Dwight Junior. His mother, Debra Hamilton, wasn't impressed with my status as a new husband. She fired back, citing my "problems with alcohol and drug abuse" and my arrest after the police beating in Tampa. She got to keep custody.

I went into salary arbitration in early 1988. After I missed two months of the previous season, the Mets weren't too thrilled with the $150,000 bump my agent Jim was asking for, lifting me to $1.65 million. But given my 15–7 record and a 3.21 ERA, the ninth best in baseball, we thought we deserved it. On the other side, the Mets were asking for a 10 percent cut in salary and were refusing to sign a multiyear deal. As soon as Jim Neader and I sat down with Mets assistant general manager Al Harazin and the arbitrator, Al pulled out a news article where I'd told a reporter that if I'd been around the whole 1987 season, we'd have won it all. That was an instant death blow for my case. I was lucky to get out of there with a $100,000 cut in pay.

The erosion of the 1986 bad guys continued into 1988, though that season was still our last, best chance to get back to the World Series. You can't say we didn't have talent, especially on the mound. Ron Darling had seventeen wins. I had eighteen. David Cone went 20–3. But we lost the National League Championship Series to the Dodgers, including a heartbreaking game four loss that I pitched. Mike Scioscia's ninth-inning home run is still one of my most painful baseball memories. Kirk Gibson won the game in the twelfth with a home run off of Roger McDowell, but the win happened only because of the one Scioscia hit off me. Mets fans were right when they called it "the season that got away from us."

11

Burning Out

NO TEAM LASTS FOREVER.

By 1989, the tension that had once translated magically into on-field electricity was turning into poison off the field. March 3 was team picture day. But instead of happy smiles, the big crowd of media got a barroom brawl, transported to our spring training field in Port St. Lucie. Things got off to a testy start when manager Bud Harrelson began calling out the seating order for the first row. "Johnson, Carter, Hernandez, Strawberry . . ."

Instead of taking his place in the row, Darryl said to Bud: "I only want to sit next to my real friends." Everyone knew exactly who Darryl meant to exclude from that club.

Things had been brewing for a couple of weeks.

Darryl had been complaining to reporters about how unfairly he was being paid. To show his displeasure, I guess, he'd shown up fifteen minutes late for practice one day. Keith, our team captain, had warned him: "Let your agent handle that stuff. You can't pull this crap on these guys. Don't let it happen again!"

Now at picture day, the simmering dispute was suddenly boiling over. Darryl started moving down the line to sit between Gary Carter and Sid Fernandez. Glaring back at Keith, he asked, "Why you got to be saying those things about me?"

"Grow up, you crybaby," Keith shot back.

That was it. Darryl turned around and took a swing at Keith. Gary Carter and Randy Myers jumped up to restrain Keith. Bob Ojeda and I grabbed Darryl.

"Let him go!" Darryl yelled at Gary before turning his attention back to Keith. "I've been sick of you for years," he said.

Ron Darling tried to make light of the brawl. But you could hear his frustration when he said, "Another day in Barnum and Bailey and the Great Traveling Show." Darryl didn't stick around after pictures. He just complained to the reporters again about his contract and stormed off the field.

Yes, we were all supposedly grown adults — playing for the same team, no less. Sitting by my locker at the end of practice, I was thinking just how tense things had become. Big, tough athletes, ready to explode at each other. Gary said he felt like he was walking on eggshells.

By May, both Keith and Gary were out for a huge chunk of the season with injuries. By July, I was also learning how it felt to be hurt. In the early years I was a Met, Mel, Davey, and lots of people always said I had the perfect pitching mechanics. I had the ability to throw forever, they said. I didn't seem to wear myself out. I'd been hearing that since high school. "Doc has the perfect mechanics." So I threw and I threw and I threw. When I started, Davey would pull me out, saying he wanted to rest my arm. But as time went on, my pitch counts got high and stayed there. One hundred pitches — that's considered a high number to throw in a game. I was often 130, 140, even 150.

That summer of 1989, all those fast and breaking balls were finally catching up with me. First, I felt a dull ache in my right arm and shoulder. The ache wouldn't go away. Just before the All-Star Break, I was having trouble raising my arm above my head. The doctors looked me over and agreed. I needed a break. On July 2, they put me on the shelf for what would wind up being two months. The issue was eventually diagnosed as a small muscle tear. I was scared. I was depressed. I didn't know how serious this was. Would my arm ever be the same? Those were the kinds of thoughts going through my head. Getting injured was a whole new experience for me. Except for going to Smithers, I had never been on the disabled list before. The doctors kept working on me. I did some physical therapy, then toward the end of the season, I thought I was ready. Davey agreed to let me try. After a couple of innings of warm-ups in the bullpen, he sent me in as relief to face the Phillies. I threw forty-five pitches in three scoreless innings. But when I got off the field, I had to admit that my arm didn't feel better. If anything, it felt worse.

I was devastated.

I exercised through the off-season with Larry Mayol, a trainer in St. Petersburg who'd worked for the Mets in the early 1980s before going into private practice. Trainers like Larry are geniuses. And with some of the painful exercises they put athletes through, they are torturers too. But the results are undeniable. I think Larry knew more than most doctors did about the mechanics of the human body. He and I spent months strengthening my arm and shoulder. And the effort paid off. I won nineteen games the following season.

I was doing well staying away from drugs. I was still drinking — plenty. But I was being drug tested regularly, and I wasn't touching cocaine. To their credit, my Mets teammates didn't try to tempt me to start using again, not even the ones who were using themselves. It took some respect and understanding on their part, and I really appreciated it. I supposed they recognized that for any addict, even for one who's been clean a while, staying that way is always a daily struggle. So they indulged in whatever ways they chose to, and in those years I kept my distance. Dr. Lans often went on road trips with us. His main job, it seemed, was making sure Darryl and I stayed productive and healthy. Clearly, this hadn't been a smashing success for him or for us, although I really don't think I could blame him. When Dr. Lans was on a road trip, I didn't even like to go out drinking. I didn't want him seeing me hungover in the morning. And I didn't want to plant any new suspicions in his mind.

Still, partying remained a big part of the Mets' identity — too big to continue without serious repercussions in seasons to come. When Darryl emerged from rehab and returned to the team, I think we all knew that 1990 would be his last season with the team, given his public troubles and his legendary contract disputes. What was difficult for me to stomach was how abruptly the Mets got rid of Davey Johnson. Winning the National League East in 1988 and finishing second in 1989 didn't buy Davey much protection. Our slow start in 1990 was too much for Frank Cashen to accept. Davey was fired by the end of May. Looking back, I can see that he was always too much of a player's manager for the Mets brass. I'm convinced he sealed his fate when he ripped up that bill for the damaged airplane. Bud Harrelson replaced Davey. My repaired arm kept performing. I stayed clean. And we were in contention for much of the second half of the season before fading to the Pirates.

By then, I began approaching seasons more conservatively. I wasn't nineteen anymore. I'd thrown an awful lot of pitches in my career. I went from being Dr. K to plain-old Doc again. When I talked to the media, I made a point of saying, "Just call me Doctor now." Early on, I craved strikeouts. Now I just wanted to win games, whatever that might take. Now my focus was pitch location, not trying to overpower the hitters.

Without guaranteed strikeout pitches, I began luring the hitters to put the ball in play, trusting our fielders to get the job done. I probably should have been thinking that all through the 1980s. I'm sure that would have lengthened my career. But Dr. K was all about the strike-outs.

By the early '90s, our fielding had become a patchwork of talented guys playing out of position. We had Gregg Jefferies at second base and a constant rotation of players at third. Dave Magadan shifted from first base to third base. Howard Johnson spent a year in the outfield then came back to third. Bobby Bonilla played at least four positions before spending a season at third. On top of that, we probably had a dozen different shortstops. I'm not making excuses. There were many reasons we weren't the '86 Mets. I didn't have the stuff I'd had before my arm troubles. But our fielding was part of the reason my ERA was creeping up. Often, the fielders just couldn't get to the ball to make a play.

Going into the 1991 season, I didn't stick with the off-season regime Larry Mayol had prepared for me, and I suffered because of it. On opening day, I went eight innings in the rain against the Phillies. That wasn't my call. Bud Harrelson, starting his first full season as manager, really wanted that first win. In spring training, I hadn't been throwing more than sixty pitches a game. I might have pitched twice that in our 2–1 victory.

Pitching had begun to hurt. The only thing that kept my mind off of my pain was our newborn daughter, Ashley, who arrived shortly after the 1991 season had started. Monica and I set up a room for her in our house on Long Island. I loved Dwight Junior. But he was living with his mother in Florida. For once in my life, I had something that brought me daily joy other than baseball. By mid-August, we were fifteen games out of first place. So after Shea games, I was thrilled to drive home and just be a dad.

My father's health had deteriorated so much that he spent a chunk of 1991 in New York City at the Hospital for Special Surgery, where more attention could be paid to his kidney function. It wasn't easy seeing him in such poor shape. But we got to spend more time together than we had in years. I was maturing. He got to see his granddaughter. And we could talk baseball in person in the middle of a season, which is something we hadn't done in years.

At the same time, the Mets weren't giving me much to smile about. It wasn't fun being at the ballpark and not in the pennant race. Hearing guys talk about their off-season plans in August was depressing. And I could tell something was really wrong with my arm. By September, the doctors determined I had a partial tear of my rotator cuff and labrum. I'd have to undergo surgery if I wanted to play again next year. The defeatist talk around the clubhouse was that if we didn't make the playoffs, at least we would probably be in second place. I started wondering what it might be like to play for some other team.

Looking back, I can see now that spring training of 1992 was the beginning of the end of the Mets for me. I had a rush of bad news early that year. My mom's mom passed away, which was tough on my whole family. Then Darryl Strawberry's first autobiography, *Darryl,* came out in March. In it, he basically accused me — falsely — of getting high during the 1986 playoff series. "If he was using cocaine during the series, I wouldn't have been surprised in the least because the pressure was so intense it made everyone do crazy things," Darryl wrote about me. The media were all over that loaded sentence.

Thanks, man. I thought we were friends.

Now a new season was about to begin. And instead of answering questions about baseball and our hopes for the season, I was being grilled about stuff that happened six years earlier, propelled by the false allegations of my supposed good friend.

Yes, I'd gotten high *after* the Series. No, not *during* the post-season play.

That may not have seemed important to Darryl. It was very important to me.

In the course of 342 pages, Darryl credited himself for most of the good things that happened on the team in the eight years he was a Met and blamed his teammates, the front office, racism, you name it — anything but Darryl — for the shortcomings. And to make the book even harder to swallow, he'd asked me to write the introduction, which I did before I ever read the book, saying a whole bunch of nice things about him.

"A person I came to rely on as a friend . . . Darryl stood up for me . . . stormed out on the field to help me" — *blah, blah, blah.* "Everyone who reads this book can now meet the Darryl Strawberry I know — the real Darryl."

Um, not quite.

I spoke to Darryl after the book came out. I told him I was really pissed. "You don't say these kind of things about your friends," I said. "Stuff that's not even true." He got all sheepish with me and apologized. That was just Darryl. He was constantly doing that. He'd say something terrible about one of his teammates, then feel bad about it. Or he'd get confronted about what he said. Quickly, he'd apologize. Then, soon enough he was out trashing his teammates again.

When reporters asked him why he wrote that about me, he admitted that he hadn't seen me using during the playoffs or the World Series. "I was talking about my year in '86 being involved in heavy drinking and partying," he said. "The issue came up about other players." He said his coauthor, Art Rust Jr., asked him about coke and me: "Did you think he was using?"

"I said I wouldn't be surprised because the next spring he checked himself into Smithers," Darryl said, hedging yet again. "Now what's wrong with that?"

Darryl's literary hand grenade wasn't the biggest challenge of that ugly spring. A woman I had sex with during spring training in 1991 decided a year later to tell local police that she'd been raped — setting off another media frenzy and shaking my whole world. Jeff Torborg, our new manager, must have been wondering why he'd ever accepted this crazy job.

Here's what happened: on March 30, I'd been out for drinks with outfielders Vince Coleman and Daryl Boston at a nightclub in Jupiter, Florida, called Jox. It wasn't far from our spring training facility in Port St. Lucie. The whole area was fairly sleepy back then. Every spring, the Mets were about the only attraction in town. At night, we'd go out drinking and looking for women, and women would go out drinking and looking for Mets. The hookups were never hard to come by. This particular night, I met a thirty-one-year-old woman, and we started talking upstairs. It was getting late. Vince and Daryl decided to go back to the house I was renting and crash. The woman and I stayed at the club, dancing and getting to know each other. Then she drove us back to my place. When we got there, Vince and Daryl were on the couch in the living room, playing *R.B.I. Baseball* on the Nintendo. We walked past the two of them and into the bedroom, where she and I had sex. When we came out, she hung around for more drinks.

"You ever been with three guys in a night?" Vince asked, jokingly.

"Two," she said. "Never three."

Vince then asked if she wanted to go into the bedroom with him, and she said yes. Before the night was over, all of us had had sex with her.

I was married. This was wrong. But it wasn't rape.

The following day, players were comparing notes on their nights out. Daryl Boston told Ron Darling what had happened back at my house. When Daryl described the woman, Ron said, "Oh, man, didn't you know? She's going out with David."

Nothing happened for a long time. Then, suddenly, a whole season later, she went to the cops. And Frank Cashen, yet again, was calling me into his office for a serious chat. I truly had no idea this one was coming.

"Do you have an attorney?" he asked.

"No, why?"

"You're being accused of rape."

This wasn't the first time Frank had to make a speech like this to a player. David Cone had been the focus of a sex-assault investigation in Philadelphia toward the end of the previous season. From what I heard, he'd shunned an "old reliable" and chosen a different groupie, leaving the first woman upset enough to accuse him of assaulting her. Wasn't that what Hubie Brooks had warned about my rookie year? Frank told David he could be arrested at any moment. In the end, he wasn't. Fairly quickly, the authorities decided not to charge him at all, but not before the woman's allegation was all over the media.

I told Frank I'd get a lawyer. In Port St. Lucie, I was concerned about how the local folks would react as word spread that three black ball-players had been accused of raping a white woman. I was also concerned about spending the next decade or two in a Florida prison. All of the New York papers sent more reporters down to cover the story. They began to fight with one another over scoops on the case. For six weeks, what was left of my reputation was debated and trashed.

Vince, Daryl, and I all passed polygraphs, and the woman's case began to fall apart. It turned out she had some history making similar allegations. On April 15, State Attorney Bruce Colton announced the cases were being dropped. Citing "an accumulation of problems" with the evidence, Colton said that prosecutors had come to doubt "whether there was a likelihood of a conviction."

But I definitely didn't get off free. Nor did those who loved me. Monica, pregnant with our second daughter, was crushed by the whole episode, as was my mother, who was still dealing with the grief from her own mom's death. They always believed I didn't rape the woman.

But Monica wasn't buying my story that nothing had happened between me and the woman. I never admitted anything to Monica. I just counted myself lucky the case never went to trial. For sure, I would have had to testify.

Nineteen ninety-two turned into 1993. Jeff Torborg was replaced by Dallas Green, the John Wayne of major-league baseball. Dallas looked at me and saw the last of the bad-boy Mets, and I think he wanted me gone. By 1994, I certainly made that easy for him.

12

Sliding Back

OPENING DAY AT WRIGLEY isn't supposed to feel good. Winter is always slow to pack in Chicago. On this day, April 4, 1994, the temperature said fifty-three degrees. To a pitcher raised in Tampa, it felt more like forty-three, maybe thirty-three with the wind chill.

But I wasn't worried. I took pride in my ability to handle the Cubs, no matter what the circumstances. Going into this game, I was 26–4 against them, my best against any team in baseball. I'd beaten them at Shea to get to the playoffs in 1986, hadn't I? Okay, so it wasn't 1986 anymore. The Mets had lost one hundred games in 1993, and it was hard to say why '94 would be much better. Dallas Green was our third manager in four years, fourth if you count the seven games in 1991 with interim Mike Cubbage. I'd lost fifteen games in '93, the most in my career, and I'd lost thirteen the season before. Though I was only twenty-nine, the injuries to my arm and shoulder were forcing me to reimagine my whole pitching style. I was entering the final year of my contract with a team of semi-unknowns behind me. I was going to start the season by handling Chicago.

I took the hill and went 3 and 2 on leadoff hitter Tuffy Rhodes before he hit one over my head and I watched it sail on the wind out of the ballpark. It didn't feel like a very good omen. But we got a couple of runs back, turning their 1–0 into our 2–1. In the bottom of the third, the Cubs got the first two batters on base and up came Tuffy to the plate.

Bang! He did it again. Out of the park in center field.

As he trotted around the bases, I felt like maybe he was admiring his work a little too long. Another home run? Who the hell was this kid? A twenty-five-year-old semiscrub who'd played in barely one hundred games across four major-league seasons, clubbing all of five home runs combined, with a career average in the mid-.200s? In the top of the fifth, the Mets didn't pinch hit for me, and I helped my cause with a two-run single. By the end of our half of the inning, we were up 9–5.

Opening the bottom of the fifth Tuffy was back again. My plan was to drill him. Show him I wasn't happy about his recent performance and that long diva gaze at his last home run. I didn't want the ump to toss me from the game. So I had to make it look good. My first couple of pitches would be unhittable curveballs, just a little wild. Then I'd find a home for one in Tuffy's rib cage. That was the idea.

Well, plans don't always work out like you expect. Tuffy hit my second curveball into the center-field bleachers, exactly where the other two shots had gone. Some guy no one had ever heard of had just made major-league history hitting home runs off of me in his first three at bats on opening day. At the end of the inning, I was furious with myself. I marched into the dugout and, in my frustration, did something stupid. I kicked a bat rack and injured my right big toe. I pitched a couple more innings. I hobbled right to the ice bucket.

I didn't want anyone to know the truth about how I hurt my foot. It was too embarrassing. And the media had fun with the minor mystery. Even the *New York Times* jumped in: "Is a bent spike jamming into the big toe a common baseball injury?"

I missed my next start, trying to ignore the pain. I was sure my toe was fine. By the end of April, as I pitched in Los Angeles against the Dodgers, the pain became too much. People were starting to talk about my limp. After the game, I went on the thirty-day disabled list. An MRI revealed ligament and cartilage damage.

Kicking that bat rack was really childish.

I was too injured to play, but not so hobbled that I was immobilized. My rehab schedule was to go easy on the foot and wait out the pain. Without a ball and a glove, my drinking and carousing went off the charts. And, with that, other temptations crept back in.

I wasn't using yet. But my mind was opening to it.

When I started feeling better, the Mets decided I should get back in shape by pitching a couple of minor-league games. At the end of May, I flew down to Virginia and played a few games with the AAA Norfolk Tides at Harbor Park.

When I got there, I couldn't help but notice that there was no drug tester around. Maybe it was the minor leagues. Maybe they were starting to trust me. Maybe they shouldn't have.

I was scheduled for a Friday night start in Binghamton, the AA affiliate in upstate New York. Then on Saturday, I'd be back in the big game when I'd meet the major-league team in Ohio. But that wasn't for a couple of days. Before I headed upstate, I decided to celebrate my return at a sports-themed strip club in Queens called Scores.

I had a wife, a son, and two young daughters by then, plus another son on the way. But my addiction was taking me out on the town again. This time, it wasn't a steakhouse with Rusty. It wasn't beers with Keith or Ron. It had nothing to do with miniatures on the team plane. This time, I figured, I'd just go out alone. As far as I was concerned, no one could keep up with my drinking. And no one had to know what I was doing.

This was a world before Twitter, blogs, and cell phone cameras. It was possible to go to a strip club with no fear of Page Six or TMZ.com. Some of the dancers knew me. One of them gave me a lap dance. We were just having fun.

"How about a more private dance?" she asked me.

I nodded.

"It'd be nicer up in the manager's office," she said.

Okay. She took my hand and led me upstairs. Another dancer followed. It wasn't long before both girls were totally naked, playfully rubbing up against each other and me. All three of us were laughing and doing shots. Pretty soon, the coke came out.

"Let's do a line," one of them said.

"No, thanks," I answered. I had willpower. I had limits. "Sorry, ladies. Enjoy yourselves. I'm getting tested. Can't share."

They kept snorting. I got more drunk. The seed that was planted in my brain in Norfolk was flowering now.

"Hmmm, they didn't test me down there," I thought.

One of the strippers chopped the cocaine with a razor blade on the glass-top desk before snorting the powder through a plastic cocktail straw. She slid the straw slowly and seductively.

I thought some more: "They must not be testing at minor-league parks. They probably won't test me in Binghamton. And anyway, that's forty-eight hours from now."

I began to make some drunken calculations. Creative accounting, fueled by many shots of Absolut vodka.

The addict in me began to bargain. I could probably metabolize the coke and piss it out quickly, I told myself. I'll bet I could be peeing clean by Binghamton. Right about then, my attention was drawn to the eye-popping scene unfolding in front of me. Looking through one stripper's legs, I could see the other one tap-tap-tapping more cocaine from the baggie to the desk.

"I doubt they'll have a tester in Cincinnati over the weekend," I told myself.

"Oh, that's fuckin' good," the baggie girl said, answering my unspoken thought and Hoovering the powder into her nose. I heard her swallow, powerfully, as she let the coke drip from her sinuses down into the back of her throat.

I knew that feeling.

I liked that feeling.

I missed that feeling.

I wanted that feeling.

Now.

More math: "The soonest my next test could be is over ninety-six hours!"

I was sold. "Maybe I'll try just one or two," I said.

I snorted a line. The disease reawakened instantly. I was right back where I was in 1986. It was like a carnival worker had just lowered the metal protective bar on the roller coaster car. I settled in and waved good-bye.

I snorted another line. Then I had another gulp of vodka. It all felt good. My mind started reeling. All I was feeling was satisfied. "I've got some drinks," I was thinking. "I've got some strippers. I've got some coke."

In other words, I wasn't thinking at all.

I was no longer worried about when the next drug test might be coming. "That's so far away," I thought. And the plans kept coming.

"I'll get someone else to take it for me."

"I'll duck the guy."

"If it comes back dirty, I'll claim, 'Screwup at the lab.' "

I stayed out all night. I called a number I had never forgotten. I bought more coke. I did more coke. After seven years clean, I was back in business again.

It was already dawn, and I was totally wasted when I drove back to my house in Roslyn, Long Island. I sobered up. I drove to Binghamton. I guessed correctly. No tester appeared. I pitched. I felt great. No one had any idea where I'd been.

I just felt like I'd been lucky and had gotten away with something cool. No harm, no foul. There was just one problem: getting lucky proved to my addict's mind that I could do it again.

I flew to Cincinnati, reaching the ballpark around five p.m. The game was scheduled for seven. At about five forty-five, one of the trainers came over to me and casually said, "Your guy is here."

Boom! There he was. The tester who'd stood next to me as I peed into dozens of cups already. He was one of several, but I recognized him immediately. Short, stocky, friendly, totally clueless about my recent whereabouts. "Hey Doc!" he said cheerfully.

I could hear my heartbeat in my ears.

"How you doin'?" I answered with a smile.

I could feel my insides shaking. My breathing seemed strange. I was already in my uniform, but I was ready to run out of the stadium. Call for a taxi, claim a family emergency, hop on a plane, and hide somewhere.

"Doc Gooden got kidnapped"; "Doc Gooden fell asleep behind the concession stand." Any excuse would be better than filling a cup with coke-heavy urine.

"Be with you in a minute," I told the tester, standing and walking toward the locker-room door. "I've got BP," batting practice, I said. "But I'll be right back."

I didn't know what I was going to do. I needed time to think.

I sprinted across the outfield a few times, not really knowing why. Maybe I could sweat the cocaine out. That made no sense. Maybe one of the clubhouse kids would pee in the cup for me. Wait, that made no sense. The cup had a temperature gauge to make the sure the urine was recent. The tester worked for Major League Baseball. He wasn't about to look the other way. I knew I was doomed.

I went back inside, took the test, and hoped for the best. Maybe something magical would happen. Maybe the specimen would get lost in transit. Maybe the commissioner's office wouldn't want the bad publicity. More hoping. More bargaining. The tester screwed on the lid. I put my initials on the cup. I signed the paperwork, and off he went.

I kept pitching. More time passed. Not a word from anyone. I was tested again. It had been more than a week since I used cocaine. I was starting to wonder if maybe I'd passed the Cincinnati test. I showed up in Miami without a Father's Day present for my dad, who had come to watch me pitch live for the first time in years. We beat the Marlins — that would have to be his gift. Thankfully, there wasn't any news until the following day.

I was napping in bed at the team hotel when my phone rang. It was Dr. Lans.

"I'm coming down to Atlanta," he said. "We're going to have to talk."

If the walls of my hotel room had fallen right then, I don't think I would have felt any more shaken. Dr. Lans's trip to Atlanta could only mean one thing.

"We have a positive test, Dwight," he explained softly when he arrived at the hotel.

"That's crazy," I said instinctually. "I never used!"

I was getting so predictable.

"Crazy or not, we have to explain it," Dr. Lans continued. "And deal with it. We've got to meet with the league in New York. We can go now or when this Atlanta series is over. Your call."

"Let's wait," I said. Of course I said that. If I left the team midseries, everyone would know something was up. Word would spread immediately. And a chance to delay? I always preferred to delay.

When we flew to New York, Dr. Lans and I met in the Major League Baseball office with three men. Lou Melendez was a lawyer for the Player Relations Committee. Dr. Robert Millman was baseball's medical director. Dr. Joel Solomon had a similar position with the players association.

My first strategy? Lie again. It didn't work any better this time.

"Dwight, you've got to take some responsibility for this," Melendez said. "Let's face it head-on and work on your issues."

I confessed. "It was a mistake," I explained. "A onetime slip-up. I've been clean for seven years. It won't happen again."

They were sorry, they said. But because of my prior transgressions, this time it would have to be a sixty-day suspension. If I tested clean moving forward, I could salvage what was left of the 1994 season after that.

I went home and told Monica. "I messed up," I said. "We'll be spending more of the summer in St. Petersburg."

"Very funny," she said. As my crooked smile gave way to an expression of profound sadness, she realized I wasn't joking at all.

I tried to downplay the situation. "I missed a test," I told her. "This is my punishment." Inside, Monica knew. She just knew. Maybe she hadn't expected the cocaine, but no husband goes out all night and comes home at dawn fish-eyed and smelling like stripper if his life isn't spinning out of control.

It was time to break the news to my parents. As I sat there revving my courage and staring at the telephone, a rare moment of clarity kicked in. All I'd been giving them, I could see, was shame, pain, and embarrassment. I could barely punch the number into the phone. Yes, I'd achieved the dream my dad had for me. I'd achieved the dream he had for himself. But what was the cost? Foolishly, I tried to soften the blow.

My mom answered the phone. "I missed a test," I told, giving the lie that hadn't worked on Monica another try. "They say they have to suspend me again."

"Oh, Dwight," my mom said sadly. Her voice was filled with disappointment. "This isn't good. This isn't good at all."

My dad took the phone. When I was suspended in 1987, he was shocked and silent. He wouldn't or couldn't talk to me. In the time since then, we'd settled into a "hear no evil, see no evil" relationship. When he'd ask how I was doing, I'd always say, "Fine." He'd say, "Great, take care of yourself," and we'd move on. This time, he took a different tone.

"Listen," he said, "you gotta get right for you. Whatever it takes. Forget about baseball. That's not important right now. Work on beating these demons or there won't be any baseball left." He paused for a second and introduced a thought that must have just dawned on him. I could hear the worry in his voice. "There won't be any *you*."

"Dad — " I tried to say.

"Son," he cut me off. "You've had a great career. If and when you get back to it, great. Think of your family first. Do this for them."

I think it was the first time I'd ever heard my dad shift his priorities away from baseball. As far back as Little League, he'd always said, "If you want to be a pro, you gotta put baseball ahead of everything else. It has to be number one in your life." The sad part is that, for a long time, we'd both known what my top priority was. It wasn't family, and it wasn't baseball.

Dad's words meant a lot to me but not enough. The commissioner's office had suspended me but not ordered me into treatment. Faced with nothing but shame and embarrassment and with a lot of free time on my hands, I went back to drinking and drugging almost immediately. I could have reached out to my parents for support. It wouldn't have been hard to find them. They lived a few doors down from Monica, the kids, and me in a house I had bought for them on our St. Petersburg cul-de-sac. Instead, a few beers led me over the W. Howard Frankland Bridge into Tampa and back to cocaine. I was still being tested regularly, but I didn't care. I was tempting Major League Baseball to suspend me even longer. After a few high-pressure phone calls from the Mets and from my agent — and with my dad's heartfelt words stuck my head — I agreed to go back into rehab.

At the end of July, out of shape and looking like a phantom, I flew out to the Betty Ford Center in Rancho Mirage, California, where I stayed for twenty-three days. Betty Ford was a great facility. It was staffed by people who tried to focus and challenge me. I was polite, but I never really cooperated with them. This may sound like an old cliché. But you have to be in treatment for the right reasons, not because someone is forcing you to. Even the greatest treatment facility just gives you the tools. There is no magic. There is no instant cure. You have to accept your powerlessness and work every day at recovery.

I wasn't even close to there.

I saw what I'd done as a minor slip-up. I was only going through the motions of recovery. I knew I had to navigate my way, going through the motions, back to baseball. But never did I think I needed to change myself fundamentally. The best way to help myself and my family, I thought, wasn't to dive into recovery. It was to put all this behind me and get back on a baseball field.

I left the Betty Ford Center feeling like I'd just had my ticket punched. I had done what I'd been asked to, now let me get back to work. I secretly knew I was probably not done drinking. I told myself I would do my best to stay away from cocaine. I also left the Betty Ford Center without a job. Baseball players had gone on strike two days earlier.

I didn't fly back to Florida immediately. I had to stop in New York to check in with the Mets brass. I also had to see Drs. Solomon and Millman and Lou Melendez. I spent a few days in meetings, trying to convince everyone how well I'd done at Betty Ford. "When the strike and my suspension are over," I told everyone, "I'll be ready to join the team again and contribute to Major League Baseball."

"You're looking good, Dwight," Dr. Solomon said.

"I'm feeling good," I said. "You know, it was honestly just the one mistake. I think it was just the depression caused by my injury that triggered it. I've dealt with a lot the past few years. But I've got a new perspective now."

The people at the team and league did their best to appear hopeful. But they also had a backup plan. The biggest piece of advice I took from our meetings was: "For God's sake, if you're tempted to do anything, just drink. Just do not, under any circumstances, do cocaine."

That flew in the face of what I'd heard at Betty Ford. I say "heard" — not "learned" — because my mind wasn't open enough for learning. I probably should have realized what a bad idea "just drink" was for me.

I got on my flight to Tampa International Airport. As soon as we hit cruising altitude, I downed five Absolut miniatures. When the plane landed, my defenses were already lowered and I was thoroughly drunk. I didn't think twice about calling my dealer from the terminal. "Who needs a taxi?" I thought. He picked me up and I didn't go home for three days.

There was no doubt I'd get caught and pay dearly. But the immediate gratification of the booze and the coke was too strong to resist. Barely forty-eight hours out of rehab, I was way, way out on thin ice. I had no plan to test clean, or even call Monica and let her know my New York meetings were done. I'd figure all that out once I came down.

Normally, once I got back to Tampa–St. Pete after the season, I'd call the commissioner's office in New York to say I was back home. Someone in New York would set up a place for me to go for testing, usually at a walk-in clinic in a strip mall. This time, it took me a week to call in. I said a sick relative had taken me out of town. Really, I was my own sick relative, giving my system time to pee out the cocaine. I passed one or two tests before I went on the bender that would cement my place in the annals of self-destruction.

For weeks, it was the 1986 off-season all over again. Only instead of sneaking into my parents' house in the morning, hoping my mom was already at work, now I had more responsibilities. More baggage. Kids and a wife. I wasn't a hotshot athlete spiraling out of control, too young and too dumb to understand what was happening. I was a dad and husband dragging everyone down.

I wasn't looking for running mates like I had back in '86 or '87. The few people I spent time with were the ones who assured me what I was doing wasn't so bad. But most of the time, I just wanted to get my drugs and do them alone. I spent a lot of time in the bathroom with the door locked. I lay alone in bed for hours in the daytime with the curtains drawn. The word "partying" didn't apply anymore.

When I was at home, I was terrible to my wife, Monica, two months away from giving birth to our son Devin. I sulked around the house. I hated to be disturbed. I considered my own family a bother. Then I'd disappear for days. In early September, she planned a third birthday party for our youngest daughter, Ariel. I was out drugging the night before. I couldn't even make it to an afternoon party.

I called with another stupid excuse.

"I spent the night with friends in Orlando," I lied. "Now I'm stuck on the highway with a flat tire."

I knew Monica wasn't believing a word of it. "I'm sorry," I said. "It's a special tire. They can't get a new one until late this afternoon."

"So you're really not coming to your daughter's birthday party?" Monica said, no longer concealing her disgust. She'd invited friends and relatives, many of them mine. I was cooking up fresh excuses.

"I'm trying to do everything I can," I told Monica.

"She'll never have another third birthday," my wife said. I could hear the hurt in her voice.

"I said I was sorry!"

She hung up the phone.

My disappearing acts had gotten so frequent, all Monica came to expect was the occasional phone call to let her know that I was still alive before I stumbled in at dawn and went to bed. She wasn't worried I was being unfaithful to her. My only romance was cocaine. And the deeper I got into addiction, it was becoming more of a job than a fling.

When Monica hung up on me the day of Ariel's party, I wasn't in Orlando or stuck on the side of a road. I had driven to the edge of our cul-de-sac and saw all the cars parked around our home. I decided I couldn't face all those people, not in the condition I was in. The party had already started. Everyone was there. Our friends and relatives would take one look at me and know. I was paralyzed by guilt and paranoia. The best I could hope for, I thought, sitting in the car, was that everyone was having so much fun in there, they wouldn't miss me at all.

Once the guests left, I told myself, I could slip inside and spend some time alone with the birthday girl.

I finally crept in after dark without a present in hand. Ariel met me near the door. She was still awake and happy, surrounded by her birthday toys.

"Daddy was at a meeting with a baseball team," I said.

She didn't need to hear the truth, and I didn't have the courage to tell it.

Major League Baseball was actually fairly lenient with me. They gave me a comfortable cushion after rehab to start turning in clean tests. I just couldn't do it, no matter how flexible they were. I was in a Tampa hotel room on a $2,000 eighteen-hour binge with some fellow degenerates when a thought somehow cut through the fog of cocaine.

"Oh, shit," I said out loud. "I have a drug test in the morning."

Even my zonked-out friends could see this might be a problem.

"I don't even know what the point is," I said glumly.

"Relax, Doc," one of my associates said. "I know just the thing." He explained that if I took enough diuretic pills, I'd pass the test no matter how much coke I'd taken in. The only problem was that we were in no shape to go to the drugstore. He made some calls and eventually a friend showed up with a bag full of bottled water and a few packs of pills. I popped a handful and began guzzling the water. I peed and peed, and after a while my heart started racing. The diuretics must have had a jolt of caffeine mixed in. I put a wet washcloth on my forehead. I lay on the bed unable to move, feeling like my chest was going to explode. I spent the rest of the night peeing into a plastic garbage can. More than once, I thought about calling 911.

Nothing could stop morning from arriving.

When I felt well enough, I drove to the clinic, gave my sample, and cooled it with the drugs for a while.

I didn't have much faith in the pills. But I was hoping if I could quickly follow the dirty test with a couple of clean ones, maybe I could somehow avoid the trouble that was heading my way.

Sure enough, a week later, Dr. Solomon was on the phone. The league, the players association, and the Mets, he said, had been studying my test results. Everyone was extremely concerned.

"When can you fly to New York?" he asked. "Can you fly to New York? Are you in any condition to do that?"

"Sure," I bluffed. "I'm doing great."

I arrived in New York and met with a larger group this time. It was Drs. Millman, Solomon, and Lans, as well as Lou Melendez and Gene Orza, a lawyer for the players association. All of them appeared deeply concerned.

"Looking at your test," Dr. Solomon said, "we frankly have no idea how you are still alive."

Gene Orza sighed and shook his head. "You know," he said, "you're worse than Steve Howe." Until that morning, I guess, the hard-throwing left-handed relief pitcher had set the standard for substance-abusing ball players.

I started tearing up. Once I did, I couldn't tell anymore if I was really crying or acting. My head was that messed up. Either way, the situation was somewhere far beyond sad. "I tried to overdose," I said. "I wanted to die." That was a lie. They were getting ready to throw the book at me. I didn't know what else to say.

"Dwight," Dr. Solomon said, "that's very serious." He paused and raised his eyebrows in gentle concern. "Maybe you should think about giving rehab another try?"

"I don't know that it helped," I said.

I didn't mention that I hadn't given it much of a chance.

On September 15, Major League Baseball and the New York Mets, in a joint announcement, said I'd failed my third drug test, an offense that would add additional time to my 1994 suspension. And the clock wouldn't start running until the strike was through. The idea that I'd be playing at all in 1995 was rapidly slipping away.

Within a few days, Mets manager Dallas Green mentioned to the press that I wasn't in his plans for the 1995 season anyway. Joe McIlvaine, the man who had drafted me, echoed that to the papers. It felt like a final kick in the teeth. Too bad I had no one else I could possibly blame.

13

Suicide Squeeze

TOOK THE BULLETS out of the gun. I pointed the weapon against my forehead. I held it there until Monica and the girls got home from Grandma and Grandpa's house. The gun was a semiautomatic 9-millimeter Glock, more than enough to do the job if I'd had the balls to leave it loaded. But this was suicide theater, not a suicide attempt.

"Dwight!" my wife screamed when she opened the bedroom door. "What's wrong with you?" She was eight and a half months pregnant.

"Mon—," I pleaded. "Just leave. It'll be much easier this way. For everyone."

"No!" she howled. Her face was a twist of fear and confusion. "Please put the gun down! Please!" She was crying now. "Why are you doing this?"

"I can't tell you," I answered. "You don't want to know."

"Whatever it is," she said, forcing a layer of calm into her voice, "we can work it out."

"I don't know."

"Promise me you won't pull the trigger," she said. "I'm going to go get your mother. This is crazy!"

I'd been unable to manipulate Major League Baseball and the New York Mets and their stern-faced doctors. But at least I was getting some traction at home. If anything, this sick show was crueler and more selfish than real suicide. It sent terror into the hearts of those who loved me without putting myself at any actual risk. It was a horrible and shameful game. But in the grip of my addiction, I swear, it seemed perfectly reasonable to me.

My mom marched into the room and came to the side of the bed where I was sitting. Mom never fooled around. She snatched the gun from me. "Gimme that," she said. I put up no struggle. Then, she and Monica and I huddled together and cried.

This was early November of 1994. A week earlier, I had filed for free agency, one of nineteen players that year to tell their teams "I'm outta here." When I next pitched in the majors, I'd make them sorry they weren't nicer to me. In fact, I had no plan for actually pitching any time soon, since it would mean I'd have to get off drugs. But now, as I held that gun to my head, even the far-fetched notion of playing ball again was being pushed back yet more.

I'd gotten a registered letter in the mail that morning. Baseball Commissioner Bud Selig said he was very sorry, but I was being suspended for the entire 1995 season, 168 days on top of the 15 days I already had to make up for 1994. Even my coked-up brain could understand: this meant I would have no job, no salary, and nothing to do all day. I would be failing my father's most basic test of manhood: Do what you want to. But make sure your family is taken care of.

Here's how sick I was: The letter didn't make me want to kill myself. It made we want to put on a show of self-destruction so dramatic that my family would sympathize with me instead of being angry I'd messed up my life again. I would trump their anger with depression. I would show them I was more upset than they were disappointed. It was a shitty, shitty thing to do. But initially at least, it got the response I was looking for.

"I'm sick," I told my mother. "I have to change my ways."

She'd heard that before. "How?" she said.

"Mom," I said, "I'm not really sure."

The announcement of my yearlong suspension wasn't released to the media until Friday, November 4. With it came a statement from Joe McIlvaine. I had never imagined, as he and my father played that game of chicken over my rookie signing bonus almost thirteen years earlier, that my professional baseball career would come to this.

"Dwight Gooden needs to get his life in order," Joe's message read. "He has been offered the best assistance baseball and the New York Mets have to give for his problem and has not taken advantage of this guidance and help. All of us who love this man urge him to get the help he needs, put God into his life, and exhibit the same tenacity he showed on the mound, especially in the early years of his career, when a lead in the seventh inning meant a victory in the ninth. Dwight needs to demonstrate that same degree of competitiveness to defeat a far more insidious enemy that is sucking the life out of him both personally and professionally."

Wow. If that didn't shake me, nothing would.

The announcement of the suspension had one good effect. It staggered me enough to keep me home for the final days of Monica's pregnancy. I was there at four a.m. on November 10 when she let me know it was time. I put her in the car and raced — not over the W. Howard Frankland Bridge to the clubs and the dealers of Tampa but to All Children's Hospital in St. Petersburg, where she gave birth to our son, Devin.

That kept me home and sober for one more week.

Then I decided I had to share the news with friends in Tampa. A drink or two turned into a day or two and a long coke bender. Another hotel room. Another line. Another lie.

Joe McIlvaine's lecture wasn't enough. Neither was fresh father-hood. I was starting to think I should just let the cocaine kill me. Not an empty-gun threat but a sad, easy way to end everything. I could retire from baseball, let Monica and the kids live off what I'd earned already, then go ahead and overdose. Why keep embarrassing myself and my family with failed drug tests?

I told Jim, my agent, to get the retirement wheels rolling. I asked the league to start the paperwork. One night as we barbecued in the neighborhood, I told Gary my plan to quit playing.

"I know you're not going out like that," he said, not even taking me seriously.

"Look," I said. "I've accomplished everything I set out to do in baseball."

He didn't want to hear it. "Somethin' ain't right with you, Doc," he said, shaking his head. "Somethin' ain't been right with you for a long time."

"So," I answered, "it's time to fix that." Then I took another sip of my beer.

Gary knew whatever I said, it was just another excuse to keep using cocaine. Retirement was code for more time to get high without anyone checking up on me. Killing myself might not have been my real intention. But it could certainly be my real result.

It was no more than a few days later that I got a call from Bob Klapisch, a baseball writer in New York. "You're looking at a year away from the game," Bob said. "What are you planning to do?"

"Get into shape," I lied. There was no sense pouring gasoline on the fire and filling the papers with stories of my retirement at age thirty.

"I know a guy down there," he explained. "Ray Negron. Worked for the Yankees for a long time."

"The Yankees?" For the first time since the birth of Devin, something made me smile. If by some miracle I didn't retire and I ever played again, I loved the idea of finishing my career in New York.

"Yeah," Bob continued. Then he quickly reeled me back in. "But with the players on strike and you being suspended, nothing's happening there. You gotta just talk to Ray. He wants to meet with you. He's got a lot of connections sending American ballplayers to Japan."

The conversation continued, but after "Japan" I heard nothing else. I called Ray Negron and set up a meeting.

When he was seventeen, Ray was caught writing graffiti on a wall at Yankee Stadium. George Steinbrenner screeched up in a car and busted Ray, spray-paint can in hand. But instead of turning him over to the cops and forgetting about him, George offered Ray a job as a Yankees batboy and a chance to turn his life around. Growing up in the Bronx, Ray had been around some tough people. He definitely had that street-smart way of carrying himself. But he'd gone from vandal to sports executive to well-connected middleman, and now he lived in St. Pete.

"So you think I can get a deal in Japan?" I asked him.

"Sure," Ray said. "But come on, man." He looked into my droopy eyes. "You've got to pull yourself together first. You can't just rely on your name."

"I'm willing to do the work," I said.

I wasn't, of course.

I wasted a couple of weeks of Ray's time, showing up at his house after night-long binges, promising I was cleaning up, constantly bugging him about the Japan deal. "I can't help you if you're gonna continue using," he told me one morning after we finished eating breakfast with his kids. "There's no way right now that we could get a deal. If you want to put in the effort, we can do something. If not, leave. You're stressing me out."

His anger, I admitted, was justified.

"When you feel like doing drugs, Doc, call me before it happens," he said. "When you've already done them, I can't do shit."

"I should have gone back to treatment," I told him. "I need something bigger than I am."

He told me about a buddy of his named Vincent, who used to work on Wall Street. "He put his future in a crack pipe and smoked it," Ray said. Ray always talked dramatic like that. "Then he came down here. Got in a shitload of trouble trading other people's cars for drugs."

"And he's your friend?" I asked. I wondered what sorts of people Ray associated with.

"Yeah," he said. "And so are you. But you've gotta put in the effort. We're gonna go to an NA meeting with Vincent. We'll go today."

The Narcotics Anonymous meeting at Freedom House on Tenth Avenue North in St. Petersburg was a long way from Betty Ford. There were no supermodels or Hollywood actors in the room when Ray and I got there. The only ballplayer was me.

We met Ray's friend Vincent and listened to a man named Ron Dock. Like Ray, Ron was from the Bronx. He was a Marine in Vietnam who learned to calm the stresses of war with opium and then heroin. He sunk into addiction, PTSD, jail, and the streets. "When you're eating out of trash cans, and you're okay with that, you have a problem," Ron was saying to the group. "I know. I was cool with that for a long time."

Our backgrounds couldn't have been much more different. But listening to Ron, I could tell we had a lot in common. We had both left home at an early age and got a taste for high-pressure adrenaline — his M16, my fastball. Then we both moved quickly to drugs. When Ron got done speaking and the meeting broke up, Ray introduced us.

"That was some speech," I said, holding out my hand.

"Who are you?" Ron said gruffly.

"I'm Dwight Gooden, sir."

"He plays baseball," Ray said with a smile. "He was a pitcher for the Mets, in your old stomping grounds."

Ron shrugged. "I don't know shit about baseball."

"That's cool," I said.

"And I don't give a shit about baseball." He furrowed his brow and looked at me. "What are you doing here?"

"I gotta get clean," I said.

"Gotta? Or wanna? Two different things."

I looked at Ray nervously. Who was this guy? Wasn't he supposed to be supportive? Ray nodded back at me.

"I want to get clean, Mr. Dock," I said.

"Why?" Ron said. That was the only time I saw him smile that day. He was pressing me.

"I'm pretty sure I will die if I don't," I said.

"Keep coming back for meetings, and we can talk," Ron told me, his voice sounding compassionate for the first time. "Show me you're invested in this."

I started going to the NA meetings. And unlike at Smithers and Betty Ford, I wanted to be there. I gave the Narcotics Anonymous meetings the same focus I had given my drug runs. In early 1995, Ron became my NA sponsor.

Five days a week, Ray started picking me up in the morning and driving over to the baseball fields at Eckerd College, where I would throw. Then, I'd hit the weight room with trainer Larry Mayol. After a quick shower, we'd stop for an NA meeting. Sometimes Vincent or Ron would meet us for lunch. I spent afternoons with my family, trying to repair some of the damage I'd done. And I'd go to bed early. Even though I knew I was suspended for the entire season, when the teams finally started playing in '95, I asked Major League Baseball to begin testing me again.

I could feel myself getting stronger. But I also hit a speed bump on my road to recovery. Actually, it was more like I was pulled over by the cops. In March, I was stopped for driving my Mercedes at 117 miles an hour on Interstate 275 with an open beer in the car at four a.m. I'd been out with friends late and shouldn't have driven home. That was a dangerous thing for me to be doing, dangerous to other drivers and dangerous to my recovery. The cop gave me a breathalyzer. I wasn't anywhere near drunk. We argued over whether his machine was broken. I got off with only a speeding ticket.

"You're not out of the woods yet, Doc," Ron said when I told him what happened. Just telling my sponsor was a good sign, I thought. Hiding had always been part of my problem. "You're never out of the woods. Be vigilant. Pick yourself up. Don't listen to the negative people. Keep working."

I stayed straight. At nine months, I felt ready to move ahead. One day when my arm was feeling great, I started pressing Ray about Japan again.

"Nah," Ray said. "Let's not worry about that. You don't want to go over there. I was mainly dangling that out there so you'd clean up and get into shape. Let's focus on getting you back in the majors."

I felt duped at first. But it wasn't long before Ray was bringing agents to watch me pitch. The White Sox seemed really interested.

That summer, I started going to church on Sundays with my mother. I turned to her after one service and asked, "Was I ever baptized?"

"No, son, you weren't," she said.

When I was growing up, I guess you'd call our family religious. But my parents weren't too strict about the formalities. Mom went to church while Dad got his spiritual sustenance from NBC's *Game of the Week*. Now getting baptized suddenly seemed important to me. I wanted to feel like I belonged to a church. Up to then, I'd only belonged on teams.

A few Sundays later at the end of the service, the pastor said, "If anyone would like to turn their life over to God . . ." When I left the pew and walked toward the altar, the whole congregation stood and cheered. I'd been cheered in ballparks for various achievements. I'd been cheered at baseball card shows and sports award dinners. I'd never been cheered simply because I was human and recognized my connection to God.

The scouts kept coming. The Pirates, the Blue Jays, more White Sox, some Independent League scouts. I even called the Mets to see if they'd be interested. I had never wanted to leave our relationship the way we'd left off. I had never wanted to leave New York. I hated the circumstances I'd left under. I considered New York my second home. The fans there had just been great to me. The Mets declined.

By this time, Ray was unofficially representing me. He got in touch with Commissioner Selig to see if he'd reduce my suspension and reinstate me. "If Dwight passes all the tests he's taking," he told the commissioner, "and is doing everything right, you should take him back." Ray assured him that I'd been "doing all the right things" and regularly attending sobriety meetings.

Gary got me a tryout with his team, the Marlins, at the end of the '95 season. Ray, my dad, and I drove to Miami. I threw on the sidelines for their pitching coach, Larry Rothschild, and then we watched the game in a luxury suite with owner Wayne Huizenga and Dave Dombrowski, the general manager. Playing on the same team as Gary would be a dream come true. "Let's work something out soon, Doc," Dombrowski said. "Looks like you're back." My dad looked so proud of me.

Just a year earlier, I'd been contemplating retirement, even dying. But now playing again seemed like a real possibility. Ray said he'd been in touch with George Steinbrenner. Before anything was final, he said, George wanted to speak with me. When the Yankees got knocked out of the playoffs, George flew down to Tampa, where he lived in the off-season. Ray arranged a dinner with the Boss at Iavarone's.

Before we could get down to the business of my comeback, though, one small problem had to be resolved. This was more than just a career issue. This was personal. Just as my suspension was coming to an end on October 1, the players association told me they were decertifying Ray, who'd been acting as my agent. Gene Orza said the union had sent a memo out to teams not to negotiate with him. But no one ever told me. Here I was, on the verge of achieving my comeback, and I got that news. Ray had been with me ten hours of every day for the past year. I knew I wouldn't be clean without him. I wouldn't be talking to anyone in baseball, definitely not George Steinbrenner, without Ray Negron.

I was mad. I even threatened a one-man "strike" until the matter was settled. Ray just told me to stay calm and focused. "It'll work out," he said. "We just need to keep talking to people."

Ray was right. Somehow or another, all the technicalities were resolved.

For years, I'd heard stories about what a hard-ass the Yankees boss was. But when Ray and I got out of the car and walked into the restaurant in our nicest suits and ties, we saw George and pitching coach Billy Connors sitting there in sweat suits. We had a friendly three-hour conversation and a very tasty meal. George asked about my wife, my children, my recovery, my community work. I told him how much fun I'd been having coaching Dwight Junior's Little League team. We even talked about Darryl Strawberry, who'd signed with the Yankees the year before. The subject of Dwight Senior in a Yankee uniform never came up.

In the car ride back to St. Petersburg, I let Ray have it. "What the hell were we doing there?" I asked him.

"Don't worry about it," Ray said.

"He has no interest in signing me," I scoffed. "You just wanted to meet with him, right?"

"No, that's BS," Ray countered. "Give it time. He just wanted to feel you out. I have no doubt they'll call back."

Sure enough, the next day Ray got a call from George, asking us to meet at his hotel in Tampa, the Bay Harbor Inn. This time, my dad came along too, almost an echo of our very first contract talks with the New York Mets. Two hours later, George offered me a deal: one year guaranteed with options for a second and a third year. He wanted me to play winter ball before the 1996 season.

Right there at the table, I agreed.

George looked at me and said, "I know you've had a great career so far. I think you'll also have a great career with us."

"I think you're right," I said. "Yes, sir."

14

No-Hitter

WENT TO NEW YORK WITH my head on straight. I moved back into my place in Roslyn, which was a long commute to Yankee Stadium in the Bronx. But I felt comfortable on Long Island. I had a purpose again. I was playing major-league baseball and lucky to have the chance. I was staying out of nightclubs. I wasn't using cocaine. I was happy being drug tested two or three times a week. I wanted no gray area when it came to people's opinions or curiosity about me. My attitude was, "Don't take my word for it. Just check the test."

As soon as school got out for the summer, Monica and the kids joined me in New York. If the Yankees had a day game, we'd all go out to dinner at Pizza Hut or Chuck E. Cheese's. Being together like that without so much chaos was a huge relief for all of us. I felt like a dad as much as a ballplayer.

Too bad I got off to such a lousy pitching start.

By the time I won my first game for the Yankees, on May 8 against Detroit, I'd already lost three and collected two no-decisions. The reporters were wondering when I'd be bounced to AAA ball. Mel Stottlemyre, the old Mets pitching coach who'd come over to the Yankees, was working hard with me. Even George was feeling some pressure. After my third straight loss, he wouldn't even stop when I tried to introduce him to Monica in the players' parking lot. "When are you going to win a fucking game?" he grumbled as he breezed by. He did approach me the next day with a heartfelt apology. "Sorry, Doc," he said. "I was just caught up in the game." And he sent a huge bouquet of roses to Monica.

I was really getting jumpy. I had this second chance. Slowly, steadily, then quite dramatically, my pitching improved. It didn't come a minute too soon. David Cone, who'd come to pitch for the Yankees the year before I did, was out with an aneurysm in his right armpit. I was in the rotation to stay.

Back in Florida, my dad's health was falling apart. He was on dialysis three times a week for four hours a pop. But his kidney ailments were aggravating his hip replacement. His diabetes and gout were off the charts. As doctors prepped for another hip operation, they discovered he'd need open-heart surgery.

"I'm so scared, son," my mother said on the phone. "They're telling me he has two weeks to live if they don't do the surgery. If he has the surgery, there's no guarantee he'll make it through."

My father had at times been a challenging husband. From my early days sitting outside his girlfriend's apartment, I'd witnessed some of that firsthand. But he and my mom had been together so long — and shared so much — she could barely imagine life without him.

"When do they want to do it, Mom?"

"They could decide on a moment's notice," she explained. "As soon as they think he's ready, they'll wheel him in."

"I'll come home if you need me," I said, my eyes filling with tears.

"Your father needs you more than I do," my mom said. "It may be your last chance to see each other."

A few days later, my mom was on the phone again. "Dwight," she said, "your father's having surgery on Wednesday morning."

On Tuesday night, I was scheduled to start against the Seattle Mariners. I discussed my dad's condition with Joe Torre, the Yankees' manager. Seeing my dad, Joe said, was bigger than baseball. George told me to do whatever I felt was right. I made afternoon reservations to fly to Tampa and skip the start.

But when I woke up on May 14 and started brushing my teeth, I didn't see myself in the mirror. I saw my dad playing catch with me. Teaching Gary how to swing. Showing both of us how to run the bases. I saw him in the stands at my Little League games, smiling next to his friend who first called me "Doc." Then, my dad was on the front steps bluffing Joe McIlvaine.

My dad wasn't a great communicator, not in the usual sense. But he always had his own ways of letting me know what he thought. He loved me. I never doubted that. And he loved baseball.

"If you want to be great," he told me, more times than I could possibly count, "everything else comes after baseball."

So what did that mean? Should I stay and pitch against Seattle and have my dad die before I got home? Should I fly down to Tampa immediately? What was my father telling me?

I thought about that for just a few seconds, then the answer was perfectly clear to me.

"Take the baseball and pitch," my father would say.

I couldn't perform the surgery that would save his life. What I could do was honor him in the only way I knew how to, playing the game he had taught me, living the dream I had learned from him.

"I think I'm staying," I called and told Monica.

"What in the hell are you talking about?" she gasped. "Your mother is beside herself. Your family needs you."

"I know it sounds crazy," I told her. "But Dad wants me here. Even if he only sees one inning on television. He'll know why I'm on the mound."

We hung up the phone, agreeing to disagree.

My mom called approximately forty-five seconds later. I wasn't budging. We hung up simply disagreeing. But part of me started doubting myself. There was still plenty of time to change my mind. I could get right out to LaGuardia Airport and hop on a plane. I called Joe.

"It's totally unnecessary to stay, Dwight," he said. "Listen, you go to Tampa. Take as much time as you need. Your job with the Yankees doesn't depend on this start. We do this one hundred and sixty-two times a year. You only get one dad."

"It's okay, Joe," I said. "I'll be there."

The hours flew by. I packed some clothes because I knew I'd be traveling to Tampa, one way or another. The next time I looked at the clock, I saw I had twenty minutes if I wanted to catch the two p.m. flight. I drove to Yankee Stadium instead.

If I could get the thoughts of my dad out of my head, I figured, I'd be okay on the mound. If I couldn't, I'd be cooked. I really needed to focus my attention on the Mariners' lineup.

Once I got to the stadium, I tried to put my dad totally out of my head. I put on my uniform and went out to the bullpen to warm up. Mel came out to watch me.

"You all right?" he asked.

"I'm good," I said, not knowing if I was or not. But there was no turning back now. Mel, Joe, and even George were in my corner. I knew I couldn't exactly dress, warm up, and then announce that I'd decided not to pitch. No other starting pitcher would be loose or warm. I'd gotten back some confidence after my past few starts. But this was a whole new kind of pressure, the kind that barely a year ago would have had me thinking, "I can't wait to get out of here and go get high." But I'd been changing. I was going to withstand that pressure and give this game my all. I didn't stay behind to get rocked for four lousy innings. I was here to pitch the absolute best I could.

That thought came back to me when I took the mound and walked the Mariners' first batter, Darren Bragg. The count went to 3–2, and I threw a curve to him that looked good to me but not to the ump. The first batter of the game was now on base, and the Mariners' young superstar Alex Rodriguez was at the plate.

Three years into his pro career and only twenty, A-Rod would have a breakout season in 1996, hitting .358 and crushing thirty-six home runs. For any pitcher, this kid was trouble. His line shot to dead center sent Gerald Williams sprinting toward the wall and my heart sinking.

At the last possible second, Gerald stabbed his glove skyward and hauled the ball in like he was scooping ice cream out of the sky. I could barely believe it, I was that unnerved. If Gerald's Willie Mays act didn't happen, I'd have no one out in the first and a runner on second or third. Nothing that followed would have happened without that catch.

Gerald wasn't done. After he caught the ball, he pivoted and threw a laser beam to Derek Jeter at shortstop. Jeter turned and fired the ball to Tino Martinez at first base to double-up Bragg, who by then was confidently approaching third base. Lifted by 31,000 cheering fans, I thought of my dad in Tampa in his hospital bed. I hoped he was watching. I knew he'd be smiling if he was.

When the Yankees were at bat, I didn't even watch for the first three innings. I walked halfway down the tunnel to the clubhouse and just stood there by myself. I thought about my dad and got teary-eyed. Did I make the right decision? I thought I had.

In the top of the sixth inning, Gerald came through again, swooping underneath an Edgar Martinez line drive as it was about to hit the grass. That ended another potentially troublesome inning. Due to a Tino bobble that was ruled an error, the Mariners already had a runner on second base. But I still hadn't really processed what was happening here.

Going into the top of the seventh, my teammates were all clued in. Joe Girardi, our catcher, had stopped talking to me. Derek, Wade Boggs, even the other pitchers — none of them would say a word. The only guy who would speak to me was the assistant trainer, Steve Donahue. He spent the early part of the game keeping me calm and letting me know the whole club was there for me if I needed anything.

The fans were on their feet, cheering loudly. But I figured that was just because they were psyched we were holding our own. This was the first time we'd faced the Mariners since they'd knocked us out of the playoffs the year before.

That's the first time I remember looking at the scoreboard. Only zeros up there. My heart really began to pump. For the first time, I allowed myself to focus on the fact. I had a no-hitter going. I was six innings deep. Could it last?

In the seventh and eighth, I retired batters in order. But my pitch count was getting higher. Could I get through the ninth before the Mariners got to me? Would my aching arm hold out?

I locked in and went as hard as I could. I didn't know when I'd ever be in this position again. Problem was, I was just about on empty. I had one inning to go.

I put A-Rod on with a walk. Then Griffey hit a grounder that sent first baseman Tino Martinez in motion. A-Rod made it safely to second. As Tino went after the ball, I should have covered first base for him. He could have flipped the ball to me for an easy out. For some reason, I was frozen, transfixed, watching Tino make the play.

Griffey motored down the base path. In a split second, I saw my no-hitter going out the window on an infield hit in the ninth inning. Tino fielded the ball and sprinted toward first base to try to make the play himself. Griffey was flying. Tino wasn't going to make it. At the last second, ball in glove, Tino dove toward the base. Arm outstretched, he slapped the bag an instant before Griffey's foot landed.

One out.

You'd think I could breathe a sigh of relief there. No. I walked Edgar Martinez to put runners on first and second. Mel came to visit me.

"Got anything left, Doc?" he asked me. Before I could speak he said, "I know the answer."

"The answer," I said, "is no. I don't have shit left. But I'm not coming out. No chance."

Mel went back to the dugout, convinced I was either going to throw a no-hitter or cost the Yankees the ball game. We were only winning 2–0. He'd done his part in asking. No one would blame him for leaving a pitcher on the mound eight and one-third innings into a no-hitter. The people were on their feet. They wanted me to stay in.

Jay Buhner came up, and I threw a wild pitch. The runners advanced to second and third. Now I was one mistake from blowing the no-hitter and the game. I took Buhner to a count of 2–2 before he went down swinging.

Two outs.

The Mariners' first baseman Paul Sorrento came up. At two balls and a strike, I threw him a curve that hung a little too long. Five times out of ten, that's a home run for a halfway decent hitter. I got lucky. Sorrento was too far underneath it and popped the ball up to Derek Jeter at short. Derek had to step back into the outfield, waving everyone else away. The ball hung up in the nighttime sky for what seemed like forever. Then I heard a small pop when it landed in Derek's firm glove.

That was three.

I'd thrown my first no-hitter. In my wildest dreams, I'd never dare imagine this. It was beyond sweet.

My teammates hoisted me up on their shoulders, a major-league first for me. They knew what this one meant to me. All of us together were celebrating the long and difficult journey I had so recently come off. We were celebrating the father who for me had launched it all.

When they put me down, I went straight to the clubhouse and called my dad's hospital room.

"How's Daddy?" I asked my mother when she picked up the phone.

"He's kind of out of it," she said. "We had the game on the TV, though."

"Did he see me?" I hoped to God the answer was yes. Mom didn't hesitate.

"Yes," she said. "He was in and out of consciousness for most of the game. But when you got the final out and they carried you off the field, he knew what was happening. He could hardly speak but he said, 'Our boy did it. A no-hitter, oh my God.' And he cried."

I was on the first flight the next morning.

The news of my no-hitter was everywhere. People kept coming up to me — at LaGuardia, on the plane, again when we landed in Tampa — wanting my autograph. At the hospital, people were shaking my hand on the way to my dad's room.

Dad's surgery had just started when I got there. Four hours in the operating room felt like a million years. Finally, I got to see my father and do what I'd known I'd do from the moment the no-hitter was done.

I handed him a ball from the game. Together, we clasped our hands around it. I told him how much I loved him. He closed his eyes and held the ball. He nodded. He was on life support. He barely came off it for the next seven months, his last.

One of the doctors walked into the room as I was leaving and said: "He doesn't have much left, Dwight. But he was so proud of what you did."

15

Pushing It

THE FINAL STAGE of a baseball career can be very frustrating. I know mine was. The little bursts of brilliance are separated by wider and wider gaps.

After my 1996 no-hitter with the Yankees, I went on a glorious 11–1 tear. It's amazing what a single confidence boost can do. For a couple of months there, I was the best starting pitcher in the Yankees rotation. But in September, my arm completely wore out. The pitches I'd thrown that year — on top of the pitches I'd thrown for the past twenty — had taken an undeniable toll on me. However much I wanted to keep on going, my body had other ideas. I sat through the victorious playoffs and World Series, consoling myself with the knowledge that my eleven wins that season had helped to get us there.

My father died that next January. I know he loved me. I know he was proud of me. I know I caused him a giant load of unnecessary heartbreak and pain. A few days before he passed, George Steinbrenner postponed a day of meetings to sit in the hospital with a dying man. George had bumped into Ray Negron and asked how my dad was doing. "Not the greatest," Ray said. "They're all over at the hospital. He could go at any time."

George stayed with my dad for almost three hours. The Yankees boss did most of the talking. Dad could barely speak. That simple kindness was a side of George few people ever heard about. I believe the visit prolonged my father's life at least a couple of days. That spring, I went back to baseball — I tried to, anyway — for the first time ever without my father to call.

I started 1997 thinking I'd pulled a groin muscle. The golf ball knot inside my leg told doctors the problem was a hernia. That meant more surgery, more recovery, more rehab, another trip down to the minors — and, when I finally got back to the Bronx, sporadic and unpredictable starts. At that point, I could only dream of surprise no-hitters and glorious 11–1 tears. The Yankees started me twenty times, and my 9–5 record was not what I would have liked. After David Cone got hurt in the postseason, I pitched well against Cleveland in game four of the playoffs. I was good, but not good enough to secure a spot on the roster of such a talent-packed team. When the Indians expressed an interest in picking my contract up in the off-season, I left the Yankees with George's full blessing.

One of the biggest things to come out of my time with the Indians was what happened one night in Detroit. Over the years, I had kept in touch with a guy from childhood who'd grown up to be a flight attendant. Randy and I traveled in different circles, but when we happened to be in the same city, sometimes he'd come out to a game. At dinner after we played the Tigers, he introduced me to another flight attendant, a feisty and beautiful woman named Monique Moore. She was attentive. She liked to laugh. She seemed to hang on every word I said. I wasn't looking for a new relationship. Monica and I were having our problems, but we were still married. My cycle of use and relapse, use and relapse, had left her exhausted. Monique and I didn't jump into anything immediately. But we did agree to stay in touch.

After two seasons in Cleveland, I knew I was nearing the end. This getting older as a pitcher — I was thirty-three, and older than that if you went by pitch count — really did stink. But it was tough to accept my baseball mortality. I sent some feelers to the Mets before the 2000 season. No thank you, I heard back. I signed with Houston but flamed out quickly after a single, rotten start. I just didn't have the stuff I once had, or even the stuff the good young pitchers had now. I asked to be traded home to Tampa Bay. I knew manager Larry Rothschild from when he coached with the Marlins. He'd always had an interest in me. With the Devil Rays, I figured, I'd be closer to home. And as a local guy with family and friends in the area, I could probably help fill some seats as well. As troubled as our marriage was, Monica even jumped in. On April 21, when I debuted my Devil Rays number 16 jersey, she packed two SUVs with sixteen of our friends and relatives for the short drive to Tropicana Field. Dwight Junior, who was fourteen years old, looked pretty sharp in his Rays batboy uniform. I pitched three scoreless innings and, thankfully, didn't embarrass the Gooden family name.

But that was about as good it got during my big hometown return. With a 2–2 record, I started on a Wednesday night in late May against the Oakland A's. In four painful innings, I gave up seven runs. The whole Rays team was terrible. It wasn't just me. There were three errors before I left the game, and I didn't commit any of those. All of Tampa–St. Pete knew how awful the Rays were. Only 13,000 people showed up that night to watch us get slammed 9–2. Immediately after the game, Chuck Lamar, the general manager, called me into the office. I was still in my uniform, sweating. Larry was also sitting there.

"We think you should retire," Chuck said. Those were the first words out of his mouth.

"Retire?" That was a little abrupt, wasn't it?

"Listen," Chuck continued. "It's for the best. Retire and come to work with us."

His plan was to take the money the team owed me and spread it out over a few years, while I worked in the Rays' front office. The way I heard that was: "Quit pitching, get your money late, and work a boring job for free."

"No thanks," I said. "Why don't you release me?"

They were fine with that.

I was thirty-five years old. In less than four months, I'd been dumped by two lousy teams. There didn't seem to be a next stop. I had nothing to do but sit at home and stew. For three weeks, my phone didn't ring. "This really is it," I thought. I could already feel myself getting out of shape. Then Ray Negron called.

"Would you like to come back to the Yankees?" Ray asked.

Who said my life had no surprises left? Three weeks later, I was about to pitch in a Yankees uniform at Shea Stadium in the first game of a home-and-away doubleheader against my old team, the New York Mets. I was nowhere near ready. But I couldn't say no. When would I ever get that chance again?

My thought was, "I'm going to pitch the game and probably get killed. But at least I get back to Shea one last time." I went down to the bullpen thirty minutes early to shake the emotional stuff out of my head. Even after I calmed myself, my warm-up pitches were refusing to cooperate. My curveball was breaking in the complete opposite direction. My fastball looked more like a changeup. Mel was standing next to me. He offered a few suggestions. Then, he just stopped saying anything. The look on his face said it all.

This ain't gonna be pretty today.

I noticed Mel had a whole posse of relievers warming up in the bullpen. That was not a vote of confidence.

Right before I went onto the field, Joe Torre said: "Just give me whatever you got. Whether it's one, two, or three innings, just give me whatever." I was starting to think George was the only person in the whole Yankees organization who believed I had anything at all in the tank.

But when I stepped onto the familiar mound at Shea, it was like I had suddenly come home. Something about my cleats in that dirt, it just felt natural. My breaking ball clicked in. Batters came up, and they were actually having trouble hitting me. I gave up two cheap runs, but I'd held the Mets in check. My pitches were legitimately big-league. After the fifth inning, when I came off the mound, Joe asked me: "You have another inning or two left, Doc?"

I didn't give him the answer I'd given him during the no-hitter. I didn't need to.

"Nah," I said. "That's enough."

It really was. The Yanks won 4–2. The fans from both New York teams could hardly believe how strong I looked out there so late in my troubled career. I know I could hardly believe it. I'm still not sure what got into me. I'm just glad it did.

"I really can't explain it," Mike Piazza said later in the Mets locker room. One of the best hitting catchers in baseball, Mike went 0–3 against me that day. "He just threw strikes. That's the bottom line."

I stuck around for the rest of the season. I pitched out of the bull-pen and had a couple of playoff appearances en route to the Yankees winning the World Series over the Mets. But picking up that July win against the Mets — that was one of my last, best moments playing baseball.

Too bad I couldn't just gently fade away.

I had stayed off drugs since I started working with Ray Negron. I'd chosen baseball over cocaine, and I had the lab tests to prove it. But that didn't mean I was working hard on my recovery. I'd stopped going to NA meetings. I didn't think I needed them. I had stopped checking in with Ron Dock. I was drinking a fair amount, mostly beer and vodka. The drinking should have been a warning. Booze has always been my gateway to more.

I went back to the Yankees during spring training of 2001 as a nonroster player. I was thinking, "I probably should have retired at the end of last year." Then my body proved me right. A week before the season started, I tore my knee during warm-ups. The doctors said three months minimum of rehab. When George heard that, he offered me a $100,000 job as his special assistant if I was ready to retire. I loved the idea of working for George and the Yankees. And frankly, the way I'd been pitching, how much longer could I really play? Plus, I had a more sinister reason for accepting George's offer. If I quit playing, I wouldn't have to worry about being drug-tested anymore.

Hmmm, I thought.

I told George yes. The addict sleeping inside me was waking up again.

My family organized a big dinner in Tampa to celebrate the end of my playing career and my new front-office gig with the Yankees. I really felt like I had something to celebrate. Afterward, all of us would go watch my daughter Ashley play softball. But just as we were ready to leave for the restaurant, my cell phone rang. It was Ron Dock. He said Darryl Strawberry was somewhere in the Tampa area and no one could locate him. I knew Darryl had been spiraling downward. The fear now was that he had relapsed or worse.

"Can you help?" Ron asked. "We're really worried about him."

"I have my retirement dinner tonight," I said, wondering how long this would take. But my family could start the celebration without me. "Yeah, sure. Anything for Straw."

"Ray will pick you up," Ron said.

Ray and I drove all over St. Petersburg. We scoured dicey neighborhoods in Tampa. We swung by the projects, where I asked old drug buddies: "You seen Strawberry anywhere?" After a couple of hours, I called my mom and apologized.

"Are you okay?" she asked.

"I'm fine," I said. "Ray is with me."

"Just be careful," she said. "We can do the dinner another night. What you're doing is the right thing."

Ashley wasn't as understanding. Just ten years old, she wasn't happy I had to miss her game. This wasn't the first time I'd disappointed her. She played outfield and shortstop, and I'd missed a lot of games. Being retired now and closer to home, I thought I'd finally have the chance to be there more often for her and for all of my kids. I knew I was ready to try. But here we were, on the same night we were celebrating my retirement, and I was already off to a questionable start. For five or six hours of family time, Ray and I drove around looking for Darryl. We never found him.

The part that went unspoken was that, as I was trying to rescue Darryl, my own life was about to spin out of control again.

I loved working for George. He gave me special assignments and was always available to me. "Go check out a young pitching prospect on our AA team," he'd tell me. "What do think of this guy?" That would lead eventually to "Go sign Sheff" and, "See if Darryl wants to come back." God knows, he showed real faith in me when hardly anyone else was willing to. When he first welcomed me to the Yankees, George told me, "This will be tough. But you won't be alone. I'll be right there with you." And he also said, "But you better never fuck with me, because if you do, I'll get ya. You'll be sorry you ever heard my name." Especially after my father died, George's approval was hugely important to me. I took my Yankees work seriously.

From Monday to Friday, anyway.

Weekends were my drug time. I was using again, and my use was getting more frequent. My dealer knew to expect a call from me late in the week and often a refill call or two over the weekend. I started staying out late again, sometimes until Sunday night or Monday morning. I wasn't with other women. I was off doing coke. But that old, familiar cycle was spreading a new cloud of tension across my family life. Monica and I were arguing a lot. I'd withdraw, she'd get madder. I'd been burning through her patience for a good long while. My kids were disappointed by my no-shows. I was disappointed in myself. When I retired, I'd planned to make up for all the school events and Little League I had missed over the years. But now the drugs were gobbling up more and more of me. The more Monica and I argued, the more I wondered whether the kids would be better off if we split.

In early 2003, I told Monica I wanted a divorce. She knew this was a cop-out and saw it for the cowardly move it was. Mainly I was bailing on the pressures of my life. Work and family take a lot of time and energy. Add regular drug use into the equation, there isn't much left. Many times before, I'd threatened to leave without actually going. I didn't know if Monica took me seriously. But this time I actually moved out. I convinced myself again that peace and quiet were waiting for me in a fresh line of cocaine.

After I got my own place in Tampa, Monique came to visit on one of her flight-attendant layovers. She had no idea how out of control my life really was, that her famous athlete boyfriend was actually a drug-addicted mess. Had she known, she probably would have scheduled a much quicker TPA turnaround. My apartment was being remodeled the weekend of her first visit. I had a connection for rooms at the Hyatt, so I told her we'd be staying there. I'd promised to pick her up at the airport. But I'd started using cocaine before she landed and was in no condition to meet her plane. I called her cell phone from a different, fleabag hotel.

"We're working on a big trade," I explained about three lines in.

"The negotiations are crazy. Can you just go to the Hyatt? I'll meet you there as soon I can."

Since I was using again, I was lying again. This time, I was poisoning a relationship that had barely even begun.

I didn't show up at the hotel until the next day. For many months, I was able to hide from Monique just how severe my drug use had become. Later that year, she moved from Maryland to live with me in Tampa. She was quickly becoming the next woman in my life.

Before Christmas, I drove Monique to St. Petersburg to meet my sister for the first time. We weren't there for a half hour before I slipped into the bathroom to use. When I came out, I was obviously lit up. Betty called me out to my face, then pulled Monique aside and warned her: "You know, he's struggled with drugs a long time."

She probably didn't need the warning by then. She was already catching on. My habit led me to do all kinds of strange things. I'd climb out of bed at three a.m. for a shower when I really just wanted to slip into the bathroom and get high. Or I'd intentionally pick a fight with her so she would go sleep in another room and leave me alone to use drugs. Monique was smart and stubborn. One angry night, she kicked in the bathroom door and caught me snorting. At this point in my addiction, I wasn't into going out and partying. All my drug use was alone. I couldn't stand the thought of sharing my stash with anyone. Every now and then, Monique would get angry enough to flee back home to Maryland. Things were never smooth and easy with the two of us. We broke up and got back together several times. I was on the verge of turning forty but was still acting like a sneaky, sulking fifteen-year-old. Except, when I was fifteen, I was never this bad.

When Monique became pregnant with Dylan in late 2004 and was really showing, she and I rode to St. Pete to visit with my mom. At that point, Monica and the kids were still living on my mom's block. Monica and I had separated nearly two years earlier, but the divorce had still not been finalized. When Monique and I walked in, Monica was there — and obviously not thrilled to see her soon-to-be ex-husband and his very pregnant girlfriend. Everyone was chilly and polite. But for the next two days, I had a series of angry phone conversations with all three women. Once again, Monique stormed out and went home to Maryland. That's where our son Dylan was born in November 2004.

As my life grew more chaotic, I kept finding my refuge in drugs. I was turning up less and less often at the Yankees' complex in Tampa. I was climbing on the roller coaster again. Hal Steinbrenner, George's son, had an office next to mine. He was friendly, but noticed how distracted I seemed. One day, without calling first, Ron Dock, who was now the team's drug-intervention coordinator, showed up at my office door.

"Doc, level with me," he said, pulling up a chair even before I invited him in. "What's going on?"

"I had a relapse," I said. "I'm gonna put it back together. I will." I meant it when I said it. I did.

But that next Friday, I drove out to get sandwiches for some of the office crew and remembered I had some coke in the car. I'd gotten very good at dipping the corner of a credit card into a baggie of cocaine, then doing my thing in a parking lot, even at a red light. I never made it back to the office that afternoon. I caught a glimpse of myself in the rearview mirror. I was horrified. I couldn't let anyone see me like that. I hightailed it straight home. I'm sure my coworkers are still wondering what happened to their turkey and roast beef subs.

The next morning, Saturday, I got a phone call I didn't pick up. It was from someone in the Yankees' front office. The message on the voice mail: "George is concerned."

I ignored it and kept using throughout the weekend. By Monday, I was in even worse shape. My phone rang again. It was Ron Dock again. "You gotta get in here today," he said.

"I'm sick, Ron," I told him. That was sorta true.

"If you don't come in today," Ron said, "George is gonna fire you. You just bailed on him, and you won't tell anyone why."

"All right," I promised, letting out a sigh of frustration. Or was it exhaustion? I couldn't tell. I only knew I hated this feeling of harsh reality closing in. It felt like a thousand-pound door shutting on me. "I'll be there," I said.

I wasn't. I skipped two more days of work.

On Wednesday, Ron Dock was back on the phone. I thought he was calling to say I was fired. But I wasn't through yet. "George is giving you until five p.m. today to report to work or else he's going to fire you," Ron said.

I didn't know what to do. This was beyond awkward. I couldn't face George. Too much time had passed already. But the Yankees were throwing me a life preserver, and for some reason I was swimming away from it. I took the coward's approach. I just withdrew. I didn't get fired. I didn't quit. I didn't go back to the office for the next couple of weeks. I had no communication with the organization at all. I increased my weekend drug use to full-time drug use. I just pretended I had no responsibilities in my life.

I'm not sure why George didn't fire me. He could have. He had every reason to. But he had a philosophy not everyone shares. He once told me, "Drug and alcohol dependency is a sickness. It isn't like sticking up a gas station. It isn't like committing a crime, even though many Americans view it that way." On that topic at least, George was way ahead of his time.

I'm also not sure why Monique and Dylan moved back down to Tampa. She realized right away how bad off I was. She called Ron Dock, who had far more patience with my constant relapses than I deserved. He and Monique decided a forced intervention was my only hope. They came up with a plan. Monique ordered a pizza and sent me down to the security gate to pick it up from the delivery guy.

When I got there, there was no pizza — just Ray and Ron waiting for me. As soon as I made eye contact, I slammed the gate shut, ran to my car, and began driving away.

My cell phone rang immediately. "What the hell are you doing?" Ray demanded.

"I just gotta make a run, guys," I said as calmly as I could manage. "Lemme do this. Then I'll come back and listen to you."

Ron got on the phone. "If you don't pull over," he said, "I gotta call the cops. I don't want you to hurt yourself or hurt anybody."

I laughed. Wasn't it a little late for that? But as soon as I heard the word "cops," I did pull over. I didn't need any more of them in my life.

Ray and Ron pulled up behind me. Ron got out and walked to my window. "Listen," he said. "Steinbrenner wants you to keep your job. But he also wants you to go to rehab. Will you agree to that?"

In the crazed state I was in — just when I needed it most — the whole idea of rehab seemed totally unnecessary. That's how messed up I was.

"Let me think about it," I said. "I'm gonna sleep on it."

I drove home and went back into the apartment. Fifteen minutes passed. I looked out the window. As I should have expected, Ron and Ray weren't going anywhere. I was craving more drugs. I wanted those pushy friends of mine out of my way. I called Ron's cell and said, "I see you. You guys can leave now. It's cool. I'm on the couch."

"Go to sleep, Doc," Ron said with a laugh. "We're not leaving."

The next morning my mom, my sister Betty, Ron, and Phil McNiff, George's right-hand man in Tampa, all came to my apartment and gave it one last try.

"George is ready to let you go if you don't," Phil said solemnly.

"I don't need rehab," I said defensively. "I'll just go back to work. I'll get into the swing of things. I'll be — "

"Dwight!" Ron cut me off. "No rehab, no work."

I still wasn't ready.

The next day, Betty and Harold came over and tried to convince me to go. Betty called my daughter Ariel. She got on the phone. She was hysterical. She wanted me to go. Somewhere inside, I knew she was right. I knew all of them were. It took my daughter to cut through my stubbornness and remind me how much I was going to lose. "I love you guys," I finally told her. "Everything's okay. I'm going to rehab."

I could hear Betty and Harold cheering in the kitchen. I could hear Ariel crying on the phone.

Ron Dock agreed to drive me immediately to a treatment center in West Palm Beach. When we stopped for gas, Ron took the keys out of the ignition and put them in his pocket.

"What did you do that for?" I asked him.

"Why do you think?" he said, laughing.

I checked into the program and immediately quit using drugs. I felt physically ill for the first few days. At my level of addiction, the body reacts strongly to not getting what it is used to. But I pushed through detox and withdrawal, and I stabilized. I wouldn't say I was there for all the right reasons. It was outside pressure that got me there, the fear of losing my job and the heart-wrenching pleas from some of those I loved. I reacted to that in a way that helped to save me, though I wouldn't say I was committed yet to changing my life. But my time inside did clean me up and allow me to work again.

After twenty days in the program, I told my counselor I was ready to go home. He was a tall, jovial, older guy. He'd seen addicts come and go. I don't think he was too impressed with my progress so far. "I'd actually like to keep you another week to ten days," he said.

"I'm fine," I assured him.

"Bullshit," he snapped. "You're like a turkey in an oven. You're getting brown and juicy, but you're not quite ready yet. You gotta let it cook, even if you're convinced it's already done."

"I gotta go home," I insisted. "You can't hold me here any longer."

"Fine," he said. "It's your decision. When you relapse, don't tell anyone I was your counselor."

16

Some Dad

I WAS STARTING TO ACT like a dad again.

Being away from drugs made me far more available to my children—and far more engaged in their lives. I wasn't constantly rushing off on my own reckless adventures. When I was at home, I wasn't just sitting in my bedroom and staring into space. Now I was actually going to my children's soccer games, not just hearing reports later. I hit a couple of parent-teacher conferences. I think the teachers were surprised to see me there. The kids and I were spending lots of time together—comfortable, casual, hang-out time—even when we weren't doing that much. I was finally being the parent I always knew I could be. I just wished it hadn't taken me so long.

We had missed so much together—Dwight Junior, Ashley, Ariel, Devin, Darren, and me. We had so many gaps to fill. Either I'd been high or I'd been traveling or I'd been juggling the demands of baseball. One hundred and sixty-two games a season, half of them road games, plus a roller-coaster habit of drug abuse — that's like two full-time jobs right there. Finally I was present and engaged like I'd never been before. And now with little Dylan on the scene, maybe I could start off on a better foot with him.

But as I was becoming a more active father to my older kids, Monique often felt isolated at home. I was running off somewhere with Devin or Darren or the girls while Monique was home alone with the baby, Dylan. None of it was easy. Dwight Junior lived with his mom, Debra. The next four lived with their mom, Monica. There was no road map for any of this. Coordination was never easy. It was doable only if everyone was on board. But it seemed like every time I'd be out with one of the older kids, my cell phone would start to ring. Monique would be frantic. "Something's wrong with Dylan." I'd apologize to the kids and go racing home. Once I got there, almost always everything would seem fine.

One Friday night in March 2005, I got a call from my second-oldest daughter, Ariel. She and a friend were ready to leave the skating rink. They were spending the night at our place, one of the nice things about the closer relationship she and I were beginning to share. When we got home, Dylan was asleep, but the girls still wanted to have fun.

"Dad, can we order pizza?" Ariel asked.

"Sure, why not?" I said.

No one was being loud or silly. But when the pizza arrived, the doorbell woke four-month-old Dylan. Dylan was cranky. After a long day, Monique was cranky too. I thought I heard her say, "This is why I don't like it when your kids come over here!"

To this day, Monique insists that she didn't say that. She said she was just grumbling about the kids waking up the baby. But the tension between us was thick. I had no idea how to diffuse it. When I heard her say that, it was like she'd lit a match in a room filled with gasoline.

"What do you mean you don't like my kids coming over?" I asked.

Before Monique could respond, I kept going. "You crossed the line,

Monique!" I said. "My kids are a part of me. They're part of the pack-age. Tomorrow, you're out of here!"

I began packing Monique's bags. She started slapping me. Ariel and her friend scrambled out of the room. I could feel the argument es-calating. Monique was already out of control, and I was getting there too. I didn't want to hit back. So I let her fire away at me, slapping me several times, me trying to push her hands off. Then, she picked up her cell phone, poised to dial 911.

"Hit me!" I recall her screaming.

"No," I said. "Tell you what. In the morning, you'll just go. Even if I have to call the cops."

I turned to walk away. She slapped me again, and then she threw her cell phone at me, smacking me in the head.

I spun around and smacked her in the forehead with the side of my hand.

God, I wish I could take that back. A man should never do that, no matter what.

Monique looked at me a little stunned. Then she picked up her phone from the floor and punched in three numbers.

Nine. One. One.

I couldn't believe how quickly this had blown up. I knew that when the police arrived, I'd be cooked.

I could hear Monique giving instructions to the dispatcher about how to get in the gate. "Just give me the phone," I said, giving the cops step-by-step directions. After I hung up, I went to the room where Ariel and her friend had retreated from the mayhem. I gave Ariel all my jewelry.

"Call your grandmother," I told her. "Tell her what happened. The police are coming, and I'll have to go with them. Tell Grandma to call Dave, the attorney. Can you remember that? Dave."

I walked back to the front of the apartment. Two uniformed Tampa police officers were already in the living room.

"What's going on?" the short, stocky one asked. Then a strange look crossed his face. "Are you Dwight Gooden?"

"Yes," I said.

"So what happened?" he asked calmly. I told the two cops everything, including the fact that I struck Monique. I was hoping when they heard the full story, they would understand this was a two-way battle, and it was over now. A minor domestic dispute, nothing we needed the police for.

"Wait a sec," the first cop said. "You hit her?"

That was all he needed to hear. "Put your hands behind your back."

This being a Friday night, I ended up spending the whole weekend in the Hillsborough County Jail. I felt so defeated. I'd been staying off drugs. I'd been a round-the-clock dad. I'd been taking care of business at work. And now I felt like I was back at square one.

The lawyer, David Stamps, got me out of jail on Monday. Ron Dock drove me home. He started to speak as soon as we got in the car. I cut him off. I knew what was coming.

"George wants to know what's going on," I said. "Right?"

"Yep," Ron answered.

When I walked into George's office, he held up his hands like a school crossing guard. Before I could say anything, he said, "Slow down, Doc. Just slow down." George didn't fire me. I don't know where the man got his patience.

I couldn't return to my apartment immediately because the cops had given Monique ten days to get her stuff and move out. I stayed with my mom until then. But our separation didn't last long. After a month, Monique and little Dylan moved back in.

I pretty much stopped working for the Yankees at that point. George never fired me exactly. I never quit. I just had so much else going on in my life, I wasn't getting any work done. My duties sort of faded.

On Sunday night, August 21, I had a couple of beers at home. I wasn't close to drunk. I didn't use any drugs. I hadn't planned on going out.

My sister Betty was having a party at her house in St. Petersburg, and she had asked me to come. On the spur of the moment, long after midnight, I thought maybe I would go by. I knew the party would be running late. It was after two a.m. when I left home.

My apartment complex on Harbour Island in South Tampa usually had its own security guard at the gate. But this time, as I drove out, I saw a Tampa police car idling at the guardhouse. That struck me as strange. Then I noticed the cop was following me. At a dark section of Cleveland Street, the cop threw his lights on. My car was familiar to the Tampa police, a little 2004 BMW convertible coupe. I pulled over. The squad car pulled up behind, lights still flashing.

After what seemed like forever, an officer walked up and rapped his knuckles on my window. "License and registration," he said.

"Uh-oh," I thought. "Here we go again."

Before I could even hand him my license, he said, "Mr. Gooden, where are you headed so late?"

"To my sister's house," I replied calmly. Inside, I had a bad feeling about this.

"Where's that?"

"St. Pete."

He squinted, leaned back, and stared in at me. "You sure you're all right?"

"Yeah," I replied. "Everything's good."

"Little late for a family visit, no?" I figured he was looking for a reason to get in the car, rip it apart, and find any drugs I'd stashed. I knew the car was clean. There was nothing to find. He could search away if it came to that.

"She's having a party, Officer, that's all."

He peered in again and walked around the car, sizing it up and down. "This is really your car?"

"Yes," I said impatiently.

"Okay," he said, shrugging. "Just give me a second."

He went back to his car for another ten minutes then came back to my window with more questions for me. I don't know if he was trying to tell if my speech was slurred. I had no idea what his plan was.

"I just don't get why she would have a party so late," the cop wondered aloud.

"It's been going on a while," I explained. "I'm just getting a late start."

"Oh yeah?" he asked. "Have you been drinking tonight?"

"Just a couple beers, but I'm fine," I told him.

The cop nodded. "Okay," he said. "Give me a second. I'll get you out of here." He went to his car again. Within minutes, cop cars came flying in from every direction.

If he'd asked me to step out of the car and take a Breathalyzer when we were by ourselves, I probably would have done it. And I would have passed. I didn't know what he was waiting for. But when a bunch of police cars screeched up, I got nervous. I had no idea what might happen next. My mind filled with memories of flashlights in my face and me on the ground being beaten by the Tampa police. "This time," I thought, "there aren't even any witnesses."

I'd been warned more than once by my friends in law enforcement. "Be careful in Tampa. The cops are still pissed at you." I was starting to believe all that. This was not paranoia. I'd had years of experience.

The first officer came back to my car. He leaned in my window and said, "I need you to get out of the vehicle."

That sounded risky to me. If I made one wrong gesture or took an unexpected step, would all these cops suddenly jump me?

"I'm fine," I insisted.

"Sure you are," he said. "I just want to make sure you're okay."

"I really only had a couple of beers," I said again. "I'm okay."

"I need you to get out of the car," he said again.

I didn't budge from the seat. No other cars had driven past us since we'd been there. I tried to think of some way out. I picked up my cell phone. Who could I call? My lawyer? My sister? Monique? None of them could get here fast enough.

"Get out of the fuckin' car!" the cop yelled.

In that split second, I panicked. What I did made no sense at all. I didn't analyze the consequences. I just did what I did. I turned on the engine. I threw the car into gear. I stomped on the gas. And I flew out of there. They tried, but there was no way those Tampa police cruisers were going to catch my BMW. Within half a mile, I was taillights to them.

Once I crossed the bridge into St. Petersburg, I was afraid to go to my sister's house. I'd already told the cop I was heading there. That was outside the Tampa police jurisdiction. But they could certainly radio across the bridge.

I called a friend who lived in the area. When he picked up, instead of "Hello," I said, "Open your garage."

"Doc?" he asked. He sounded confused. "What's going on?"

"Please, just do it," I said. "I'll explain when I get there."

I parked the BMW and lowered the garage door with a mixture of relief and fear. Inside, I told my friend the whole story, which freaked him out even more. I had run from the police and was hiding out at his house. I don't think he'd harbored too many fugitives before. The whole thing was totally surreal. I sat on his sofa and turned my cell phone off. "They might be able to track me through the signal," I told him. "But don't worry. No one knows I'm here."

The next morning, we turned on the TV. The local news was showing my picture and describing my escape. For the two days that followed, the local papers and TV treated my road stop like a manhunt of major proportions. *America's Most Wanted* asked the public to help find me.

"We've got nothing," said police spokeswoman Laura McElroy, urging me to turn myself in at once. "It's not like he's been in touch with us." Then she turned the heat up a notch. "He's in serious trouble," she said.

My old Little League coaches, even my mother's pastor, spoke to reporters and pleaded with me. "Go ahead and turn yourself in," said Monty Bostick, my coach when I was thirteen. "We love him," said the Reverend Gordon Curry of the Greater King David International Church in St. Petersburg. George Steinbrenner said through a spokesman, "I feel very sorry for Dwight."

All that time, there were helicopters hovering over my mom's house, cops in front of my kids' schools and my apartment. I kept checking my voice mail as it filled up with messages from Monique, my mom, Betty, Sheff, Ron, Ray, George, and almost everyone else I knew, including my attorney, Dave, and his partner Peter Hobson. "It's not as bad as you think," they said.

I used my friend's phone to call the lawyers back. There was a warrant for my arrest, they told me, on charges of driving under the influence, eluding police, and resisting arrest without violence. "Relatively minor stuff, if you turn yourself in," Peter said. "If you make the cops find you, it's gonna be ugly. Meet me somewhere. We'll go to the precinct together."

A decision to go to a party at my sister's house had turned into the plot from a bad car chase film. In this one, the cops followed for a minute but then they just let the hot-rodder go. I hid in the backseat of my friend's car to meet my attorney in a mall parking garage. I was still nervous, afraid of getting caught. But my lawyers convinced me I had to turn myself in. I switched cars, and we drove together to the warrants facility at the county jail. My lawyers were right. As a criminal case, running from the police that night was a not a huge crime — despite all the public uproar. But in a life as tumultuous as mine, bad decisions somehow get multiplied.

Once Dave had cleared up the fugitive issue, he reminded me of another problem I had. While I was at my friend's house, I had been scheduled to take a mandatory one-hour class on domestic violence. It involved the case I had with Monique. I needed to do this if I had any hope of getting the charges against me dismissed. When I was on the lam, I missed the class.

As a result, I was sentenced to ten days in the Hillsborough County Jail — with some unexpected company.

As I was being processed, one of the corrections officers mentioned something to me. "We have your son," he said. "Dwight Gooden Junior." He was being held in another wing of the jail on a probation violation stemming from a crack cocaine sale to an undercover cop.

In jail with my own son? It was devastating for both of us.

Dwight Junior was nineteen years old. He was a little shorter than I was at his age and at least as thin, maybe 150 pounds. With a name like "Dwight Gooden Junior," I worried that he would be a target — for other inmates and for the guards. It had happened before at school, forcing him to transfer from Kings High to Hillsborough when the taunts about his troubled baseball dad turned into threats. But that was kids' stuff, and this was jail. So I was concerned.

As Dwight Junior was growing up, I wasn't around nearly enough. When I was there, I didn't always set the best example. The years I was suspended from baseball, we got to have an almost normal father-son relationship. I even coached his Little League team, the North Seminole Marlins. I was a proud dad, but his pitching talent was genuine. He even joined my old team at Hillsborough High. But as long as Dwight Junior was playing baseball, there was no stepping out of his father's long shadow. I think he found that tough. A couple of colleges offered him baseball scholarships. A couple of the Yankees scouts asked me about him. But he had the courage to tell me what I already knew.

"I don't think baseball is for me," he said. "It's your game. Not mine."

I wasn't upset at all with that. I respected his independence. I still do, although I don't like some of what he chose to do instead. He turned his attention to music, which was great, but then he stumbled quickly into drugs. When he got busted in 2003 as part of a Hillsborough sheriff's sting operation, he was charged with selling and possessing crack cocaine and did a short stint in jail. I was heartbroken. He could have done fifteen years. And it was hard for me not to feel responsible. When he got out, he moved into my Tampa apartment. But that didn't turn out too well. The day he arrived, he asked to borrow my car and disappeared for two days. That sounded familiar. When he finally showed up, I told him to go stay with his mother. I was the designated screwup in that household, and I wasn't sure I could handle another one. Within three months of being released, he was busted for marijuana possession. Just like me, he was taking the lessons of his father and expanding on them. I had set a powerful example.

My lawyers were pushing me to enter a hard-core treatment facility in Tampa. I'd had two run-ins with the law in two months. But I didn't think I needed such an intense program. I was drinking, but I hadn't started using again. Still, with the domestic and fugitive charges hanging over me, Dave convinced me I needed to show the judge I was actively confronting my problems. In this case, it was alcohol — though all of us knew where the booze frequently led me.

On November 3, Hillsborough Circuit Judge William Fuente sentenced me to three years' probation and community service with the agreement that I'd stay in treatment the rest of that year and into 2006 at HealthCare Connection. As spring training approached, I learned that, even after a year, George Steinbrenner still hadn't given up on me. When I got out of HealthCare Connection, he invited me by for a chat. "You ready to come back to work, Doc?" he asked.

I thought it over for a minute, how nice it would be. But I believed I was making progress in rehab. I was scared to juggle baseball and aftercare.

"I think I gotta stick to my program a while longer," I said to George. "Believe me, I'd love to work for you. But I have to get my life together first. I'm tired of embarrassing you and myself."

17

Behind Bars

HOW LOW DID I GO?

Counselors and addiction experts are constantly talking about "hitting bottom." At drug-treatment meetings, someone will describe a struggling friend: "Before he can pull his life together, he has to hit bottom first." On daytime talk shows, people are "hitting bottom" left and right.

To me, bottom is the cemetery, and I'm not looking to hit there any time soon.

On my winding trip through addiction, I have arrived at some low spots, lower than I could have ever imagined when I first showed up in New York to pitch. Bouncing in and out of treatment programs. Relapsing time and again. Missing the World Series parade. Leading police on a three-day fugitive hunt. Being held in the county jail with Dwight Junior. In my life, I've had big ups and big downs. But the closest I've ever felt to the bottom was turning around in a Tampa courtroom — and seeing my mother age right in front of my eyes.

My three-month stint at HealthCare Connection — ninety days of tested sobriety — had gone well. I was settling back into my life as a husband and a father. The older kids were coming to visit again. I was glad I hadn't gone back to work for George. He wouldn't have liked what happened next. I was about to wash away all my progress with what I rationalized as a few harmless Budweisers.

In March 2006, Ariel, Ashley, Devin, and Darren spent a weekend with Monique, Dylan, and me. It was a blast having them all together. Driving home Sunday night after I dropped the four older kids back at their mother's place, I started feeling sorry for myself. I knew I wouldn't see them again for another couple of weeks. And when I did, they would soon be leaving again. They didn't live far from me. But I hated that they were doing so much of their growing up without me.

As I thought about where my life was and what I could do about it, for some reason a can of beer sounded like the answer to me. I'd been taught to call my sponsor when I felt that way. Call someone! But I wasn't a very good student. So I didn't.

I pulled into a convenience store and bought a can of Bud. Just one. That was all I would be having, I convinced myself. I sat in my car in the parking lot and — *pffft!* — cracked open the can of beer. Christ, it tasted good. Cold. Crisp. Sliding down my throat so smoothly. Leaving a perfectly balanced aftertaste.

I crumpled the can, got out of my car, and walked it over to the garbage can. See, I told myself. I knew I could handle that. In fact, I handled it so well, I went right back into the store and bought another can of Bud. My tolerance was low after abstaining so long, I didn't feel a thing after one beer. Midway through the second beer, I had nice buzz going.

The beer buzz, of course, ushered in a predictable craving. And it wasn't for another beer.

The familiar old feelings resurfaced in the time it took me to down the second sixteen-ounce can. You could set a clock by my patterns. They're that predictable. My defenses washed away, I put in a call to my old coke dealer, whose cell number I had conveniently forgotten to delete. He didn't answer. I decided to buy one more beer, drink it in the parking lot, and see whether he'd call back. He didn't.

At that point, I decided to just go home. If the dealer didn't return my call, I'd do the right thing. I'd go inside and go to bed.

By the time I made it to my house, my dealer still hadn't called. But the parking lot pact I'd made with myself was already losing out to weakness. So instead of going to bed, I decided to drive by his house, just to see if his car was there. If it wasn't, then I'd go home and go to bed. That seemed like a better deal.

I drove by his house. His car wasn't parked there. I decided to drive by one other place I knew he sometimes went to. If he wasn't there, then I'd go home and go to bed. For real.

By the time I got there, he finally texted me. He said he'd just gotten home. So I drove back to his house and bought some coke from him. I sampled some in the car. On my way home, I picked up a couple of more beers.

When I finally walked in the door, Monique took one look at me and could see I wasn't right. She told me so. I told her she was crazy. The argument gave me a reason to storm away and finish the rest of my coke. I stayed out all night getting high, coming back home at dawn when the coke had worn off. Now I was even more depressed than when the kids had left. Monique had already packed her bags to leave.

"I'm going back to Maryland," she said. "I can't have Dylan here."

That hurt, as it was meant to.

Here I was, depressed I couldn't have my kids with me. And Monique was taking my youngest son nine hundred miles away. Only then did I call one of my counselors from HealthCare Connection.

"I relapsed," I said.

"That's okay," he told me. He actually sounded upbeat. "It's good that you recognize the situation. Why don't you come back in for a few days, and we'll evaluate you and see where you're at?"

"That's a good idea," I said.

In the light of day, I knew what had triggered the relapse. But I'd caught myself quickly, and I was feeling good about that. I even called my probation officer and filled her in.

Her tone was slightly different from the counselor's. "You relapsed?" she asked. "What's that?" I guess she thought she was being funny.

"I used drugs," I said. "I'm going to go back into treatment though. I didn't want to be hiding. I wanted you to know. I'm being aggressive about it."

"What exactly did you use?"

Why the interrogation? I was coming clean with her like I was supposed to. And all she wanted were the details of my slip-up. But I told her the truth.

"Cocaine," I said. "It's over now. It was just a mistake."

"Why don't you come down here so we can talk?" the probation officer said. Now her voice sounded genuinely concerned. I don't know why I was so trusting of her. For years, my paranoia had protected me from that kind of trap. It turned out her only real concern was catching me. One dirty test later, my conditional release was violated. I was back in the Hillsborough County Circuit Court, dressed in an orange jumpsuit, standing before Judge Daniel Perry. I knew I'd screwed up. When the judge asked if I had anything to say, I was honest.

"I have a problem, sir, with cocaine," I said. "I had a cocaine relapse."

But the judge didn't seem too moved by my comments. He said I had a choice to make.

The judge could reinstate the five-year probation I'd violated.

Or I could do a year and a day in prison.

If I took the probation and I screwed up even once, my lawyer, David Stamps, explained, I'd be looking at five years in a Florida state prison.

"But if you take the year and a day," the lawyer said, "you won't really do a year in jail." He said he was confident I'd be sent to a treatment facility instead. That's what the judge had often done in similar cases.

"The choice is yours," the lawyer said. "Totally up to you."

My mother was sitting in the front row of the courtroom. I turned around and looked at her. I hoped she could give me some guidance. She looked terrible.

"What do think, Mom?" I whispered. "What do you think I should do?"

"Dwight," my mother said quietly with the flattest, saddest tone I'd ever heard in her voice, "I can't make that decision for you." After years of moral guidance, she sounded exhausted, spent, just through. She looked as defeated as I felt, maybe more.

I rolled it over in my head. If I took the five years' probation, could I really stay out of trouble that long? I had never done that. There was always something derailing me before. I was living in Tampa. Wouldn't the police find something on me? Then I'd definitely spend five years behind bars.

If I took the other option, Dave kept assuring me, I was a shoo-in for extended rehab. "The rehab might do you some good."

I had to make a decision. The judge was waiting to hear.

"I'll take the year and a day," I said.

The judge looked stunned. "Did you hear me correctly?" he asked. He repeated the options.

"Yes," I replied confidently. "I'll take the year and a day."

"A year and a day it is," the judge said. "Custody of the Florida Department of Corrections."

I turned around and looked at my mother. She was sitting perfectly upright, like she was always. But it was like the life was passing out of her, she looked so old. Right in front of my eyes, she seemed to age ten years. If there was a bottom for me outside the graveyard, that was the bottom right there.

I wanted to go over and hug her and tell her everything would be okay. I wanted to tell her that I loved her and I wouldn't really be locked away. I was going to get help. I'd do well in treatment. I'd get better. I'd get cured. But with a bang of the gavel, I was taken immediately from the courtroom and back to my cell.

I didn't hear anything at all for a couple of days. The wait was taking longer than I expected. My lawyer was also waiting. But when he saw me, he said he didn't have any news. Not yet. Then, a cop I knew was making his way through the lockup. He stopped at my cell.

"How ya doin'?" he asked, sounding genuinely concerned.

"As good as can be expected," I said.

"Yeah," he said, shaking his head. "That was a strange decision. I guess you know what's best."

"What do you mean?" I asked. He didn't seem to know the plan, how taking the sentence was really just a way of getting treatment. What did he know? "I'm going to rehab, and when I'm done, I won't be on probation anymore. My record will be wiped clean."

"I don't think so," he answered. I could tell he thought I was confused or misinformed. "I saw your file, Doc. You're going to prison. Nobody told you that?"

I was stunned. "What?"

"You're going to prison for a year and a day," he said with a shrug.

"I gotta talk to my lawyer," I told him, truly panicking for the first time. All the times I'd stepped in front of a judge up to now, they had shown such understanding. They seemed to know I wasn't a criminal. I was an addict. Or they had stars in their eyes from my baseball career. Why would that have changed? I didn't even want to wait for my lawyer to fix it. I was getting scared. "We've got to get the judge to switch this around. I want the probation!"

"That's gonna be tough, Doc," my cop friend explained. "You don't get any do-overs, my friend." He shook his head. "I'm really sorry, Bud."

I had to do my time. And I did.

After a few days in the county jail, I was put on a modified gray school bus with grates on the windows and driven to the Department of Corrections' Central Florida Reception Center outside Orlando. I wouldn't call the reception hospitable. I was a rookie again in a whole new ball game.

"You're Gooden?" one of the guards on the intake unit said as I stood with a dozen new prisoners in a large, open room.

"Yes," I said quietly.

"No!" the guard exploded. "It's 'Yes, sir,' motherfucker!"

"Yes, sir," I responded.

"Are you Gooden?" he asked again.

"Yes, sir," I responded again. This could have been a joke, but I didn't think he was joking.

"No," he said this time. "No, you are not Gooden. You're a number now, All-Star. You're" — he read from a clipboard — "DOC number T47272. That's who you are. You're a number now."

I looked at the floor and nodded. I could hear the footsteps and shackles of new prisoners joining us. No one else was saying anything. I wasn't looking for trouble.

"You were a Yankee," he said. "Right?"

"Yes, sir."

"Fucking Steinbrenner," the guard sneered. "I can't believe he gave a sack of shit like you a chance."

I didn't respond.

"Steinbrenner's a fucking loser, just like you, right?"

"No," I said. I quickly corrected myself. "No, sir. He's an all-right guy."

"No, he's a loser," the guard corrected me. "Tell me he's a loser."

There was no way to win this game. I wasn't saying anything more.

"Helloooo?" the guard pressed on. "Come on, prisoner. Steinbrenner's a bad guy, right?"

I lowered my eyes and kept my mouth shut. That seemed to agitate him even more. The other prisoners were shifting on their feet. I noticed a couple shaking their heads.

"I can't hear you. You can't fucking talk, now? You mute? Tell me Steinbrenner's a bad guy. It's the truth, right?"

He had everyone's attention now. He had shown he wasn't taking any attitude from any of us. Especially me, it seemed. "Look at me when I am talking to you," he said.

Just then, a second guard, oblivious to the grilling, materialized. He began calling out numbers of prisoners, sending us one by one to other school buses and, blessedly, away from reception. Next stop for me: the Florida State Prison at Lake Butler. I spent fifteen days at Lake Butler and the rest of the my time at the Gainesville Correctional Institution.

Lake Butler was a maximum-security facility. It had its own death row. Lake Butler had fights and gangs and some scary, violent inmates. These guards had seen it all. But this was where my addiction had taken me.

I tried to follow the advice that I heard. I didn't join in any teams in prison, not even something as innocuous as softball. I didn't lend anyone money. I didn't react at all when a short, muscular guard tried to frighten us like a scene from *Scared Straight!*

"Make no mistake," he shouted at the fresh fish. "There's no guarantee you'll even make it out of here! And I ain't talkin' about the length of your sentence. The reality is some of you will not make it outta here alive." I felt pretty safe in my eight-by-eight-foot cell, where I was locked up day and night. But I was cut off from everyone. I couldn't go to the rec yard. I couldn't call my lawyer. I had no way of knowing how my kids or my mom were. Suddenly, the Hillsborough County Jail wasn't looking so awful. My cell had no clock and no windows. I could only guess what time it was by the meals being served. I had nothing to read. It was just men, the walls, my bed, a steel toilet, and my thoughts, twenty-four hours a day. I did sit-ups and push-ups to wear myself out. I tried to sleep as much as I could.

I thought if I just kept to myself, I would be left alone. Wrong. Four guards showed up at my cell and stood there together, berating me. "You're a loser. . . . You fucked up. . . . Look at you. . . . Pathetic." I felt like a member of the visiting team again at Fenway or Wrigley. They went on like that for a good long while until, I guess, they finally just got bored. Then, twenty minutes later, one of them returned with a manila envelope. He pulled out a stack of photos and baseball cards. "I'm a big fan," he said. "If it's not too much trouble, do you think I could get you to autograph some stuff? Sorry about that thing before."

I was relieved when they sent me to Gainesville. The environment there was different from Lake Butler, in a good way. Gainesville was a minimum-security facility, specializing in drug rehabilitation. We lived in open, seventy-two-man dorms that resembled an army barracks with double-decker bunk beds.

It wasn't quite Smithers or Betty Ford — or even Narcotics Anonymous in St. Petersburg. But at least they were trying, and the counselors seemed to care. We spent six days a week in group meetings, talking about our problems, getting called on our bullshit, revealing ourselves. It was a regimented program with lots of rules. I was impressed this was happening in prison. This was at least a little closer to the deal I thought I was making in court that day.

Inside the dorm, there was no privacy at all. The common bathroom had half a dozen toilets without stalls. Bottom bunks were trophies for guys who had proven themselves. Like everyone, I started on top. Eventually, I made my way to one of the coveted lower bunks in the center of the room. Even in prison real estate, it's location, location, location.

Gainesville's rehab program was more about building social skills than teaching people to stay off of drugs and alcohol. There was an older counselor, Mr. Sellers, who'd really lay into prisoners.

He'd say "you fuckin' loser" to inmates the way fans liked to call me "Doc." It was a full-fledged nickname. Even he would try to be helpful to people who sought his advice, though I don't remember too many people seeking his counsel on their social skills.

I hated being locked up. But I tried to make good use of my time. Once the guards saw I didn't expect special treatment and wouldn't make extra demands, most of them treated me with respect and decency. "We've seen pro ballplayers before," one of them said to me. "Your teammate Strawberry was here. He was a diva. He treated us like the help." I laughed and said, "He was like that in the locker room."

A lot of the other inmates were extremely down on their luck. Some guys never seemed to get any visitors or mail from the outside world. It was like they'd been totally forgotten. Despite all I'd dragged them through, my family and friends never forgot me. Monique and my daughters were great about writing to me, as were hundreds of baseball fans. Hearing from people on the outside was a hugely important connection that kept me from going insane. I couldn't imagine being one of those forgotten souls. I hoped I never would be.

One night a couple of months into my sentence, a younger guy strolled up to my bunk just before lights out. He looked like a true thug. Tattoos, a scowl, a practiced swagger. But one-on-one, I could tell he was hurting. He spoke to me in a whisper, not wanting anyone to overhear.

"You get so much mail," he said with a soft smile. "Could I maybe read some of it?"

I didn't think I'd heard him correctly.

"Oh, nothing private," he said, laughing. "I don't want to pry into your life, man. It's just that, I got nothing, you know." He held up his empty hands, making his case.

I looked at my stack of letters. I didn't want to hand over anything from my family. I did have some nice words from fans. That seemed harmless. Still, it was personal stuff.

"It'd give me something to do," he said. "My kid's mom won't send any pictures. I got nobody."

Cautiously, I handed him a stack of fan letters. "Don't go passing this stuff around," I warned him. "This is important to me. Read 'em, then give 'em back."

My mother came to see me once. But watching her go through the metal detector and get patted down was just too horrible. I told her I appreciated her coming, but I didn't think she should come back. I'd see her as soon as I got out.

It was the same with Monique and Dylan. They came to visit a couple of times. But I didn't want to put them through that. Flying from Maryland to Atlanta and then to Gainesville, renting a car and a hotel room, then being allowed a two-hour visit—I missed them terribly, but that was more than I could ask. And more than I could shoulder. The extra guilt was a heavy part of my sentence.

Before I left Gainesville, I was supposed to speak to my small therapy group and tell the personal story of my own addiction and what I'd done to fight it. But there was a violent storm that day, and we couldn't leave the dorm. Someone decided it might be a good idea for the celebrity-athlete inmate addict to address a much larger group, the whole dorm. Now I was really nervous. The whole dorm? But when I shared the story—my first cocaine experience at my cousin's house, my missed parade, the ways I'd hurt my family and my own career—I think everyone realized I was just another guy who had messed up a lot of things he cared about, who didn't have all the answers but was trying to do the best he could. I wasn't Dwight Gooden, star pitcher. I was just another struggling person who wanted his life back.

18

High Low

THE CALL CAME AS A total surprise. It was January 2010. Jeff Wilpon, the Mets' chief operating officer, whose family owned the team, had some big news for me. Four new people, Jeff said, were going to be inducted that August into the Mets Hall of Fame, the first time anyone had been added since Tommie Agee eight years earlier.

Ever since the Mets had moved to Citi Field in April 2009, the sportswriters and the fans had been expressing a nagging complaint. They said the team was failing to celebrate its own amazing past. At the new ballpark, the history of the Brooklyn Dodgers seemed to get more attention than the history of the New York Mets. The exterior design of the stadium resembled Ebbets Field. The rotunda at the main entrance was named for Dodger great Jackie Robinson and featured a quote of his: "A life is not important except in the impact it has on other lives." No dis on Jackie. Mets fans revered him. But soon enough, a new Mets Hall of Fame was installed right off the rotunda. The Hall of Fame Committee, which hadn't met in years, had now decided the time was right for a new class to go in.

"We're revving it up again" was how Jeff described the plans to me.

All four of the new guys, he said, were closely connected to the 1986 World Series Mets: Darryl Strawberry, Davey Johnson, Frank Cashen. "And the fourth person being inducted into the Mets Hall of Fame," Jeff said, "is you."

This wasn't Cooperstown. This wasn't the Hall of Fame people once expected me to be part of. Ever since my rookie season in 1984, I'd been hearing talk about the Baseball Hall of Fame. How likely I was to get there. How long I'd have to wait. Then how I'd tragically blown my opportunity. Once in a while, some friend or fan or baseball numbers geek would pull me aside — this still happens — and talk Hall of Fame statistics with me. "You really should be in Cooperstown," these people would say. "Your numbers are better than a lot of the guys who are there." The running theory from my boosters seemed to be that I had created such gigantic expectations in my early playing days that my failure to meet them — not my actual performance — was being held against me. That might or might not be true. I don't know. I'll let other people argue about that.

All that said, no one was more surprised or more pleased than I was to get Jeff's call. My eyes welled up with tears even before I had hung up the phone.

We'd had such a wild ride together, the Mets and me. Now the team that I had started with, the team I cared most about, wanted me in their Hall of Fame. I was just so honored.

In 2006, I'd been invited, along with the entire '86 championship team, to the twentieth-year reunion of the 1986 Mets at Shea Stadium. The media had been making a big deal about how Darryl and I and the rest of the guys were finally being forgiven for the partying that some people thought cost the Mets a four- or five-year dynasty. Unfortunately, "the still-partying Doc," as one of the stories described me, couldn't be there for the anniversary celebration. I was four months into my one-year prison term. But two years later, another invitation had come. The Mets asked me to the closing of Shea Stadium, the Shea Goodbye, in September 2008. That was the first time I'd actually appeared at the stadium in eight years — the only exception being for the 2000 World Series when I'd been wearing a Yankees uniform. For the Shea Goodbye, the team didn't even announce in advance that I was coming. Until I got there, team officials weren't convinced I was actually showing up. I could hear the relief in their voices when I arrived: "Oh, good. You're here." I certainly didn't know how the fans would receive me that day, but I went. And the ovation I got was overwhelming. I smile just thinking about it.

I had so much fun at the last Shea game, I went to Opening Day 2009 at the new Citi Field, watching my nephew Gary in his first game as a Met. It was unreal, seeing that little kid from the backyard on New Orleans Avenue now a grown-up man in a Mets uniform. The fans seemed to understand the full circle that represented, and they couldn't have been friendlier to me.

I went up to the Ebbets Club, one of the restaurants in the new stadium and another cap tip to the Dodgers. "Will you sign the wall?" the general manager asked me. "And write in a couple of stats?"

"No problem," I told him as he handed me a Sharpie.

DOC GOODEN, I wrote. 84 R.O.Y., 85 CY YOUNG, 86 W.S. CHAMPS

The next day I got a call from Jay Horwitz. "Doc," he told me, "you can't just be signing your name on the wall. The Wilpons are upset with you."

I explained to Jay that I wasn't just writing graffiti. The general manager of the restaurant had asked me to sign. "It wasn't like I was walking around with a Sharpie in my pocket," I told him. But when word leaked that the Mets were going to remove that section of wall and that the manager might be fired, the story blew up in the papers and sports-talk radio. Suddenly, the Mets front office had a change of plans. They didn't want to get rid of my signature anymore.

"We've listened to our fans on this," Jay told the reporters. "The last thing we want is for them or Doc to be upset. We just didn't want everyone to think it was okay to start writing on walls all over the stadium."

Jay came up with a brilliant plan. He said the section of wall with my name on it would be moved to a spot off the outfield where fans could easily see it. Other popular ex-players would be asked to sign the wall too. Honestly, I didn't care what happened to the autograph. I just didn't want the hard-working restaurant manager to end up losing his job. But this showed how popular the '86 Mets still were. Oh, and the following year, the team even picked a new name for the restaurant, the Champions Club.

Ya gotta believe!

Whatever the hard feelings of the past, the new good feelings seemed to continue. That spring, the Mets even asked me to go down to Florida and speak with the minor-league players about the pressures of life on and off the field. I definitely appreciated the offer, although with Monique being pregnant, I had to say no thanks.

I wasn't in great shape, mentally or physically, when I got that call from Jeff Wilpon. I was living in New Jersey. I had put on weight. I was sitting around a lot and not exercising at all. Even worse, I was gradually slipping back into my addiction. By early 2010, I was drinking. I was hanging out in strip clubs. So of course, I found my way back to cocaine. Alcohol, strip clubs, cocaine: the pattern was as predictable as "three strikes and you're out." I could clean up enough to handle an autograph signing or a basic public appearance, but that was about all.

Grabbing a moment of clarity at that foggy time, I realized that being inducted into the Mets Hall of Fame was a really, really big deal for me. A Major League Baseball team was recognizing my achievements in the most public way imaginable. And not just any team. It was my team. The New York Mets. I felt like the franchise had forgiven me for my many sins in the 1980s and 1990s. Or at the very least, the front office was saying to me, "For better or worse, you are one of us. Forever."

I had missed the parade after our World Series season, too wasted to attend. I'd missed the twentieth-year reunion of that championship team, serving my one-year prison term at the time. I wasn't about to miss the Hall of Fame.

I was only sorry my father couldn't be there too.

Jay Horwitz organized a conference call with the sportswriters. It was magical, like an instant time machine back to earlier days. Darryl said he regretted leaving the team in 1990 for the Los Angeles Dodgers. We complimented Davey for his ability to control the '86 wild men. We gave Frank props for putting together such an amazing squad. Davey and Frank said what great players Darryl and I had been. "I'm very honored and humbled, and you guys know it's not easy to humble me," Davey joked.

I was totally open about how I felt.

"In '94, when I left because of my own personal issues, I was crushed, heartbroken," I admitted. "I understood the Mets wanted to go separate ways. Not that I felt betrayed, but I had let them down and never got the opportunity to correct the situation."

I made a point of being gracious to Darryl, even though we'd had our difficulties.

I didn't mean to be too serious, but I wanted people to know how I felt about this honor, the Mets especially. "For me, being inducted, it's like a homecoming," I said. "Everything has come full circle for myself. I'm just honored and overwhelmed for this day to come."

That was as plain as I could say it.

"Deep inside I was always a Met and I always will be a Met," I said. "I'm just blessed to be in this situation."

Drugs hadn't taken over my life again. Not yet. But I was definitely heading down a dangerous path. I wasn't using every day. But I was using often enough. I was going out at night. I was fighting with Monique. I was spending long hours alone in my room. And when I got high, I noticed I wasn't bouncing back as quickly as I used to.

I told my doctor I needed something to help me sleep. I didn't mention the coke, of course. "What can you prescribe that will help me sleep and relieve some of the stress I'm feeling?" I asked him.

He gave me a prescription for Ambien.

Ambien is one of the most popular anti-insomnia drugs on the market. I wouldn't call it a magic drug. But it did help to calm me down and lull me off to sleep. I've heard people say Ambien can be addictive if you use for a while. I didn't take it long enough to say. I just know the pink-colored oblong tablets helped with both the stress and the lack of sleep, and they did absolutely nothing to make me face the underlying problems in my life.

March 22, 2010, was a Monday. I got high that night. Not a lot. Not a little. Just a normal amount for me. I used until almost midnight. At about one a.m., I took four Ambiens, the five-milligram size, about what I usually took, and I got ready for bed. That was my new pattern. The cocaine had me going. The Ambien settled me down. I had done it many times before.

I climbed into bed. I drifted off to sleep. I had no idea how my life was about to change.

Monique shook me awake around six a.m. and said, "Can you take Dylan to school?" She hadn't slept much in the month since our baby daughter, Milan, was a born. I was groggy too.

"Yeah, sure," I said.

I pulled myself out of bed. I climbed into a pair of sweats. When Dylan was ready to go, he and I walked out to the driveway and got into the SUV, a black 2007 Chrysler Aspen. Dylan, who was five at the time, climbed into the backseat, where he usually liked to ride. I put on my seat belt. I don't remember asking Dylan if he'd put his seat belt on. I backed out of the driveway and onto Old Mill Road toward the Academy of Most Blessed Sacrament on Franklin Lake Road, where Dylan was in kindergarten.

It had been seven hours since my last line of cocaine. The effects from that had long since faded. It was six hours since I had taken the four Ambien. They lingered longer.

The next thing I remember, we were half a mile from home and Dylan was asking me, "Dad, why are you riding in those people's yard?"

What?

His question startled me. It was like I had just woken up and opened my eyes. I was in a familiar residential area. But clearly something was wrong.

"Uh-oh," I thought. "This is not good. I must have been blacking out."

Right there, I should have slammed on the brakes and gotten Dylan out of the car. I should never have been driving in that condition, especially not with my child in the car. I know now how crazy that was, driving with my five-year-old, dozing and driving off the road. But when Dylan asked me that question, my reaction was more like, "That's not good. I have to correct that." It wasn't, "Holy shit! Oh my God!"

In my messed-up judgment, I immediately started calculating in my head. "He has to get to school. The school's not too far. I should be able to make it to the school."

I went another fifty feet or so. Then, I rear-ended a 2009 black Mercedes-Benz driven by one of our neighbors, a seventy-one-year-old architect named Ronald Schmidt, who was heading to his office on Englewood Road.

I wasn't hurt. Thankfully, Dylan seemed okay. And so did Ronald Schmidt, who got out of his car and, under the circumstances, really didn't even seem all that upset. I believe he recognized me.

"I'm fine," he said. "There's no damage to the cars." He said he didn't think there was any need to call the police. We shook hands. We agreed we were all very lucky. He drove off, and so did I.

Even then, it hadn't hit me how screwed up my judgment was. I still hadn't gotten it into my head that something really bad was happening here. All I could think was, "My wife asked me to drive my son to school. I have to get Dylan to school."

I was driving across people's yards. I had no idea what I was doing. My mind was racing. I was trying to stay focused. "I'll drop him off," I said to myself in the calmest tone I could muster. "Then I'll figure out what's wrong with me."

Apparently, one of the neighbors called 911. By the time I got back in the car and drove another half a block, we were stopped by the Franklin Lakes Police. I might have also hit a gate or jumped a curb or bounced off a utility pole — I don't know exactly what. I was zoning in and out. What I do know is that the cops came. They took one look at me and at Dylan. They didn't think any of this was minor at all.

"You all right, Doc?" one of the cops said. It seemed like everyone in Franklin Lakes knew me.

"Yeah," I said.

"What's going on?"

I didn't know what to tell him.

He looked at Dylan and asked, "Are you all right?" Dylan said, "I think so. I might have hit my head."

Thankfully, Dylan's head bump was minor. He wasn't even crying. We were all so lucky no one was badly hurt or killed. Truly, I could have killed three or four people that day.

A police officer asked if I would take a breathalyzer.

"Okay," I said.

I blew into the little device. It came up zero alcohol.

I didn't like doing any of this in front of Dylan. But the cop didn't seem like he wanted to wait. He went away and then came back a few moments later. He asked me to blow again.

Another zero. I heard one of them say to another. "No alcohol."

The police didn't know what I was on, if anything. But they could tell something wasn't right. "I can't just let you go," the cop said. "Someone called 911. There are too many people around."

I could see the officers talking to each other.

"What's going on?" one of them asked me. "Are you high?"

"I took an Ambien before I went to sleep," I said, beginning to slump in the seat. "That's all."

"Okay," he said. "You have to take a field sobriety test."

I was pretty sure I couldn't pass anything that required manual dexterity. "I can't stand up," I said. "My balance isn't good."

"We'll have to take you in," one of the cops said.

By that point, it didn't surprise me. I knew I was in no condition to drive.

"Can I call my wife to come and get my son?" Even in my woozy condition, I was thinking I didn't want my son to ride in a police car. But they put us both in the cruiser and drove to the police station on DeKorte Drive. I remember the officers talking to me. I remember parts of what they were saying, but I kept dozing off.

"Are you high on coke?" one officer asked me back at the station before Monique got there.

"No," I said.

I thought, "If I was high on coke, I wouldn't be falling asleep like this. I'd be alert and wired."

"Just something to help me sleep," I said. "Ambien."

"Can you give us some urine?"

"Sure." I went into the bathroom and peed in a cup.

The urine came back with evidence of Ambien and lingering traces of cocaine.

They charged me with a long list of crimes. Being under the influence of a controlled dangerous substance, driving under the influence of a controlled dangerous substance, endangering the welfare of a child, driving while intoxicated with a child passenger, leaving the scene of an accident, reckless driving, failure to keep right, and failure to change my address on my driver's license. They didn't miss much.

I was released on my own recognizance without posting any bail. But because Dylan was in the car with me and my driving had put him in danger, the police notified DYFS, the New Jersey Division of Youth and Family Services. These are the people who investigate child abuse and endangerment cases.

I was free to go. But now I wasn't only facing serious criminal charges. The state was taking a serious look at something I cared about at least as much as my freedom — my fitness as a father to my kids. Actually, I cared about that even more.

19

Room Service

CAME OUT OF THE HOUSE the next morning in my usual
baggy gray sweats. About a dozen reporters were waiting for me
in the driveway. I had never ducked reporters, not since Rusty
Staub lectured me in my rookie year. But the accident had happened
just twenty-four hours earlier. I'd barely had time to speak to a lawyer.
There wasn't much I could say.

"Now is not the time," I said. "Sorry."

Since I wouldn't comment, the reporters called Ron Goldstein, who
had been booking me for public appearances and had become my
manager and close friend. Ron tried to put the best possible spin on
what led up to the crash. "Doc would never deliberately do anything to
put his children at risk," Ron said. "He is a very good father and a very
good friend."

The Mets got calls too. My arrest was yet another Gooden embarrassment for them. Even my old friend Jay Horwitz, who was always

looking out for me, would say only, "The Mets are aware of the situation." He did make clear that my planned induction into the Mets Hall of Fame was still on the team calendar in August.

My old teammates mostly just winced. "This is very sad because I care about Doc and I worry about him," said Keith Hernandez, who'd moved into the Mets broadcast booth.

My old pal Bob Klapisch wrote a piece for the *Bergen Record* in New Jersey quoting someone who claimed to be one of my closest friends: "As much as I hate to say it, whatever Dwight's got coming to him, he deserves it this time." I didn't know for sure who said that. But knowing the star player Bob had talked to in the past about me, I thought I had a pretty good idea.

Waking up and looking at Dylan asleep in his bed, seeing the look in Monique's eyes, then reading those quotes in the paper — I felt like I'd let everyone down all over again. Over the next days and weeks, I tried to construct in my mind how the accident had happened. Was drowsiness a common side effect of Ambien? Had the coke I had taken many hours earlier somehow made me ripe for a blackout? Had I seemed out of it to Monique as Dylan and I walked to the driveway?

I wracked my brain.

The charges were forwarded by the Franklin Lakes Police to the Bergen County Prosecutor's Office. The most serious was child endangerment. Under New Jersey law, my lawyer told me, I could go to prison for ten to twenty years. My freedom and my role as a father were both in serious jeopardy. All of this was weighing on me, and things were getting even more tense around the house.

"What the hell were you were thinking?" Monique demanded.

"I'm sorry," I kept saying. "I'm sorry. I don't know what happened. I thought I was okay to drive. You think I wanted to put Dylan's life at risk?"

Monique and I had fought before, but now we were arguing all the time. I started sleeping down in the basement. I'd leave the house and stay out for hours. I'd come home and sit in the dark and not talk to anyone. "We just had another baby!" she yelled. "And now this?"

I had to try to make some changes, as much as I was capable of. After the accident, I knew I had to stay away from cocaine. And I did for a while. But I was still self-medicating with alcohol, with the same predictable consequences. I was using the alcohol to dull the guilt and the shame. That made things even worse. Then I would feel more guilt and shame, which I tried to drown in more alcohol.

My marriage was pretty much over.

Every time Monique and I would get into it, she would call the investigators from the state's Division of Youth and Family Services and tell them, "He's high around the kids again," which wasn't true. "You have to do something."

She cried on the phone.

She demanded they arrest me.

She accused me of threatening her.

Some days, she called ten or twenty times.

The truth is I never threatened her. I wasn't using drugs in the house. I wasn't acting out violently. Mostly, I was just morose. I stayed inside, up in my bedroom or down in the basement, cut off from my own family and from the outside world, depressed, withdrawn, and miserable.

In late April, state investigators ordered me removed from my home. "You can't be here," the social worker said. "You have to move out."

I didn't fight it.

On May 1, I moved to a Comfort Inn on Route 17 in Paramus. Monique took Dylan and baby Milan and moved back to her parents' house in Columbia, Maryland. We ended our lease on the house in Franklin Lakes. I was totally depressed and feeling sorry for myself. I couldn't stand all this drama and bitterness and the constant allegations. Now the thought of losing contact with my two youngest children, the only two who'd known me as a full-time live-in dad — that was almost too much to bear.

All I wanted to do was to hide from myself and the world. Behind the locked door of room 133 of that suburban Comfort Inn, at least I could find some relief in the drugs.

I stayed inside the room almost twenty-four hours a day and revved up my coke habit again. I still had some money from doing public appearances, and there was a dealer I knew who would drive to the hotel and make small deliveries. I slept at strange hours. I paced around the room. I watched TV a lot, hours and hours and hours of ESPN. I kept forgetting to charge my cell phone. The room had a Jacuzzi, but I was too paranoid to use it. I thought I might slide into the water and drown. I did more coke.

I couldn't stand the idea of anyone seeing me like this. I would sneak out at night and get something to eat. I'd go to Wendy's. I'd go to Dunkin' Donuts. There was a Red Lobster next to the hotel. A couple of times, I went in there. But that wasn't quick enough for me. No telling who might see me in there.

I'd go to the ATM when I ran out of money, but I wouldn't go inside the bank.

Sometimes, when the maids would come to the door, I'd say, "Leave the towels outside." Then later, I'd carry the clean ones into the room and leave the dirties in the hall. Several times, I called the desk clerks to change the key card for my room. In my paranoia, I had the idea someone might be sneaking in when I walked out for my Wendy's Baconator burger, fries, and Frosty.

I had a few public appearances that summer. Not too many, but a few. I turned down some jobs that people called or texted me about. I just didn't think I could do them. I tried to clean up for the ones I did, just enough to do my appearance and make a little money and get out of there as fast as I could. I did what I could to hide the shape I was in.

I don't know if the casual fans could tell how messed up I was. I hope no one saved those pictures.

A few people pulled me aside and said, "Hey, Doc, hang in there...." "I got twenty years...." "I got eighteen years...." "You can do this." They were telling me they knew I was struggling. They wanted me to know they were pulling for me.

My wife was gone. I wasn't seeing my kids. I wasn't even calling my mother in Florida. I didn't know what to say the couple of times she got me on the phone and she asked, "How are you, baby?" I had almost no communication with anyone. It was just me and my drugs, feeling sorry for ourselves. Instead of once or twice a week, soon I was using two or three days in a row.

I thought constantly about the accident. How it could have happened. How it was ruining my life even more than my life was already ruined. How mad I was at Monique for making me sound even worse than I was and taking my kids away from me. How much I blamed myself. And any time I needed more to worry about, there was the real possibility I'd be heading off to prison again — and not just for a couple of months this time. And when I'd sober up from being high, the guilt and shame would wash over me again. Which, of course, pushed me to do more drugs.

"I can't live like this," I told myself.

The only person I spoke to regularly was Ron. He'd get takeout shrimp from the Red Lobster and sit in the room while I ate it. He kept saying, "Come stay with me. I've got room. This is too depressing. We'll come up with a plan."

I wouldn't budge. The thought of staying in the room seemed horrible. The thought of leaving seemed even worse. I knew this was no good for my disposition or my sanity, hiding in a room all day with the TV on and the curtains closed. But I couldn't bear the glare of going outside. Truly, I hadn't felt this low since I was lying on the bed in my Long Island apartment, missing the World Series parade.

One day in June, Ron came to the hotel with our friend Carl and another guy. "You gotta get out of here," he said. "I'm worried about what's happening to you."

They didn't threaten me exactly, but it was close. It was like the three of them had come to move me out of there, and they weren't taking no for an answer. What gave them the right? I was really starting to think I wanted to die.

"Okay," I said finally, just to put Ron off. "I'll come and stay with you tomorrow."

"Good," he said. "That's good." For the first time in weeks, he seemed relieved.

I excused myself and went into the bathroom, glad that was over and hoping they would leave. But when I came out, the three of them had taken all my clothes out of the closet and off the chairs where I'd left them and loaded everything in Ron's car.

"What are you doing?" I demanded.

"You said you were coming over," Ron said.

"Tomorrow," I corrected him. "Tomorrow. Give me my stuff back."

Ron refused. I demanded. Ron refused some more. We argued back and forth for almost an hour.

"You have no right to take my clothes," I told him.

Eventually, Ron sent the other two out to the car. They returned to the room with my things.

"Tomorrow," Ron said as they finally left me alone.

I didn't leave the next day. Or the day after that. But the confrontation with Ron must have planted something in my head and opened my heart a little. On Sunday morning, I was lying in the king-size hotel bed. The curtains were still closed. I had the radio on. I was just lying in bed looking up at the ceiling, thinking about how messed up things were and how they couldn't possibly get any better. At some point, I started talking to God.

"Look," I said, "if you can pull me out of this mess, or at least get me a couple days to get my head right, I'll turn my life around and get back on track. I have to do something to get some focus, or I really will lose everything."

Just then, a song came on the radio. It was one of those gospel songs you hear on Sunday mornings, a song you probably wouldn't hear any other day of the week. The singer had a giant voice that sounded like it could probably blow the roof off a crowded church. I'd never heard the song before or the singer. But it will stay in my head as long as I am alive. The singer's name was Marvin Sapp.

"I never would have made it without you," he sang.

> *Never would have made it,*
> *Never could have made it without you.*
> *I would have lost it all.*
> *But now I see how you were there for me.*

It wasn't just the words. It was also the powerful way they were sung. Together, they pounded against me and cut through my fog. Hearing that song on the radio in that hotel room at just that moment, maybe that was the higher power people in recovery are always talking about. I'm not a real religious guy. I certainly wasn't at that time. But something undeniable came over me.

> *And I can say*
> *Never would have made it,*
> *Never could have made it,*
> *Without you*

The song went on for five or six minutes. It wasn't a short song. And it hammered home that message over and over again. It overwhelmed me.

I got up. I walked to Dunkin' Donuts. I came back to the Comfort Inn. I took a good, long shower and let the hot water roll over me.

I called Ron.

"What are you doing?" I asked.

"Nothing," he said. "Are you all right?"

"Yeah," I said. "But if it's okay, I'm gonna stay with you for a couple of days."

Ron didn't hesitate a second. "I'm on my way," he said.

In twenty minutes, he was at my door.

"Wow," he said when he came in. "You look great."

That's the day things began to change.

PART IV

Saving My Life

20

Fame Game

MOVED INTO RON'S HOUSE in Old Tappan, New Jersey, and started doing a little better right away. I felt a little weird, living with Ron and his wife, Angela, and their teenage daughters, Brianna and Sara — like what business did I have mooching off these nice people? But the whole family was totally welcoming to me. They didn't ask a lot of questions. They never said, "How long are you staying?" or "When are you planning to leave?" They just let me live with them and build up my confidence and figure out what I was going to do next.

I lived with the Goldsteins for several weeks. Then I rented an apartment in Edgewater and continued the slow process of trying to pull myself back up. I made myself eat more than Dunkin' Donuts. I began working out at the gym. I started checking in regularly again with my mom and my sister Betty. Clearly, they'd been worried about me. I tried to reconnect with my older kids. My son Dwight Junior moved up from Tampa and started living with me. He had been working hard building his music career, and he wanted to make some New York connections.

It wasn't all perfect. It wasn't as if I'd had a miraculous rebirth. I never stopped drinking. Every once in a while, I also used cocaine. I kept my worst instincts at bay by attending a day program in Manhattan called the Addiction Institute of New York, which was started by some people who used to work at Smithers. I definitely still had a lot of issues.

But I was far better off than I'd been lying in bed with the curtains closed at the Route 17 Comfort Inn. Most important, I wasn't feeling like giving up anymore. Ron and I started talking about what my next move should be.

I had two big events on my calendar. One I was extremely excited about. The other one I was dreading. I was only hoping the two of them wouldn't somehow collide.

I knew that on August 1, I had my induction into the Mets Hall of Fame. I could still hardly believe my good fortune with that. It felt like a vindication to me. And I also had a court date coming up. I didn't know when exactly. The case kept getting delayed. My lawyer was talking to the prosecutors. Various negotiations were going on. I was worried that the criminal case would scuttle the Hall of Fame. God, I hoped not. Who knew when I might get an honor like that again.

Since my arrest, there had been a flurry of stories in the papers recounting almost every bad thing I had ever done. I wondered if Jeff Wilpon was already regretting his call. The bad-Doc publicity seemed to be everywhere. I'd gotten used to the papers publishing long chronologies, laying out every mistake I'd made since 1986. I didn't like it, but I was used to it. But what my wife did, so close to the induction ceremony, caught me totally off-guard. Still spitting mad at me and blaming me for outrages true and false, Monique spoke to the *New York Post* and totally unloaded on me.

"WIFE: GOODEN LEFT KIDS HIGH AND DRY," the July 24 headline said.

She accused me of abandoning her and the children. She called me a deadbeat dad. She said she had no idea where I was or how to reach me.

That wasn't true. Clearly, I'd been a bad husband in various ways. But I'd never, ever, ever run away from my kids. Accuse me of things I'm guilty of. There are more than enough of those. And my recent whereabouts had hardly been a secret since I'd left the Comfort Inn. I did an autograph signing at a hotel in New Jersey. I played in a charity softball game. I appeared at a baseball fan fest. It wouldn't have taken Sherlock Holmes to track me down. I didn't want a public feud with Monique. That was a bad idea for many reasons. I knew how dirty she could fight. I did what seemed right. I made double-sure my kids had what they needed. I tried to stay positive and look the other way.

Monique wasn't the only one I thought might try to derail my Hall of Fame induction. I got a call from my nephew Gary asking me what was going on. It turned out Darryl had dropped another of his little bombs. "Straw called," Gary said. "He's worried about you. He says you're doing drugs and you're dying."

"What? I'm fine, I'm doing good. I'm gonna be there."

This was becoming a pattern with Darryl, telling stories that had a kernel of truth. But he'd make the problems sound far, far worse than anything that was actually going on. And then he'd call people like Sheff or Monique or even Dr. Lans and say what a concerned friend he was. Of course, he'd never mention that he was doing many of the same bad things I was, worse sometimes.

Darryl could be very convincing, and Gary sounded genuinely concerned. "Are you sure?" Gary asked. "He's telling people you're doing terribly. You're living in a fleabag hotel."

Now I'd had some rough days back at the Comfort Inn. But I promise you, it was no fleabag, unless fleabags have started offering Jacuzzis and flat-screen TVs and Red Lobsters next door. On Darryl's part, this felt like wishful thinking to me. I had the distinct idea — I couldn't prove it but I don't think I was wrong — that Darryl wasn't too thrilled to be sharing his Hall of Fame spotlight with me. It was "Doc and Darryl, Darryl and Doc" all over again.

And this wasn't the first time Darryl had started downing me in the buildup to a big Mets alumni event. In 2008, a few months before the Shea Goodbye ceremony, he was down at spring training in Port St. Lucie when he gave an interview to our mutual friend Bob Klapisch. The headline in the next day's *Bergen Record* summed up the piece fairly well. "GOODEN OUT OF CONTROL," it said.

Darryl admitted we hadn't spoken for a year, but he made it sound like I was totally out of control. He said I was "in the middle of a long, downward spiral," that my life "had turned into a blur of old addictions." The way Klapisch wrote it up, he made Darryl sound like a perfect little angel and me totally on the skids. "As Gooden drifts out of control, Strawberry has found structure, if not peace," Klapisch wrote.

"It broke my heart, really," he quoted Darryl as saying. "Doc is such a great guy, I love him forever. But he never got away from the people who ruined his life. He's still out there with them, doing crazy stuff. So I keep busy with other things now."

What a phony!

I certainly had my problems. But why was Darryl blasting them everywhere, with his own exaggerations thrown in? Didn't Darryl have his own issues with drugs, alcohol, and reckless behavior? I didn't feel any need to run around saying alarming things about him.

I saw him after the story was in the paper, and I asked him about it. "I didn't say that," he told me. He tried to blame our old friend Ray Negron. All I knew was that, with another big ceremony coming up, Darryl was at it again. I just hoped his stories — and Monique's — weren't getting too much attention in the Mets' executive suite.

The Mets never blinked.

If team officials ever got cold feet about putting me in the Hall of

Fame, no one ever said anything to me. To my great relief and appreciation, they didn't seem rattled at all.

My mom flew up from Florida for the Hall of Fame weekend, and it almost felt like a family reunion. My kids Dwight Junior, Ashley, Ariel, Devin, and Darren and my grandson, Emiere, all came. My nephew Gary, who was finishing out his career as a Met, was there, along with his wife, Deleon. So was my ex-wife, Monica. She and I had been married for sixteen years. She'd been with me for a lot of the things I was being honored for. I was happy to share the weekend with her. Monique was too angry to come. She stayed back in Maryland with Dylan and Milan, the two littlest ones.

The Mets put on quite a show. We had a charity luncheon on Saturday with fans in one of the new Citi Field club suites. People brought 1980s Mets memorabilia for Darryl, Davey, Frank, and me to autograph. Lots of reporters came, including many of the beat writers who had covered that World Series team. They seemed to feel as much emotion as we did. I was happy to pose for pictures in a Mets cap.

"I beat myself up over so many things," I said. "I didn't live up to expectations but nobody had higher expectations for me than me, and I let myself down a lot. But the fans never gave up on me."

I'm sure everyone knew I was still struggling. But no one seemed to dwell on that. This was a weekend for celebration.

"I am deeply, deeply honored by this," I said. "I've had chills since I was told about it. I've always wanted to come back and right the ship. The Mets have always been on my mind and in my heart. Now it feels like a homecoming. Everything feels right, and this is where I belong."

The celebration culminated at Citi Field on Sunday afternoon before a blowout 14–1 loss to the Arizona Diamondbacks. Maybe the new Mets should have let the old-timers play that game.

I wasn't quite sure what to say to a crowd like that. I thought I might have trouble containing my emotions as I talked about how blessed I felt to be getting this honor with Frank, who signed me to my first contract, and Davey, my first manager, and Darryl, the player I'd be paired with forever whether I wanted to be or not. I'd just speak from the heart, that's all.

At the stadium to support us were several other members of the Mets' Hall of Fame, fanning out on both sides of the podium. The group included Bud Harrelson, Rusty Staub, Ralph Kiner, Keith Hernandez, Mookie Wilson, and Gary Carter. A lot of talent there and a lot of old friends.

All of us looked a little worse for wear since we'd actually run those bases. And there was a lot of teasing back and forth. Keith and Mookie and Gary kept making fun of all the extra pounds I'd put on. "Hey, it's the Nutty Professor!" Mookie said. I certainly didn't think I looked like the rotund Eddie Murphy character. But they kept coming over and patting my belly and breaking out in laughs.

WFAN radio announcer Howie Rose, who was master of ceremonies, called us "truly iconic figures" in Mets history. That was nice to hear. When each of our names was called, we entered the field through a gate in the outfield as though we were coming out of the bullpen to pitch, making the long walk to the podium. Davey, looking sharp in khakis and a blazer, jogged a few steps before reconsidering and slowing to his usual choppy stomp. Frank, who was about to turn ninety, doing fine on his aluminum cane. Me in a boxy three-piece gray suit hiding at least some of my suddenly famous gut.

Each of us got a video tribute on the outfield Jumbotron. Then we each had a chance to say a few words. "There was nothing greater than showing up to Shea every night to perform," I heard Darryl say. There was no denying that. When Davey spoke, he mentioned me and how much I loved being on the mound and watching the crowd put up all those famous Ks. Cashen said how special it was to be inducted with two of the greatest players the city had ever known. That was especially gracious, I thought, given some of the grief I had caused him personally.

As I waited to speak, I still wasn't sure how the fans at the ballpark would react to me. They'd been great at the Shea Goodbye. But that wasn't about me. That was about the team and the stadium. It had been so long since I truly was a Met. When I ran across Mets fans out in the world, they were almost always friendly and encouraging to me. But this was a little different. I was standing out on the field again. I was being honored, I who had thrilled and then deeply disappointed everyone. New Yorkers are the most loyal fans anywhere, but also the toughest and most vocal. Who knew what memories, happy and sad, that might dredge up in a crowd as large as this one.

They knew about my promise as a pitcher and how imperfectly I'd lived up to it. They could imagine some of the deep, dark holes I had fallen into. No one at Citi Field needed to be reminded. The stadium was new, but the fans were not.

Then I heard Howie's voice again, and I approached the podium. I swear it was 1984 again, and Davey had just told me that I'd made the team.

"The youngest pitcher in All-Star history," Howie's baritone boomed, "and ranks among the franchise leaders in nearly every pitching category including one hundred and fifty-seven victories, twenty-three shutouts, one thousand eight hundred and seventy-five strikeouts. The Mets ace, we call him 'the Doctor,' Dr. K, pitcher Dwight Eugene Gooden."

I might have been the Prodigal Met returning at last to his family. But the cheers were so loud and so lasting, I knew without a doubt that I was home.

"Thank you," I said, looking across this gorgeous new stadium, trying to pick out the faces of my mom, my nephew Gary, and all my kids. "This is really amazing. It feels so good to be home."

The way my own voice echoed across the stadium, it reminded me just how big the big leagues are. This wasn't just a ballpark. It was also a monument to baseball.

I listened carefully to the crowd reaction. I didn't hear a single boo.

The applause from the stands was like a long, warm embrace pulling me in and holding me. These were the people who had always stood by me. They were standing by me still.

"The success I've had here in New York wouldn't have been possible without the support of you, all of you," I said. "The fans always supported me on and off the field."

That was true. They had. Even when I didn't deserve it.

"There was no better feeling when I took the mound and I had two strikes on the batter, and all you guys were standing and clapping, wanting that third strike," I said.

They were there when I needed them most.

"A lot of times, when I took the mound, if I didn't have my best stuff, you guys gave me the extra adrenaline to bring the best out of me that particular day," I said. "You are going to the Mets Hall of Fame with me."

I had a few special thank-yous that could not go unsaid.

"I have to say to my mom, I love you very much for all the support, for always being there and putting me in the best situation to fulfill my dream, and that's playing major-league baseball. Thank you, and I love you."

She had put up with so much over the years from me. I could never thank her adequately. So had my kids.

I started naming them. "Dwight Junior, Ashley, Ariel, Devin —" and then I took a breath. I could hear some laughter in the crowd, but I didn't want to forget anybody. "I have a lot of kids, stay with me," I said. "Darren, Dylan, Milan, and my grandson, Emiere. I love you guys very much. Thanks for all your support, and thank you for just allowing me to be Dad and Granddad."

I couldn't have asked for a better homecoming or a better family reunion. Now all I had to do was try to live a life that deserved it.

21

Candid Camera

DIDN'T ASK TO BE PART of *Celebrity Rehab with Dr. Drew.*

I was familiar with the program. I'd seen it on VH1. Each season, the show featured a fresh crew of semifamous people who were having problems with alcohol or drugs. I guess celebrities in need of rehab weren't too hard to find, especially in California.

Dr. Drew Pinsky and his team led these high-profile addicts through a full-blown treatment program at the Pasadena Recovery Center in Los Angeles while TV cameras recorded everything. There was no shortage of drama among the cast members. The celebrities were constantly acting out in crazy ways.

I had no idea how successful the treatment might be. I didn't know whether *Celebrity Rehab* had actually helped any of these actors and singers and TV reality stars beat their substance issues or get a new grip on their out-of-control lives. But the back-and-forth could be fascinating in a train wreck sort of way. I remember watching a few episodes and thinking, "I can't believe those people are laying out their private business for the whole world to see!"

I'd taken drugs for more than two decades. I'd made half a dozen attempts at getting clean. But I had never thought of going on *Celebrity Rehab*. I was much too private for that. The last thing I wanted to do was confront my innermost demons in front of everyone in America with a basic cable plan.

Why would I do that?

But clearly, someone must have been speaking to someone about me.

On the morning of March 4, 2011, eleven months and two weeks after my wreck with Dylan, I woke up to a headline in the *New York Post*. My picture was in the paper along with the pictures of a couple of other famously messed-up characters with ties to New York's Long Island.

"LI DETECTOR," the headline said. "HOW PROUD ARE WE? CELEB REHAB RECRUITS HERE."

The story said that the new season of the VH1 recovery show was going to be a "mostly Long Island edition." One cast member, the paper said, would be Amy Fisher, the "Long Island Lolita" who served seven years in prison for shooting Mary Jo Buttafuoco, the wife of her married lover, Joey. After her release, Amy had gotten married, had three children, and moved to California. She started her own porn site and was reportedly struggling with alcohol. Said the *Post*: "The Bellmore, LI, native joins two other troubled Long Island denizens, Michael Lohan (Merrick) and Dwight Gooden, who lived in Port Washington when he pitched for the New York Mets."

Dwight Gooden?

"Wow!" I thought. "How did that get in here?"

Lohan, of course, was the father of troubled star Lindsay Lohan, who'd been in and out of rehab at least as many times as I had. The story said he didn't drink or use drugs anymore but was hoping to improve his anger-management skills. Given all the Lohan-family blow-ups, he could obviously use some help with that.

But what was I doing in the story? Even the Long Island connection was a stretch. Back in my New York playing days, I'd had a couple of apartments on the Island. But I came from Tampa and lately I'd been more of a Jersey guy. The bigger question though was this: "What made someone think I was going on *Celebrity Rehab*?" — besides the fact that I'd been battling addiction for more than two decades, and I was, I guess, at least semi–well known? Would have been nice if someone had mentioned it to me!

Before I'd even finished the story, my old Mets teammate Lenny Dykstra was on the phone from California, frantic as usual. It was still the middle of the night out there.

"You going on Dr. Drew?" Lenny wanted to know. "Really?"

"Nah," I told him. "No way. I don't need that. I don't know where that came from."

Ron called as soon as Lenny hung up. "You see the *Post*?" he asked.

"Yeah," I said. "How did that get in there?"

Ron didn't answer.

It was only later — much later — that he confessed to me he had set up the whole thing. Talked to the *Celebrity Rehab* people, leaked the story to the *Post* — all of it. He was so worried about my downward spiral and my upcoming court date, he thought he had to do something dramatic, even if it meant sneaking around with TV producers behind my back. Without telling me, he'd reached out to someone who worked on the program and floated the idea of a coke-using, repeatedly relapsing, nice-guy former baseball pitcher for the *Celeb Rehab* cast. But that morning on the phone, he didn't let on to any of that.

Still, as we talked about the story and the idea of rehab on television, I started thinking maybe it wasn't such a crazy idea.

"Maybe," Ron agreed, nudging me in his own way.

"I'm back in my addiction," I said. "I'm in a funk right now. I've been hiding so long, it could be time to bring it all out into the open. Make myself accountable. You think they'd put me on there?"

"I don't know," Ron said. "But you'd be pretty exposed out there. For the first time, you'd be admitting to the world, 'Yes, I'm an addict. I am.'"

People had already seen some evidence. They'd concluded I was pretty messed up. But they'd never seen exactly how deep my problem went or heard me discuss it directly. "I'd also be admitting it to myself," I told Ron. "Maybe this show can give me the jump-start that I need. Maybe."

A couple of days later, a man named Ben who booked celebrities for reality shows gave me a call. He said he'd been talking to Ron. "We'd really like to have you for season five of *Celebrity Rehab*," he said.

I told him I was open to the idea but I wasn't sure it was right for me. "Listen, Doc," he said. "You'll get world-class rehab for free, and we pay you to appear. What do you think?"

I knew I couldn't afford a facility like the Pasadena Recovery Center. Nothing else was working. I had a serious felony case hanging over my head. I could be on my way to prison for a long time. I was separated from my wife and children. I was living in a small apartment alone. I was hungry for another chance, something different from the things I'd tried before. From what I'd watched on the show, Dr. Drew seemed okay, and I really liked his sidekick, Bob Forrest, a no-bullshit musician who had been a massive heroin addict for years.

But the addict in me was still negotiating. "How long will I have to be there?" I asked Ben.

"It depends on how much time they think you need," Ben said. "Anywhere from fifteen days to three weeks is ordinary."

"Let me think about it," I said.

"Okay," he said, sounding a little frustrated. "But I gotta have an answer in forty-eight hours or I move on to someone else."

I called Ron and told him I thought I wanted to do it. "Maybe I can take the mask off and go on the show and let people see me like I really am now," I said.

"Makes sense," Ron said, letting me make my own decision but still not mentioning whose idea it had really been.

"It's time for me to tell people, 'This is what I've been through,'" I said. "'This is what it's been like for me the last twenty years. And this is what I'm doing about it.' I just gotta talk to my mom first. And my kids. I can't do it unless they're on board."

I called my mother and told her what I was thinking.

"Ooh," she said with a hint of recognition in her voice. "I know that show. It's kinda trashy, I think. I'm not a fan. But son, if you think it will help you, Lord knows you could use it."

"I hear you, Mom," I said. "If I do it, I'll try not to embarrass you."

Dwight Junior and my oldest daughter, Ashley, were both in favor of the idea. "Anything you think will help, I'm okay with," Ashley said.

"I gotta warn you," I told the older kids. "A lot of stuff could come out. There's gonna be things I have to say and deal with, things that are probably going to be uncomfortable for you guys as well as me."

I didn't want them being teased by their friends any more than I wanted my mother taking grief from her church ladies. Those who love me have lives too.

"Thank you all," I told them, so grateful for their support. "I'll try to make it count this time."

Before I could give the producers a solid yes, I also needed to talk to my New Jersey lawyer, Neal Frank, who was handling the child endangerment case. He was all for it. "Getting treatment is the best thing you could do for your life — and your case," he said.

The prosecutor expressed some early reservations about my seeking treatment on a television show. But Judge Donald Venezia, who had been assigned my criminal case, gave his initial approval. He must have figured that if I screwed up, he'd know about it soon enough. My next court appearance wasn't scheduled until April 2011. By that point,

Ben-the-booker told me, I'd be back from Pasadena and in some kind of follow-up program in New Jersey.

Everyone except the prosecutor seemed thrilled when I finally said yes.

Ben told me who my fellow cast members would be, besides Amy Fischer and Michael Lohan. It was going to be a colorful group: former Guns N' Roses drummer Steven Adler, *Survivor* contestant Jessica "Sugar" Kiper, *Baywatch* young gun Jeremy Jackson, and troubled actresses Sean Young and Bai Ling. And now me.

The night before I flew to Los Angeles, the addict in me kept saying, "You know, you really don't have to do this. You could purposely miss the fight. You could fly out there, then give the slip to the people who are waiting at the gate at LAX, hop a plane back east, and figure things out from there."

I knew better than to listen. I realized I didn't have too many chances left. But I didn't know enough not to get one last hurrah in right before I left New Jersey. And I fooled exactly no one. Within minutes of walking into the Pasadena Recovery Center, I tested positive for cocaine use within the previous seventy-two hours.

I lied about it for a minute. But my urine was dirty. What could I do? The counselors knew then that they were in for a challenge with me.

22

Cast-Offs

"ELL ME ABOUT YOUR relationship with your oldest son," Dr. Drew Pinsky said to me.

We were sitting in his office at the Pasadena Recovery Center in Pasadena, California, the real-life drug-treatment center where *Celebrity Rehab with Dr. Drew* is taped. The cameras were rolling, of course.

"Little Doc," I said. "We have a lot of stuff, a lot of similarities. He was born in eighty-six, and that's right around when I started my drug abuse. So his whole life I've been battling drugs. One of the things I still carry a little guilt about is that in oh-five, we were both locked up together."

"You both were on a drug charge?" Dr. Drew asked.

"Yeah," I said. "He was on a drug charge also, and that was very tough for me to accept and forgive myself for. I had dreamed about wanting to continue my career long enough where, if he'd made it one day, we could hopefully play together."

That would have been amazing, and Dr. Drew seemed moved by the thought. "Oh, wow," he said.

"On the same team," I added. "Not ever thinking we'd be wearing the same orange jumpsuits."

Here's the real secret of *Celebrity Rehab*. It isn't that each season's cast members are willing to throw their personal business all over TV. It isn't even that millions of Americans like to watch a soap opera featuring a bunch of semifamous alcoholics and drug addicts. The real secret of *Celebrity Rehab* is that there is actual treatment going on, and some of it can be brutally intense. Don't be fooled by the cameras and the conflicts and Dr. Drew's high-fashion glasses. Despite the showbiz environment and need for ratings every week, *Celebrity Rehab* can actually change lives.

I know. It definitely changed mine.

The day-to-day process wasn't so different from the programs at Smithers or Betty Ford or most other treatment programs I'd been in. Group therapy meetings where the residents share their struggles. One-on-one sessions with Dr. Drew or Bob Forrest, the wise ex-addict who is head counselor and program manager. A real attempt to focus each of us — not just on the substances we'd been abusing but also on the reasons we kept coming back to them.

For me, this journey into treatment just felt different. There was obviously the pressure of the court case. Prison was hanging over my head. Failing this time would be more costly and more public than my previous failures. And being older, maybe I was just more ready than I'd been before. But a lot of credit also goes to the *Celebrity Rehab* team. They seemed to get me, as no drug counselors had ever gotten me before. From the day I showed up, Dr. Drew and his team kept asking me about my relationships with my family, my kids especially. They seemed to believe those relationships were key to helping me live a healthier life. If I was going to get better, my family would be a big part of the reason why.

In one of our earlier one-on-one sessions, Dr. Drew wanted to know how Dwight Junior and my kids reacted to my drug use.

"Does he blame you for this?" Dr. Drew asked.

That was a hugely painful topic.

"Um," I said, thinking for a minute. "I'm not sure. I mean, I hurt my kids, and I'm aware of that."

Drew pressed on.

"You know, one of the things that addicts often do is they isolate themselves from their kids because they don't want to hurt them with their disease. But the isolating hurts the kids," Dr. Drew said. "They want you, even if you're using. They want you to be around them."

I knew that was true. But, God, I hated talking about it.

Most addicts I've known, including me for most of my life, wouldn't think of seeking treatment in front of a national cable TV audience. Most addicts seek out the dark corners and the shadows, where they can safely feed their habits out of view. Personally, I liked to get high behind closed, locked doors. But not this crew. These were public people who seemed to crave the spotlight even at the most embarrassing moments of their lives.

And what a cast Dr. Drew and his producers had pulled together for season five of *Celebrity Rehab*. Sean Young could be calm and pleasant one minute, then fly into a random fit of rage. Michael Lohan seemed to suffer chest pains only when the cameras were on. Steven Adler got so sick of Amy Fisher's refusal to admit she was an addict, he delivered an ultimatum to Dr. Drew: "It's either her or me!"

No one could cause a scene like Bai Ling. The erratic actress began her journey to sobriety by refusing to take her psychiatric meds, then climbing onto the roof of the treatment center in her bathrobe. The staff wasn't sure if Bai was going to jump or not. But everyone had to admit one thing: she was a stone-cold master at keeping the cameras pointing at her.

These were the people I was going to get healthy with? In this crowd, I actually felt like the sane one.

Here I was, quiet, low-key, mostly sticking to myself, trying to make some progress on the most stubborn issue in my life, my quarter-century battle with drugs and alcohol. I don't mean to say I was the only one doing any hard work. I'm not saying I'm the only one who benefited from our three-week stay together. I'm sure others did too. It's just that some of my fellow celebrity rehabbers seemed far more concerned with the "Celebrity" than the "Rehab."

Sean Young was a last-minute replacement on the show for Michaele Salahi, the White House crasher who'd been featured on *The Real Housewives of D.C.* Michaele was dropped from *Celebrity Rehab* when it turned out she really wasn't addicted to anything — except publicity.

Sean couldn't seem to forgive herself for a series of bizarre public incidents, all of them fueled by alcohol. After days of moping around the group, Sean lost it big-time at Michael Lohan. She was in her room one morning when Michael began yelling about a fight he'd had with his girlfriend. Everyone could hear him. Suddenly, sad-faced Sean was leaning into Michael, jabbing her finger in the air and screaming at him.

"Shut up!" she yelled. "You're so fucking loud, you woke me up. Shut up, you loud-ass!"

Then she turned and stormed away.

Michael waited until Sean was out of sight. Then, in a much quieter voice than either of them had been using, he said, "Are you drunk? It's ten after eight. You're supposed to be up, anyway."

Sean must have excellent hearing. She spun around, marched back to Michael, and started screaming again, even louder this time.

"You sit there and talk about how you're a Christian — turn the other cheek! Turn *your* cheek. Shut the fuck up and stop sucking up all the air around here!"

Michael glared back at Sean. "Talk about your anger issues," he said. "Look at you."

"SHUT UP!" she yelled, although Michael got the last word this time. The last grumble, anyway.

"Psycho!" he said.

I'm sorry to say this, but Michael was a joke. A former cocaine user, he'd replaced the blow with alcohol and rage. He was nice enough to me, asking, "How ya doin', Doc? How ya doin'?" But he had real trouble playing nicely with others. Michael was clearly the person Michael was most interested in — that and reminding people who his daughter was. It seemed to me like he had come to Pasadena mostly to rack up TV time, which he was finding every bit as addictive as cocaine, alcohol, or anger.

One minute, he could be totally calm and normal. Then the camera light would go on, and he'd start screaming like a maniac.

"I'm gonna leave! I'm gonna leave!" he shouted in response to some imagined slight. When no one objected, he began frantically clutching his chest as if he were having a heart attack.

"My heart! My heart!"

When the cameras moved to someone else, he looked perfectly fine again.

To many of these folks, maximizing camera time seemed at least as important as getting better. Bai Ling was the gold standard at that. I'm not sure if she's really as whacked-out as people were saying. But she acted so bizarre, the patients, the staff, and the cameras couldn't help but focus on her.

Her first-night climb was just the start. Like Michael, Bai could be totally calm, talking like a well-balanced adult. Then, in a flash, she'd be weeping or laughing out loud. She seemed to do this most often when the cameras momentarily strayed from her. I don't think she liked that at all.

Jessica Kiper from *Survivor* was the same way She had battled just about everything — alcohol, marijuana, cocaine, Vicodin, Valium, and Xanax. She could turn her emotions on and off like a water faucet. Whatever their personal demons, these people are professional performers. They perform.

One morning, Jessica and a couple of other cast members were eating breakfast on the patio. She was sitting at a table. I was standing next to the table, just talking to everyone. No drama. Then Jessica looked up at me and turned dead serious. "You've got to understand," she said. "When the camera's rolling, you can't stand in front of us."

I thought that said a lot about Jessica. Here we were, confronting our deepest, darkest issues, and she was worrying about camera shots. If I was standing somewhere I shouldn't, maybe the angle on her wouldn't be right.

Among the eight of us, I think Jeremy Jackson and I were the only ones who went on the show for the right reasons — to get better and to stay that way. He was my roommate, a good-looking guy in excellent shape, which turned out to be part of his problem. Jeremy is best known for his role on TV's *Baywatch*, where all through the 1990s he played the young Hobie Buchannon, the son of David Hasselhoff's character. Jeremy had been a severe drug addict in his *Baywatch* days. He was arrested in a meth raid and did a long stint in rehab. Lately he'd been wrestling with a steroid habit. He took the group sessions seriously. You could tell he had a real shot at progress by the way he copped to his own disappointments. He wasn't just trying to suck up the maximum camera time.

Amy Fisher seemed like a nice person. She'd gotten a lifetime's worth of attention as a teenager when she shot her boyfriend's wife in the face. But she still had a knack for drawing drama. She was a real lightning rod in the group. She infuriated Steven. She could even get under the skin of low-key Jeremy.

All of us had promised to be blisteringly honest. But Amy would never say she had a problem. That infuriated Steven, who called her dishonest and kept pushing her. But Amy wouldn't use the words: "I'm an addict." She would say, "I struggle with alcohol." Steven, who'd been fired from Guns N' Roses for his heroin addiction and was now trying to get his pot smoking under control, seemed to consider all this a personal affront to him and everyone else in the group. He didn't even try to keep his frustration with Amy under control.

One afternoon, I was sitting with Steven, Amy, and Shelly Sprague, one of the program techs, as Steven berated Amy again.

"If you're not an alcoholic or an addict, why are you here?"

Shelly told Steven to calm down, which made him only madder. He redirected his anger at her. Steven grabbed Shelly's arm, and she started pleading: "Steven, Steven, please let me go. Why are you grabbing me?"

It stayed tense like that for several long seconds, and no one looked ready to back down. I just sat there quietly, as the uproar unfolded around me.

Steven clearly had problems keeping himself under control. After several outbursts at Amy, Dr. Drew tried to make Steven see how hostile he'd become. Tried. But trying to make Steven listen, even the calm Dr. Drew, in his perfectly pressed shirt, lost his cool. "Steven!" Dr. Drew shouted. "I gotta finish, goddamn it! Listen to me! When your aggression affects other members of the group, the group doesn't function. Amy maybe has shut down because you scared the shit out of her."

The Amy drama never seemed to stop. One night, she packed her bags and threatened to leave, complaining that *Celebrity Rehab* had too many cameras.

"The camera crew is like paparazzi," she said.

Didn't she know this was a reality TV show?

Another day, Amy complained bitterly about how uncomfortable the recovery center was. "It's one step above prison," she fumed. "Prison beds. Prison food."

As she spoke, Michael, Steven, and I were sitting there. Like Amy, we'd all been to real prison. "That's ridiculous!" Steven finally erupted. "I cannot believe for one bit that you shot somebody in the head, and you went to a jail that was as nice as this."

Jennifer Gimenez, a model and music video actress who is one of the rehab techs, surprised me with a request.

"I want you to write a letter to your kids," she said to me.

"Um, okay," I said.

"I want you to write the things that you feel guilty, shameful, and regretful about," explained Jenn, who'd had her own long struggles with cocaine.

It was more than just surprise I felt. More like terror. Yes, I felt guilty—about a lot of things. Shameful and regretful too. I thought I'd said I'm sorry to my kids in my own way, though maybe not in so many words. I assumed they knew how awful I felt. But putting it down in writing? For them and for everyone else to see? I guess that's what people mean when they say "Get out of your comfort zone."

Writing a letter like that was a million miles out of my comfort zone.

Jenn told me I didn't have to do anything with the letter, only write it. She handed me paper and a pen, and I began to write. "To my heart, which is my kids. I take this time to let you guys know how much I love you and that I'm very, very sorry for not being the dad that you guys deserve. I apologize deeply for being in the same house as you guys and texting from one room while you guys were in the other room because I was too high to come outside. Showing up at the graduations drunk, missing some of you guys' birthdays. That, I don't get to do over. Missing you guys' school activities and basically divorcing you guys for drugs. So it's up to me now to do all I can. My goal is to be your father again. Someone you can trust, believe in, and be proud of. Love you all, Daddy."

After I finished writing, Jenn asked me if I would please read it to her. Hadn't she just said I didn't have to do anything with the letter, just write it? But I took a gulp and began to read. Out loud. To Jenn and the cameras. And the whole rest of the world. I had never — never, never, never — bared myself in public like that before.

It was hard enough to believe I had written such a painful letter. It was even harder to believe I had read it for everyone. I covered my face as I finished, and I cried.

"That's really heavy," Jenn said.

I nodded and swallowed hard. "Yeah, uh-huh," I said. I didn't know what to say. I was trying to hold back more tears.

"You can be here for your kids," she encouraged. "You're a good person who was sick, and now you're fighting for your life."

"Yeah," I said. "Just trying to get better. Doing what it takes. Any course now. My life's on the line. For me first, then the kids."

I knew at some point all this stuff would be on television. My kids and my mom would be watching the episodes. So would their school friends and the church ladies. So would thousands and thousands of people who had seen me play baseball and followed me over the years, people who had been thrilled by my promise and saddened by my stumbles. I knew some of what was happening in my treatment would be hard to watch and listen to. It was certainly hard for me to say and do. But I hoped people would see I was digging into something honest and painful, exposing parts of my life that made me look stupid and selfish and weak. I hoped they wouldn't all hate me for it. I hoped they wouldn't judge me by that alone.

If I could finally learn to live sober and learn to stay that way, I knew there was no better gift I could give to any of those people who cared about me — or to myself. It would be the gift of saving my life.

23

Show Time

TRIED TO STEER CLEAR of *Celebrity Rehab*'s celebrity crazi-ness. That proved impossible. I was even the focus of one ridiculous eruption. About ten o'clock one night, just as I was getting ready for bed, one of the behind-the-scenes staffers came looking for me.

"Dykstra's here," he said.

How many other Dykstras are there? Lenny. Nails. My high-flying Mets teammate. I had told him I wasn't going on *Celebrity Rehab,* and now here I was.

"Doc," Lenny said, giving me a big hug. "I gotta get you out of here, man. I think they've kidnapped you. They have you hypnotized."

Lenny had driven over from his home in Encino with two burly guys. He was there to bust me out of rehab.

I tried to calm him.

"Everything's cool, Lenny," I told him. "I came here because I wanted to. I actually think this is helping me."

The producers tried to get Lenny to sign a waiver so they could use some of his footage on the show. Lenny totally refused. He didn't trust anything about the place or those people. But I was starting to think I could trust them with my life.

Bob Forrest, especially, had total credibility with me. He wasn't only the head counselor at the recovery center. He'd been through everything I was going through, maybe even more. When he spoke about drug addiction, he had lived what he was speaking about.

Bob is a brilliant musician, a respected veteran of the alternative music scene in Los Angeles. He has had long associations with Jane's Addiction and the Red Hot Chili Peppers, performing with them many times over the years. But his early career got sidetracked by heroin and other drugs. After beating his own addiction, he helped many in the music world confront theirs.

He was constantly calling me and the other residents on our little excuses and justifications.

"It's your life, take responsibility," Bob would say, peering from beneath the big floppy hat he wore almost all the time.

"Quit feeling sorry for yourself. That's just another way of hiding. Haven't you hidden long enough?"

Dr. Drew was impressive. He is an educated man and a well-trained expert. But he hasn't been through addiction the way that Bob has. Bob 100 percent knew his stuff. He was all about the treatment, not the showbiz.

One day, the three of us were discussing my childhood and my family, trying to get at the roots of why I had always felt so sad and vulnerable and insecure.

"When you were a child, do you remember any particular trauma that you witnessed or went through?" Dr. Drew asked.

"Nothing major," I said instinctively.

I thought for a second.

"I've seen a couple of my friends get cut," I said. "I've seen a couple of my friends get beat up real bad. I've seen dead bodies in the projects and stuff like that. Is that what you mean?"

"I don't know," Dr. Drew said.

"But as far as real trauma, no," I said.

Bob Forrest spoke up. "Have you ever had any family members get shot? Anything like that?"

"Oh, yeah," I said. I couldn't believe I'd forgotten.

"I witnessed my sister getting shot."

They both sat up immediately.

"Tell us about your sister getting shot," Bob said.

"Well," I said. "Her husband did it. I saw it happen. I was in the kitchen. I was five years old."

I told the whole, gruesome story of that horrible day. About being in the kitchen and G. W. coming in and firing and me grabbing Derrick and hiding in the bathroom and thinking G. W. would come after us and staying in the bathroom until the red-faced policeman came in and crouched on the floor.

I couldn't believe I had forgotten to mention that.

"You don't think that's trauma?" Bob asked.

"I guess so," I said.

"Let me ask you this," Dr. Drew said. "When you get high, don't you always go into the bathroom? Wasn't that a safe place for you? You think those two things might be connected somehow?"

That was amazing. Bob and Dr. Drew had just drawn a straight line from the fear and anxiety I'd felt as a child to the drugs I'd used as an adult. No one in any other rehab or treatment center had ever thought to make that connection. It was like a little light went on in my head.

My whole time in treatment, our conversations kept coming back to my family. "Stay on the point of greatest urgency," Bob explained.

"So your son, he was in jail for trafficking drugs?" Dr. Drew asked me in one of our later sessions. This time, he had asked Dr. John Sharp, a psychiatrist from Harvard Medical School, to join us. Dr. Sharp would be overseeing my aftercare when I left Pasadena.

"Trafficking," I said. "Not using. He sold to an undercover cop. I think that's what it was."

Drew looked a little skeptical. "So he was a trafficker, but never a user?" he asked.

"No, he never used," I said. As far as I knew, he hadn't.

Drew didn't press that point.

"Why are you guys apart now?" he asked. "Why did he move out?"

Dwight Junior and I had never discussed that directly. In fact, there wasn't much we'd discussed while I was sober. I knew he was upset with me, but I could only guess why. He didn't say, and I didn't ask. This was typical for both of us. It was how my dad and I had been.

I told Dr. Drew what I recalled. "He went to Tampa for Thanksgiving, and he never came back. But somewhere inside me, I think he moved out because of my use."

Dr. Sharp jumped in. "You might be right," he said. "But you might be wrong. So it would be good to find out."

"That's a great idea," Drew said, brightening up.

I wasn't sure what they meant. But I said, "Yeah, okay."

The door opened behind me. Dwight Junior walked in.

Looking back, I can see how Dr. Drew and his team were working almost from the beginning to hatch some kind of reunion. But when my son walked through the door, I was totally surprised. He looked good. Tall and confident. He had on a red T-shirt that said TRUST NOTHING WITH TEETH.

I truly couldn't believe he was walking through that door. "Wow," I said, getting up to give him a hug. "What's up?"

People always said I had a big smile. My son smiles just like me, maybe bigger. They probably didn't need lights in the room to catch us on camera. We provided our own Gooden electricity. But I didn't know what to say. "Hey, what's happening?" I said again.

"Hey, what's happening?" he said back. "Good to see you."

"Flight was all right?" I asked.

"Yeah, yeah, long," he said.

When people don't know what to say, even fathers and sons, sometimes they just fill up the spaces, whether it's important or not.

Dwight Junior sat down. "Thanks for coming," Dr. Drew told him. Then he got right down to business. "So, Dwight Senior was telling us a couple of things," Dr. Drew said. "What was the reason you moved out in November?"

I think Dwight Junior was surprised by the question, how direct it was. "Um, actually, um," he began. "I had to go back to Florida for some . . . um . . . personal issues. So I had to go home."

Drew always pressed hard. He turned to me. "Dwight," he said, "did you have some concerns about why he left?"

"Yeah," I said, turning to my son. "I was just saying to them that I was thinking that you probably left because of my drug use."

Dwight Junior looked both relieved and frightened to hear me say that.

"To be honest, um, hmm, yeah, it's . . . it's a hurting feeling to see that, to see what was going on," he said, clearly reaching for the right words to say what he meant. "Then at the same time, I felt like I couldn't, I couldn't, like, I felt I couldn't really help."

He spoke to Drew directly. "I wanted to say stuff, but then again I really didn't want to be hard on him because I didn't want that to be an excuse for him to try and go use more. So I really didn't say much, so it really took a toll on me inside, and then again, I really didn't want to leave him alone to be in that situation by himself either."

Hearing that almost doubled me over. Growing up, my son had felt like he had to take care of me. Not only had I not protected him, I had made him feel like he had to watch out for me. That is really, really messed up.

Dwight Junior had every right to be furious with me. But as a kid, he was afraid I couldn't handle his anger. It would add to the pressure I was under and give me another excuse to use more drugs. He had to eat his own feelings all those years. He couldn't blame his dad, although all the blame was mine.

My God, what a burden I had placed on my kids! At least Dwight Junior and I were clearing up some difficult business. My son had a right to that.

Dr. Sharp looked directly at me. "You said you wanted to apologize to him for something."

My son was on my left. I looked straight ahead, unable to look him directly in the eyes.

The two professionals were not making this easy. They'd probably say easy isn't their job.

"Yeah," I said. "The thing I wanted to apologize for was . . ."

"Direct it right to him," Drew said.

I looked at Dwight Junior, though still not directly into his eyes. "The thing I want to apologize for is, number one, going back to oh-five when we were together in the house and I was isolated a number of times. You would cook breakfast I think basically to try and get me out of the room and I wouldn't come out. I was choosing my drugs over you and your sisters and brothers. So I just want to apologize for the actions I went through with that."

At that point, I could see my grown son begin to tear up. I wanted to lean over and hold him. He had grown up with only half a father, maybe less than that. He deserved so much more. But I needed to finish what I was trying to say.

"And also that time we were both incarcerated, I know we had dreams about playing professional ball together," I said. "My deal was to play as long as I could until you got there. But then to end up spending time with you in jail. That's something I never said I was sorry for. But I'd just like to apologize for it now. You don't have to accept it now. Accept it on your time. But it's something I had to let you know. I love you for sharing with me how you feel. Even if it's something I don't want to hear, I need to hear it. I have to hear it. I do love you."

Whew.

That was a long time in coming.

It felt so right to be saying it.

I had a feeling my son was getting what I was saying. He was crying as much as I was. "I love you too," he said.

"I'm sorry," I said, patting him on the back.

We all took a minute to catch our breath.

Then Dr. Sharp spoke, to my son this time.

"It really affects you, Dwight, to hear that from your dad," he said.

"Yeah," he said, really losing it now. "It's rough because I always wanted the best for him. I always knew if he was a different person, we could've been at another level right now. I'm not trying to down him. But due to his actions he kinda slowed up the process for everyone. He was the leader. He had a name, a good name, and then I'm Junior. So I have to live everything out — all his wrongs, all his rights. I have to live it out."

Drew stepped in, now asking me, "Do you give him permission to tell you his feelings even when you're using, even when you've fallen down, even when you're in trouble?" Damn, I hoped he'd never have to do that again. But whatever happened in the future, I wanted that much to be clear.

"Yes," I told my son, "you definitely have my permission for that. Anytime you see me headed that way — "

"Even if you're well," Dr. Drew interrupted.

"Yeah, even if I'm well, or you see me slipping, or you see any signs, whatever, let me know."

I totally want that. I think my son does too.

"Well," Dr. Drew told Dwight Junior. "I think the plan is to allow him to be open and honest with you. To express feelings both ways."

Dr. Drew looked at me. "Good job with the apologies," he said.

Then back to Junior: "Good job being open with your feelings about having to struggle with his condition and how that affects you emotionally."

Family was my road to recovery. But that wasn't necessarily true for everyone. For family day, all eight of the cast members got together at the nearby Happy Trails Catering with our children, parents, spouses, siblings — anyone who would agree to visit and sign a release to appear on camera. But if the presence of family was meant to calm everyone's nerves, it had exactly the opposite effect. Happy Trails turned unhappy in a hurry. My roommate, Jeremy, introduced his sister Taylor to Amy, who said she and Jeremy were becoming good friends. Taylor wasn't sure who Amy was.

"You didn't introduce yourself as 'Buttafuoco face shooter,'" she explained.

Oh, boy!

Lou, Amy's husband, heard that and flew into a rage. "That's disrespectful," he said.

Jeremy's sister said she was only making a "sweet, funny joke." But Amy wasn't laughing and neither was Lou. Soon, Lou was up in Jeremy's face like some kind of mobster.

"Be careful the way you talk to my wife," he warned. "It's my wife, and I take it personal. Just be cool about that. Do we have an understanding?"

"I'm comfortable with my truth," Jeremy replied evenly, "and I pray you get comfortable with yours."

They might have been a little too California calm for Lou.

"I'll kill you, you motherfucker!" Lou screamed. "I'll bury you where you stand!"

That sent Jeremy's sister into a panic attack. Hyperventilating into a white paper bag, she phoned the police and reported Lou's foulmouthed threats. The cops showed up, demanding to speak with Amy's husband.

Dr. Drew, who wasn't usually opposed to a little drama for the cameras, did not seem pleased at all. This was getting out of control. The two people who'd lit the fuse, Lou and Taylor, weren't even addicts or officially on the show.

Through it all, I was sitting a few feet away with Dwight Junior. Dr. Drew came over and tried to calm everyone down.

"The last thing we want is big trouble over nothing," he told Jeremy. "You be cool."

"I'll do my best," Jeremy said.

Before we left Pasadena, Dr. Drew called together all eight of the celebrity rehabbers and asked us each to write a letter to our addiction. That seemed a little weird to me. I understood why we might write letters to those we loved and hurt badly. In my case, writing a letter to my son had helped me say things I never would have been able to say if I hadn't written them first. But a letter to my addiction?

Dr. Drew used me as an example for the group. "Dwight," he said, "your disease has had such, such a dramatic effect on your life. Knowing you now, and everyone would agree, you're one of the greatest guys anyone would ever want to meet."

I wasn't sure about that. Not after some of the things I'd done. But the other people all nodded, which made me feel good.

"You really are," he went on. "And one of the greatest baseball players of all time. And this goddamn disease deprived you of being those things that you are. It just robbed you."

"I've been in this a long time," I said. "I had to dig deep, deep inside myself. I know I have a good heart. But I haven't been good to myself."

Or to others, I might have added.

"That's right, Dwight," Dr. Drew said. "That's right, man. You deserve better."

Michael Lohan spoke up. "You've got a great heart," he said. "You're a gentle giant. You really are."

I started crying again. "Thanks," I said.

"Let it out, big guy," Michael said.

Even though I thought Michael was an attention hog, he did have a way of connecting. With his volatile daughter, he'd been around a lot of emotional uproar. He was far more experienced at that than I was, not that I wanted to use him as a role model.

"It's tears of joy," I told Michael. "This time. It's tears of joy that I don't have to get that way anymore."

Dr. Drew looked relieved to hear that.

"You've got a good-bye letter for us?" he asked me.

"Actually, this letter's to myself," I said. And then I read it. For Dr. Drew. For his team. For the others in my little group there. For my fans. For my family. Most of all, for myself.

"Dear Dwight," the letter began.

"I am writing you this letter to let you know how much you are missed. Everyone you feel you have hurt has forgiven you. It's really time you forgive yourself and understand it was your disease most of the time. You tell yourself all the time you want to get better. You want to be a better father, but it all starts with you. If you're not right, you can't be right for anyone else. So please, start right now. I ask God to forgive you and to forgive yourself and to continue to grow. You deserve it. I love you very much. Welcome back.

"Love, Me."

The others all started clapping. I was crying. Others were crying too. I was finally able to say what I had been trying to say about where my life had gone.

Not to let myself off the hook.

Just to recognize what I had allowed these drugs to do to me and to give myself the strength to begin my life again without them.

24

Staying Strong

Y OU SEEM TO BE DOING GOOD," Bob Forrest told me
before I left the cocoon in Pasadena. "But you've been doing
good a hundred times before."

He was right about that.

"I'm going to keep in regular contact with you," Bob said. "I'm very
concerned about whether you stick to it this time or fade away."

Bob was right to worry. I was worried too. More like terrified. Getting off drugs was never my biggest challenge. Staying off was. My win-
loss record in that game was 0 and some number I didn't even want
to think about. I kept coming out to the mound, and the batters kept
hitting me out of the park.

I felt a little better knowing I wouldn't be disappearing off Bob's radar. Of all the people at *Celebrity Rehab*, he was the one I left feeling the
closest to. In the fight against addiction, there is no substitute for some
battle scars. And I definitely left the show feeling as though my life

had changed. I was genuinely pumped about my ability to live clean and sober. I had confronted shame and guilt that I'd been carrying for decades. I had said some painful and difficult things. I felt like my son and I were on a positive path. I got fresh insight into why I'd chosen so often to hide in the comfort of drugs. Dr. Drew, I thought, was dead-on about me and the bathroom. For the first time ever, I could see all that plainly. I'd been given this chance to pull myself out of my downward spiral. If I didn't, I knew there wouldn't be too many rest stops between here and that cemetery at the bottom.

Not bad for a cable TV show.

But would the progress last? That was the big question hanging over me. And I was the only one who could answer it.

I knew I had to think of my recovery as a lifelong journey, and that journey had barely begun. Twenty-five years of bad habits would never be reversed in three weeks, no matter how smart the counselors or how psyched I felt now. Dr. Drew and his team were good, but not that good. I wasn't even close.

Thankfully, the *Celebrity Rehab* people were clued into that. I didn't have to push or plead with anyone. From the moment I first spoke to Ben-the-booker on the phone until our last-day send-off in Pasadena, everyone made it clear: follow-up was a vital part of what we were doing. The counselors had pushed Jessica extremely hard when she said she didn't need follow-up treatment. They knew Sean would have an extra-tough time, going home to a husband who was just as addicted as she had been. I'd been on this road before, and I knew: I would need major reinforcement for a good long time. Until I tried living on the outside, I wouldn't really know how I'd do without my alcohol and drugs.

When I got back east, I immediately checked into the Evergreen Substance Abuse and Addiction Treatment Program at the Bergen Regional Medical Center in Paramus, New Jersey. It was only a twenty-minute drive from my house. Dr. Sharp made the arrangements. He said I should think of Evergreen as a job. I went there three days a week and stayed for hours every time. The program was a lot like *Celebrity Rehab* — minus the cameras, the California sunshine, and the drama queens. We had group therapy meetings, one-on-one counseling sessions, and the same in-your-face confrontation. The one big difference was we got to go home at night.

When I wasn't at Evergreen, I attended twelve-step meetings at AA or NA, going to one or the other almost every day. Gerry Cooney, the former professional boxer, agreed to be my sponsor. His toughest fights, Gerry made clear to me, were not against Jimmy Young, Ron Lyle, or Larry Holmes — but in the ring with heavyweight brawlers like cocaine and alcohol. It was crucial for me to hear about the efforts of others, realizing that in this battle I was far from alone.

Getting back to my daily life in New Jersey wasn't easy. I knew I couldn't call my drug-using friends or the guys I used to hang out with in bars. My marriage to Monique had pretty much fallen apart. Without the rush of drugs, I worried that my days and nights would sometimes feel mundane, like I'd lost a friend who had been there for me. A very high-maintenance friend. But a friend I had counted on for company, for fun, for protection, against some of the hard things in life. Isn't that a bizarre way of thinking — that my biggest enemy was my friend? That's how drug addicts think.

I just tried to stay as busy as I could. Besides the day program at Evergreen, my manager, Ron, arranged some public events for me — autograph signings and speeches and sports banquets. It felt so great knowing people still wanted to see me. The people were always encouraging. "You look good," they'd say. "Hang in there, Doc. We're pulling for you." *Celebrity Rehab* wasn't airing until the end of June. But there'd been a few more stories in the papers and on the Internet saying I'd been there.

I did notice people checking me out, staring in my eyes to see if they were bloodshot. Gauging my focus. Did I seem distant or confused? Looking for a sign, any sign, of how I was doing off drugs. "Is he okay?" But I didn't get the sense they wanted me to fail. They were hoping, praying, and keeping their fingers crossed that I'd be able to rebuild my life. That was great to know. I really did get strength from the encouragement of others.

I kept getting regular calls from Bob Forrest. Just as he had promised, he was checking in on me.

"How you doin'?" he asked.

Nothing formal. Nothing pushy. Listening for trouble spots.

"Strange being out without the drugs?"

Bob understood what that was like.

"You talk to your mom? How's Dwight Junior? How are Dylan and Milan? You been going to the meetings at the day program? Staying busy?"

"I'm doing good, I think," I told him, trying to give him an honest assessment. "I think I am."

Clearly, this was not going to be easy.

I had to get used to leaving clean in a world where drugs and alcohol were always available. That's a big challenge for any addict. There are temptations everywhere. Living in North Jersey, where I knew lots of people, I felt a lot more temptation than I had being sealed inside a treatment center three thousand miles from home, watched by counselors and cameras twenty-four hours a day.

The fight to stay sober was constant. The lure of slipping back into the comfort of drugs or drinking was everywhere. Even with the full schedule of day treatment. Even with Ron's events. I knew that boredom was a big reason addicts often relapse. I didn't want to take any chances getting bored.

I dove back into the lives of my kids. I made a point of staying in extra-close contact with my mom. I had neglected her in that period after the accident. I didn't want to do that again. She was one of the main reasons I had for staying clean and sober, not disappointing her. I figured the more I stayed in touch with her, the more powerful my motivation would be.

I went back and forth on the phone with Monique, who was still living in Maryland. Those calls were always tense. We talked about whether I should move down there when I was finished with Evergreen so at least I'd be closer to Dylan and Milan. Or maybe she should move back to New Jersey with the kids. Or maybe we should just stay apart. I still loved Monique, but nothing was ever easy with her. Being available to my kids was hugely important to me, and I knew I had to find a way. I had been so neglectful of my older children when they were growing up. That was one mistake I definitely did not want to repeat sober.

And the criminal case was still waiting for me. If the judge decided to send me off to prison for the Ambien accident, as he had every right to, I knew that could sidetrack my whole recovery.

I was totally willing to admit what I had done. I hadn't meant to put anyone in danger. I certainly didn't mean to put Dylan's safety at risk. I didn't try to hit that man's Mercedes. But I had done all those things — I couldn't deny it. I had used the cocaine, which sent me to the Ambien, which left me dozing behind the wheel. I was ready to accept responsibility. If not me, who else could I blame? I felt like I was on a positive track now. The accident seemed so long ago, like that was almost another person at another place and time. But I knew it was me. I just wanted to put it all behind me and move on.

After months of negotiations, my lawyer, Neal Frank, worked out a deal with the prosecutors. I would plead guilty to one count of child endangerment. In exchange, the prosecutors would drop all the other counts against me. Frank said he thought Judge Venezia would probably give me probation. But there was no guarantee. My sentence was up to the judge. And no one knew what the prosecutors might say against me in court. We knew they'd opposed the idea of *Celebrity Re-*

hab. That could come up again. Even with a guilty plea, Judge Venezia could still send me to a New Jersey state prison for up to three years. Since I'd already done jail time in Florida after blowing probation down there, my lawyer warned me: prison was a genuine possibility.

I truly didn't know if I could handle that.

25

Judgment Day

O N THE MORNING OF April 15, 2011, I walked up the front steps of the Bergen County courthouse in Hackensack, New Jersey. The courthouse was a huge gray building with a large dome on top. I thought: Nothing good can possibly happen in here.

Given what was scheduled at 9:30 in room 311, I didn't want any of my family coming along. Five years earlier, when my mom heard that Florida judge say "a year and a day," I didn't know if she would ever climb out of her seat again. Now I was facing up to three years behind bars. I couldn't drag her up to New Jersey for that.

I stared straight ahead as I waited for my name to be called. My lawyer, Neal Frank, was sitting to the right of me. Ron was on my left. State Superior Court Judge Donald Venezia was coming onto the bench. The clerk called out, "State versus Gooden." My lawyer and I walked to the front. Bergen County Assistant Prosecutor Kenneth Ralph was already there.

It's funny what can pop into your head at times of huge pressure. What I noticed, as my whole future hung in the air, was that both lawyers had last names that sounded like first names. This would be a legal battle between Mr. Frank and Mr. Ralph.

Before anything got started, the judge made me raise my right hand and swear to tell the truth. He asked "was I under the influence of any narcotics, prescription medicine, or alcohol at this time?"

"No, sir," I said.

Given what I was charged with, I could understand why he might want to ask.

It had been more than a year since I'd climbed behind the wheel of that black SUV, groggy from Ambien with traces of cocaine in my blood, five-year-old Dylan in the back. I thanked God for the favor I didn't deserve, that no one was hurt that morning as I careened off the road near our house. Now, before Judge Venezia would decide my sentence, the prosecutor and the defense lawyers would both get a chance to be heard. My lawyer went first.

He began by telling the judge I had been doing great in treatment. I had successfully completed an inpatient program at the Pasadena Recovery Center in California. In the three weeks I'd been back in New Jersey, he said, I'd been attending the Evergreen Substance Abuse and Addiction Treatment Program at Bergen Regional Medical Center, where I'd been drug tested several times a week. He told the judge I'd passed every one.

That all sounded good, I thought.

Instead of giving me prison time, Frank argued, Judge Venezia should sentence me to special probation under the state's drug-dependency law. That meant probation with extra conditions attached, one of which was that I continue with my treatment.

As my lawyer got rolling, I wondered how he would deal with my long list of past screwups. He addressed that directly. I'd been in rehab before and blown it, he told the judge. But this time would be different, he said. Never before had I been so motivated — for my own sake and for the sake of my family.

"It's the first time that Mr. Gooden has really had this level of commitment and the opportunities that he's had," Frank said, saying I knew how much was at stake here. "He comes up with one dirty test, he violates probation. He comes before Your Honor. The plea agreement goes out the window."

I was not a perfect risk, Frank admitted. But I was a risk worth taking, he said. "I don't see that anybody loses by the court taking that chance," he argued. "Sure, you're going out on a limb. But I ask the court to do that because I also suggest that Mr. Gooden has gone out on a limb in his life to do what he's never ever really done before."

I believed that. But would the judge?

"To some degree, he's a changed man," my lawyer concluded. "He's forty-six. He's been fortunate thus far. I hope that the court will go along with the request that I'm making because I think it's well-founded in the evidence."

Judge Venezia seemed to listen carefully. But damned if I could figure out what he was really thinking as my lawyer talked. I had no idea.

The judge asked if I had anything I wanted to say before the prosecutor spoke. I didn't want to say much. I thought my lawyer had covered most of it. It was a little strange, my sitting in the courtroom and hearing him discussing my life. But with so much at stake, I did want Judge Venezia to hear in my voice how serious I was about my future.

"Your Honor," I said, "I've been really trying hard this time around. As my attorney mentioned, I've been in treatment before. But this is the first time I've really dedicated myself to it. I really did some soul-searching on the things I need as far as opening up and sharing stuff with the counselors, things that happened in my life and the reason why I kept going back out using drugs and alcohol. I'm trying to correct that problem going forward."

And it won't stop with this case. "Even when I'm done here," I told the judge, "I'll continue the rest of my life. I have a lifetime commitment that I continue to be involved with aftercare, even though it's a day-to-day process."

"About time, right?" the judge said when I finished.

"Yes, sir."

It certainly was.

I couldn't tell if my words had touched the judge at all. But I know I said what I was thinking, and I was glad I did.

Then, it was time for the prosecutor to talk. The difference was night and day. Bergen County Assistant Prosecutor Kenneth Ralph stood up with a stack of papers and a sad expression. He didn't seem to be buying anything my lawyer or I had said. He certainly wasn't in favor of probation. Given my history, he said, "the court has to have some pause."

His office, he said, was recommending three years in prison.

"Mr. Gooden has been through treatment before," he reminded Judge Venezia. "Mr. Gooden has been in treatment over a period of more than twenty years." Then the prosecutor started ticking off the painful particulars. Smithers, Betty Ford, Health Care Connection — it was like a whole resume of my failures. "So it can't be said that Mr. Gooden has never had a chance. He has had a chance. And in this instance, he's found himself in a situation where his conduct, his abuse of drugs, put other people at risk. Fortunately, he didn't cause harm. He put his own child at risk. He put other motorists on the street at risk. And it's time to be held accountable for what he's done."

Right there, I could feel my hopeful future slipping away. It made me sound awful. And the worst part was, I couldn't really claim any of his facts were wrong.

"The Pasadena Recovery, by all intents and purposes, is a legitimate treatment center," he said. "But it's also the setting for a reality TV show called *Celebrity Rehab,* and that's what Mr. Gooden went to do. So he somehow turned around this tragic and disastrous situation to something he could exploit for his benefit by continuing to promote his celebrity."

Now he was making me sound like Amy Fisher, Bai Ling, and Sean Young.

"I saw Mr. Gooden basically using this case to promote himself and apparently make money going on a *Celebrity Rehab* TV show," the prosecutor said. Whatever the ultimate sentence, I think the court should consider a fine so that there's not a benefit from the involvement in the criminal justice process in this case," the prosecutor said.

He really wasn't leaving anything out.

He even scoffed at the credentials of Dr. Sharp, the psychiatrist from Harvard overseeing my followup treatment, making him sound like a lightweight. "Despite the fancy titles that are on those documents, you know, a doctor from Harvard Medical School, Pasadena Recovery Center is a TV show, for what that's worth," he said. "Suffice it to say, we stand here, Judge, I think with more questions than answers."

As prosecutor Ralph finished and sat down, Judge Venezia nodded politely, the same way he'd nodded after my lawyer and I had spoken. He gave absolutely no clue at all about his choice between probation and prison time.

What was he thinking? What would he do?

What he did was to look straight at me and start talking baseball.

"You're like a pitcher who's gone through two innings, who's gotten banged around," the judge said. "By the third or fourth inning, you're looking like you're not going to get into the fifth. Very frankly, that's where you are, okay? Because if you don't get your life together now, I don't think you're finishing the game. You are, like Mr. Ralph indicated, on the brink of basically putting yourself either in jail or jeopardizing your own life and the safety of your family. Do you understand that?"

"Yes, sir," I said.

Where was he going with this? Would he throw me out of the game or call me safe at home? These baseball stories can go either way.

"I generally think you're a decent guy," the judge said. "I know who you are. But your celebrity is not the key. You're not a bad person, but you've got an issue that you just keep avoiding. And the problem with it is how long you're going to take to finally address the issue. And I think now you are at the crossroads."

Then he turned his attention to the accident.

"It could have been a disaster," he said. "I think you understand that."

He was happy I was in treatment. He said, "Hello! That's exactly what it's for! Those programs can help you, if God helps those who help themselves. I can almost hear my own mother, giving me the same advice."

I liked that he mentioned his mother. But he didn't dwell on her. He continued with the pitcher-in-trouble idea.

"I'm out of the dugout, and I'm the manager," he said. "I'm looking at you, and I'm about to take the ball from you and say, 'Into the showers you go, because you're done.' Okay?"

I wasn't about to interrupt this.

"I think you understand," he went on. "And the fact of the matter is you are finished if you don't do everything I tell you to do, assuming I do put you on special probation. You're not going to finish the game of life. You're going to end up putting yourself in the ground. You'll die a young man or cause somebody else to get injured or both, or just disgrace yourself like some of your other brethren in other sports have done."

Wait, did he say "probation"? I thought he said probation. Probation sure sounded better than prison time. I'd never heard a judge talk the way this judge was talking. But he sounded like he was going to give me that one last chance.

I glanced over at my lawyer, Frank. He had the tiniest hint of a smile. Ralph, the prosecutor, did not look happy.

The judge went on a bit longer. He covered a lot of ground. He mentioned a football player he'd represented when he was a lawyer. "He was making the news lately," the judge said. "He used to play for the Giants. I just can't believe where the guy ended up from where he started out. You know who I'm talking about." I think he meant linebacker Lawrence Taylor, my longtime friend whose troubles, like mine, included cocaine use and a hit-and-run driving case. "I don't think he yet learned his lesson," the judge said.

The judge mentioned Lindsay Lohan. I'm not sure if he realized I'd just spent three weeks with her father in rehab. The judge said he wasn't going to give me "Fifteen hundred breaks" like Lindsay got. "That's up to whatever judge she's before," he said. "I'm not doing that with you."

Next, he mentioned my weight. He was hitting on all kinds of topics.

"You lost weight, I see," he told me. "That's good, because you weren't looking so good the first time I saw you in December. I think that's an indication of what you're going through. You're killing yourself. You'll die of a heart attack. We'll read in the paper or get some *ESPN* blast that something happened to you. I don't want to see that happen to you."

The judge said he wasn't basing his sentence on my celebrity or what I'd done on the field.

"It doesn't matter if you were Dwight Gooden, former pitcher, or Dwight Gooden, maintenance guy, or Dwight Gooden, manager of the Target store," he said. He didn't want me to be "another one of these people you look up under Wikipedia online and see, 'Dwight Gooden, geez, pitched a no-hitter,' did this and that, and look where he ended up."

Judge Venezia was like no judge I'd ever seen before. At times, I had a little trouble following along with him. But I could tell he was a caring person. And definitely a baseball fan. Finally, he got to the legal business or, as he called it, "the legal mumbo-jumbo." This was the part the lawyers were waiting for. Me too.

"Per the plea agreement," he announced, going through the required legalese, "I'll sentence you as a third-degree offender. And I've decided, as I indicated before, and I read the criteria in the record, that Mr. Gooden meets the criteria under 12 2C:35–14," the New Jersey criminal statute that allows special probation for certain drug defendants, "and sentence him under that statute to a five years' special probation term based upon his drug dependency and his meeting the nine criteria listed under that statute. In addition, Mr. Gooden must also continue to attend and successfully complete an outpatient drug-and-alcohol rehab program. But it's got to be for at least twelve months' duration. I don't want any of this three-or-four-month stuff. It's got to be for at least twelve months' duration. It has to be. You need that."

He suspended my driver's license for seven months, reminding me that if I get caught driving on the suspended list, "you've got mucho problems, you understand?" He ordered regular drug-and-alcohol testing and fined me $1,500.

His special probation had a lot of special conditions. But it sure beat prison, I knew that much.

"Five years is a long time," Judge Venezia warned me.

"Yes, sir."

"So I told you," he said, pounding the baseball theme one last time, "I already made the trip to the mound. I'll keep you in. But there's no more trips to the mound. Because that next one, I take the ball. You understand?"

"Yes, sir."

Then the judge reached beneath his bench. I could see he was holding something in his hand. It was a baseball. Gently, he tossed the ball to me.

"Here," he said.

I have to admit, even after all I'd heard the past hour, I was a little startled by that. But I reached up my hand, and I caught the ball. Firmly and instinctively. It would have definitely been embarrassing if I'd bobbled it or missed. Only then did I notice something was written on the ball.

It was a note from the judge.

GOOD LUCK, the note said. FINISH THE GAME.

26

Ready Steady

As THE MONTHS ROLLED ON, I stayed with the Evergreen program at Bergen Regional Medical Center, just as Judge Venezia had ordered me to. But I wasn't going only for him. I was also going for me. The group meetings and the counseling sessions kept me focused on my recovery and kept me connected to other brave addicts who'd also decided they'd had enough.

Celebrating our triumphs. Facing our disappointments. Sharing our strategies for living clean and sober lives. On this road, it was important for all of us never to feel alone.

Even I was starting to believe I could do this.

The long-term goal of recovery, as Bob Forrest kept reminding me, isn't to live forever inside a treatment bubble. The goal is to develop the tools to allow a former user to live successfully in the world. It's a delicate balance: Move too slowly, and you aren't quite living. Move too quickly, and you're risking the progress you've already made.

Gradually, with Dr. Sharp's approval, I shifted from three days a week at Evergreen to two. He said I was showing impressive commitment and making solid progress. I had the reinforcement of NA and AA. I was going to three, four, five, or more meetings a week. I was calling Gerry Cooney, my sponsor, every day to check in.

One day, I texted Gerry instead of calling him, saying everything was fine.

"You didn't call me," he said when we spoke on the phone the next morning. He didn't sound mad. He just said it like it was a fact.

"I texted you," I told him.

"No," he said. "I need to hear from you."

"What do you mean? I texted you."

"No," he said again. "I want to hear your voice. None of this texting BS. We talk."

Gerry's older than I am by eight years. But he hasn't lost his boxer's swagger. I wasn't about to argue with him. Plus, what he was saying made sense to me. He knew how much could be hidden behind a text message. So did I. Talking's just better. My mom could always read me the same way. She'd say: "Call me." After two minutes on the phone, she knew if I was worrying about something or if I felt stressed.

From the minute I came off *Celebrity Rehab,* my attitude was: push myself hard every day, but make sure my support systems were solid and in place. I was blessed to have lots of backup, and I knew I had to use it. Too often in the past, like a lot of addicts not ready to change, I let myself get isolated. Not this time.

Ron and I spoke constantly. I surrounded myself with my kids and other relatives. I made extra efforts to be available to the fans. I stayed in regular touch with other positive friends from the recovery and baseball worlds. I had people to watch my back, and I told them I wanted them to. The more people I saw, the more I put myself out there, the more people I had helping me. That was a tool for me, knowing any one of them could point at me and say, "Hey, you're messing up again. I thought you were getting clean."

I had finally reached a point where I could be open about who I was and what I was struggling with. I could say, "This is how I feel" or "This is what I did" and I know my friends weren't going to say, "Oh my God, you're a mess. You're freaking me out. I can't believe you did that."

I'd been hiding stuff so long, I had no idea how good it would feel to be honest with people and to hear them say: "You're all right." Or at least, "We know you're working on yourself. We're pulling for you."

I'm not saying this was easy. It most definitely was not.

Even as I got steadier in my recovery, the temptations were always out there. One night I was sitting in my basement at home in New Jersey watching TV. An ad for Rémy Martin cognac came on. I hadn't had a Rémy since the late '80s. I remembered it was one of the drinks that came out in the locker room at Shea Stadium when we won the World Series that triumphant and terrible night. I remembered Rémy as a dark liquor. But this commercial had what looked like clear Rémy Martin in a clear bottle.

I saw the commercial. I thought, "Oh, it's clear now. I've never tried that."

I didn't go right out and buy a bottle. For the next twenty minutes, the thought bounced around in my head: "I wonder what that tastes like."

I knew I shouldn't be thinking like that. I knew that eventually, thoughts like that would come back to bite me. Sitting in my basement, watching TV, preoccupied with thoughts of alcohol, I knew I should call Gerry or someone else I could talk to.

I didn't.

I told myself, "Oh, that's not necessary."

Then, a couple of days later, I was driving through my town past a liquor store that used to deliver to my house. As I drove by the store, I noticed a blue-and-white Bud Light sign glowing in the window. I'd probably seen that sign five hundred times, but this was the first I'd noticed it. "You could get a Bud Light," I thought. "That would be nice. Just drink one Bud Light. Go straight home and stay home. You'll be fine."

Thankfully, I came to my senses quickly.

"Wait a second," I thought. "I can't be thinking like that. No, I can't have a Bud Light! It would never stop with one." I felt myself getting stronger, more determined. And I shook the idea out of my head.

Later that night, I was talking with a friend of mine from AA. I was telling him about the Bud Light sign.

"Something probably triggered that Bud Light craving," he said. "It doesn't just happen. Something got you thinking like that."

Up until that moment, I hadn't made the connection. But as we spoke, it suddenly occurred to me. "Yeah, I know exactly what it was. It was a commercial I saw on TV."

I described the commercial to him. "It was for Rémy Martin but it came back to Bud Light," I said. Because I didn't recognize the slippery slope I was on, I didn't reach out for support. Because I didn't, a couple of days later I was thinking about Bud Light. Probably if I'd talked about the Rémy Martin ad then, the Bud Light thought would never have come into my head.

I was learning another important lesson of recovery: the person I was most in danger of hiding stuff from was me.

All that time, Bob kept calling from California. That prosecutor in New Jersey might not have believed my TV treatment was legitimate. But Bob was as committed to my long-term recovery as any counselor I'd ever had. He checked in with me every week or so. He really did keep me connected to the boost I'd gotten in Pasadena. He was a great barometer for me. Like Gerry and my mom, he could tell in my voice when I felt concerned or something was nagging at me. The man is amazing. I would never even think of lying to Bob. He would know immediately.

Five months after we taped the show, five months into my time at the Evergreen, Bob came to visit me in New Jersey. I was really thrilled to see him, but it was more than just a social call.

"What's happening, my man?" I said, greeting him like a long-lost war buddy. He responded just as warmly to me.

He seemed encouraged by how I was doing, but I could also hear some skepticism in his voice. Did he doubt my words of confidence? I guess he did. I don't know if he was reacting to me personally so much as to my stage of recovery. Probably both. He spoke like a man who'd been disappointed before, disappointed by himself and disappointed by others.

Bob spoke very seriously to me. "The things I've been worried about," he said, "you've been worried about too. What happens at about the six-month point. The seven-month point. The eight-month point. 'Cause you've been there four times that I know of. Everybody's gonna think you're doing fine, and you could go buy an eight ball. What do you do then? I'd like to see that look in your eye like, 'Fuck coke.'"

Was he reading my mind? More likely, he had stood where I was standing now.

"I'm right there with you," I told him. "When the outpatient's over, I know that's the test."

I told Bob that working with him and Dr. Drew and the rest of their crew had given me an ideal starting gate. They made me look at myself with a new and brutal honesty. I started fresh relationships with my kids. I'd been given some direction and a firm initial shove. The people at Evergreen and at AA and NA were helping to reinforce that. But still, none of it was erasing my difficult and frustrating past.

"It still comes up," I said of the guilt I'd felt for so long. I couldn't deny it. How my use had affected every relationship in my life. With other players. With my coaches and managers. With my parents, my wives, and, most important, my kids.

"You're always gonna feel guilty," Bob said. "I still feel guilty." He'd been clean, I knew, for more than ten years. "But don't, don't give up. And don't be deterred, and don't let it sway you and take you down again. I want you to imagine something. You say, 'Fuck it' at the eight-month point, and you go back to drugs, and you die, and the obituary is in the *New York Times,* and your mama has to go to the church with her lady friends. Think about that. I'm serious."

Oh, man.

"Yeah, yeah," I said as I let that image sink in. "My mom is a big mo-tivator for me right now. I mean, I put her through so much. I can re-member the look she had when I was getting sentenced to go to prison. I looked back at my mom, and I was in this orange jumpsuit. I remem-ber that look. She seemed so devastated. The one thing I promised myself is that my mom wouldn't see me get in trouble for drugs and alcohol as long as she is living. That's not gonna happen. And that's one of my big motivations from here on out.

"But not the only one," I added.

The truth was, I had many reasons to stay clean. There were my kids. They'd put up with so much already. I had to stay clean for them. And for the fans. I'd thrilled them, and then I'd disappointed them. They did not deserve to be disappointed again. I had to stay clean for my friends, on and off the baseball field, in and out of treatment. They'd believed in me even when I didn't believe in myself. I definitely had to stay clean for them.

And for me. That was probably the biggest reason I had to stay clean. Me. Always and every day, I had to stay clean for me. I had so much to be grateful for. I still had so much to live for. I still had so much to give.

"That's right," Bob said, after I got done going through that whole long list for him. "You have some pretty good reasons to beat this thing for good."

After thirteen months at Evergreen, I shifted to their aftercare program, Bergen RENEW. The meetings were smaller, and most of the clients had been clean a while. The one-on-one counseling sessions continued, though over time we spoke less about drugs and alcohol and more about the daily issues of life. But the basic approach to staying clean was pretty much the same: Be honest with myself and others. Take responsibility for the decisions I make. Surround myself with positive people who can support my lifelong recovery. For me, the aftercare was the latest tool to support my recovery, along with the AA and NA meetings I continued to attend. I just had to keep using them. The challenges might be difficult. But this time I knew I never had to face them alone.

In one of my meetings not long ago, someone had a great way of making that point. "It's almost like having cancer. You might go in for major surgery at the beginning. That's what residential treatment was. But you have to follow that up with chemo. These meetings and staying in contact with each other, that's basically our chemo. That's what will give us the strength to fight addiction. That's what will keep us healthy and clean."

I think he got that right.

I'll be at this forever, one well-focused, hard-working, mutually supportive day at a time. But God, I was liking the way it felt.

27

Why Now?

S O WHAT WAS DIFFERENT this time? What did *Celebrity Rehab* have that Smithers, Betty Ford, and the other programs did not? I have thought a lot about that over the past two years.

First of all, there was nothing wrong with those other places. All of them had caring counselors and thoughtful treatment plans. But a couple of things did happen in Pasadena that touched me deeply. I had that reunion with Dwight Junior, which was so powerful for both of us. Dr. Drew and Bob had also had that insight about the way I'd been hiding from pain throughout my life — in bathrooms, no less. That helped me see how my early trauma and my later drugs might be connected. I have no secrets anymore.

Still, something else was different this time, something beyond what was said in all those meetings and discussion groups. That something else was me. When I went out to California for that drug-treatment reality show, I was ready to change my life. And I hadn't been before.

I was older. I was more mature. I had grown totally exhausted by the turmoil I was living in and all the problems I was causing for people around me. I was sick of disappointing everyone and sick of disappointing myself. I'd been through treatment. I'd been to prison. I'd been to the Comfort Inn. And I wasn't ready for the cemetery. I knew if I didn't get it right this time, that was where I was heading next. *Celebrity Rehab* might have sparked my recovery. But the power to make that change — and the timing of it — came from deep inside of me.

After all that I'd been through, I still had the values my parents had taught me, values that lie at the core of who I am. Do your best. Shoot for greatness. Don't make excuses. Respect yourself. Treat others decently along the way. Even in my darkest hours, I still had Dan's and Ella's voices bouncing around in my head. I was still their son. After all this time, after so much disappointment, I still wanted them to be proud of me. My dad was dead. My mom was pushing eighty. I was slouching into middle age. But I was still their son.

When the change finally came, it wasn't a famous baseball player who was changing. It was just a man. It wasn't Doc. It was Dwight. This was my life, and I'd finally decided to save it.

On one visit home, a cousin of mine, Roy White, came over to my mother's house. Roy was in his late fifties. "Cousin," he said to me. "It's good to see you doin' well. I know what you been through."

Roy had come out of prison after four years. I was glad to see him too. "People in the family," he told me, "they were worried about you, worrying since you first started using drugs. But you know what? I told them, 'When he's ready to come in, he'll come in.' And you did."

Yes, I did. I was ready, and I came back in. I think Roy got that right. It took a while. But I'm in. And I make a solemn promise to those who have loved me, to those who have stood beside me, to those who have cheered me on.

My promise is I will try.

I will try with the deepest fiber of my being. I will try with everything I have. I will try today and try tomorrow and try until the end. I will never give up again.

I hope I never stumble again. But if I do, I promise to pull myself back up again and try some more.

Everywhere I go now, people say how good I look. They see me smiling, and they remember the old Dwight, the old Doc. It's amazing how many people — in their own lives or in the lives of their relatives and friends — have been through some battle with addiction. People come up to me constantly and say, "I'm in recovery" or "I know Bill W.," or "Hey, how's it going? We've been pulling for you." People are so kind like that. It helps to lock me in. It's like their faith in me is returning.

Even with my mom — I can see I'm gradually earning her trust again. I know trust rebuilds slowly. I can still see occasional flashes of doubt in her eyes. "I'm going to the store," I'll tell her. Or, "I'm going to pick up my kids." She'll say, "Okay." But she'll still have that look in her eyes like she's wondering, "Is he really going to the store? Is he really going to pick up the kids?"

"You want to come?" I'll ask her.

"Nah," she'll say with a smile. "That's okay."

It used to bother me when I got that look from my mother or from someone else. It bothered me, I suppose, because I had my own doubts. Now I understand. I have to regain people's confidence in their own slow time. Everybody has a right to doubt me, whether it's family, friends, fans, everyone. They have a right to watch and see how I'm different this time. And I'm proud to say I've been showing them. I'll let my actions do my speaking. Time will take care of the rest.

Gerry, my sponsor, has a good way of describing this. "Days turn into weeks," he says, "and weeks turn into months, and months turn into years." It's his way of saying an addict's word means nothing. It's actions over time that count.

I have been trying hard to remove the craziness from my life and surround myself only with positive relationships. I am keeping my distance from people who could tempt me back to alcohol and drugs. I no longer socialize with my drug-using friends. I don't go to strip clubs anymore. I know they are danger zones for me. I try not to put myself into situations where, for some sick reason, my old life will seem attractive again.

Monique and I are getting divorced.

It's a mutual decision, and I really don't want to speak badly about her. With lawyers involved, I'm sure there will be some finger-pointing, but I'd really like to minimize that. Both of us love Dylan and Milan, the two children we have together. We both want what is best for them, and I intend always to be a regular presence in their lives. I still carry shame and guilt for the way I divorced my older children for drugs. Dylan and Milan have a right to a saner and more supportive upbringing. That includes not being exposed to the nuttiness of their parents' intense marriage. I have tried to make this marriage work, tried hard and tried repeatedly. It both saddens and relieves me to recognize what has been true for several years. Monique and I are not good for each other, and together, we are not good for our kids. Both of us, I am sure, will be far better parents apart.

In my sobriety, I've also had some good insights on my friendship with Darryl Strawberry. In the public eye at least, that relationship helped to define me more than any other in my baseball life. Everywhere I go, even today, people ask me, "Where's Darryl? . . . What's up with Darryl? . . . How's Darryl doing?" In people's minds, he and I are still almost a package deal, and I understand that. Darryl and I arrived in New York one year apart. He was Rookie of the Year in 1983. I was

Rookie of the Year in 1984. Two talented young players — a black out-fielder and a black pitcher — helping to revive the sorry Mets. He was hitting the home runs. I was pitching the strikeouts. Doc and Darryl, Darryl and Doc — it was a feel-good story for everyone. Our names always seemed to be linked. And the fact that both our careers got shortened by addictions — that only seals the connection for the fans. Mets fans want all Mets players to be tight until the end, especially Darryl and me.

In '84 and '85, people did see us together a lot. At one time, I thought we were pretty close. I looked at him almost like a big brother. He would tell me, "This is New York. You have to handle yourself a certain way." But starting in 1985, when that Nike billboard went up in Times Square and the K Korner was in full swing and I was getting so much attention around New York, I think Darryl began to resent me. He started saying things and doing things that weren't so nice. I saw how he treated other people, and eventually I came to figure out he was treating me like that. At first, I just shrugged and told myself, "That's just Darryl." But over the years, we've drifted further and further apart to the point where, today, Darryl and I really have no relationship at all.

I'm not sure what makes Darryl behave the way he does. We had very different upbringings, and that's probably a part of it. We just have different values, different ideas of what it means to be somebody's friend. But I think he's always been a little jealous. Before I got there, it was all Darryl, Darryl, Darryl. He was the player everyone was talking about. I'm not sure he liked it when people starting saying, "Darryl and Doc." When you're a celebrity athlete, it's hard not to feel that being the star is part of what makes people care about you. But in a team sport like baseball, no one ever really shines alone. I think Darryl cares about Darryl and not too much else.

Over the years, I never downed Darryl, even when he was downing me. And I had plenty of reasons to. Many of the things he accused me of, he was doing too.

When rumors were floating about a drug-using Mets player, he jumped in to say, "It's Doc."

When he couldn't mess around with women because his wife was there, he made sure my girlfriend found out what I was up to.

When I was about to share his spotlight at some big event — the Shea Goodbye, the Hall of Fame, this or that anniversary — he always seemed to find a reason to trash me to some reporter or to my relatives. He upset Gary, my mom, Monique, Betty — the list goes on and on.

Even when I tried to keep my distance from him, Darryl kept popping up. Saying I was living in a fleabag. Claiming I was too stoned to come outside. Warning I'd be dead in a hurry. Taking whatever was happening and making it far, far worse. I'm sorry, but I don't think that's how friends should treat their friends.

It wasn't like I hadn't been kind to Darryl in the past. Over and over, I'd gone out of my way to be decent and helpful to him. That's just what friends do, I really believe that. I showed up in court to support him before he went into treatment at Phoenix House. When he got locked up, I gave money to Ron Dock to deposit in Darryl's commissary account. When George Steinbrenner was considering hiring Darryl, I told the Boss I thought that was a great idea. I had missed my own retirement dinner, cruising the backstreets of Tampa, looking for him. And all along, as Darryl was calling Gary and Monique and my other relatives and spreading dire stories about me, I kept picking up signs that he was caught up in some of the same vices that I was. I wasn't the least bit shocked to hear we shared the very same dealer in Harlem.

"You missed your boy," the dealer told me more than once when I went uptown to score. "Straw just came through."

All these years later, the little Darryl bombs keep going off. In 2011, when we had the twenty-fifth anniversary of the Mets World Series win, Darryl had a charity event at his new restaurant, Strawberry's Sports Grill in Douglaston, Queens. It sounded like fun. I would have been happy to attend. I was there in support of him when he opened the restaurant in 2010. Unfortunately, this time I had a scheduling conflict.

When the people arranging the event called, I told them, "I'm sorry. I can't do that. I have another event in New Jersey that night I already agreed too. I wish I could be there, but I can't."

Word came back. "We'll pay you."

I explained: "It's not about the money. I just can't come."

But when the night arrived, Darryl told a completely different story to the reporters and our teammates. He told them I was insulting the charity, the Mets, and him by not being there. He finished by announcing, "Doc's not welcome at my restaurant."

The whole thing was totally untrue.

I saw him a month or so later at a bar mitzvah we'd both been hired to attend. Darryl being Darryl, he told me how sorry he was. He blamed a miscommunication. He said he'd gotten bad information. He said he felt bad.

"I hope you'll accept my apology," he told me. "I should have called you myself. I shouldn't have taken these other people's word."

"I accept your apology," I told him. "But understand. I'm not gonna forget what happened. I'm not doing that anymore."

We won't be calling each other on holidays and birthdays to say, "How ya doin'? What's up with you?" That hasn't happened for years between us. I doubt it will ever will again. Losing the friendship of someone I once trusted and cared about has hurt me more than I realized. But I don't see it changing. We all need good, positive relationships to be the best people possible. At this point, we have no relationship at all.

The next time I see him, I will speak to him and say, "Hello." I will wish him well with whatever he's doing. But I know what friends are and how they treat each other. I won't make the mistake of thinking Darryl and I are friends.

28

Forward March

I AM MORE THAN TWO YEARS CLEAN NOW.
I am a loving son, a doting father, a loyal friend, and a totally out-of-control sports fan. I have a TV about the size of a movie screen in my basement, and I sit down there for hours watching game after game until I can hardly keep my eyes open. Sports may be my last un-treated addiction. I love the Mets and the Yankees. They are two very different ball clubs, but I feel deep connections to them both.

I know the Mets could use a few fresh stars these days, especially after trading R.A. Dickey to Toronto. But I got a real thrill when Sheff finished his career with the team, especially hitting his 500th home run. When he got to 499, I followed him around like a groupie, hop-ing to be in the park when he crossed the magic line. David Wright is still a joy to watch, and hope springs eternal at Citi Field. I was just so sad when Gary Carter died. What a true class act he was. And I'm still in touch with quite a few guys from the 1986 World Champion

Mets—the solid Keith Hernandez, the fun Wally Backman, the forgiving Kevin Mitchell, the sweet Mookie Wilson. I love talking to Bob Ojeda. I see David Cone at the ballpark. I'm on the phone with other teammates—not Darryl Strawberry so much. I definitely miss seeing my oldest friend from that crowd, the lovable and maddening Lenny Dykstra. In 2012, Lenny went to prison in California for auto theft and bankruptcy fraud. That just seems so wrong to me, Lenny being in prison. If anything, he belongs in a psych ward, not a prison cell.

I still get excited watching the Yankees on the field. I love how Derek Jeter and Mariano Rivera play the game. The organization George Steinbrenner built truly lives on beyond him.

I like to watch the Knicks play basketball, and I may be the biggest football fan of all time. The New York Giants are my team. To me, Lawrence Taylor is still the greatest player ever. He was at the top of his game as I was reaching the top of mine. He redefined the pass rush, line play, and offensive formations in the NFL and totally deserved his ten straight Pro Bowl appearances. Ever since I came to New York, he and I have been good friends.

Yes, I grew up in Florida, but clearly my rooting loyalties were forged in the big town. Really, I just love sports, any sports. I could watch a wrestling match between two junior high schools I never heard of. Five minutes in, my heart will be pounding, and I'll be jumping up from the couch.

But most of the time, I'm a pretty laid-back guy.

I like family barbecues. I like hanging out with really old friends. I love cheering on my children at their practices and games. I never yell at the ref or the coaches. I try not to be the crazy parent in the stands.

I don't drive Camaros or BMWs or Benzes anymore. I have an SUV big enough to haul my kids and a lot of their gear. It's a safe, comfortable vehicle, and it gets terrible gas mileage. After the 2010 wreck with Dylan in the backseat, everyone wears seat belts.

I don't drink. I don't use cocaine or any other recreational drugs.

I can prove it if I have to. As part of my five-year probation from the Ambien wreck, I still get drug-tested regularly. Every single one of my tests has been clean, and I expect them all to stay that way.

Some people resent having to pee in a cup every week. I try to recognize it for what it is: another tool that will help to keep me sober. If I start using again, the New Jersey Probation Supervision Services Division — and therefore Judge Venezia — will know in a hurry. After what he said in court that day, I can't imagine the judge will be feeling much sympathy for me and my dirty urine. I would hate for him to demand his baseball back.

Clearly, I've always been ripe for addiction. My whole life, whenever I had something I liked, I wanted more of it — way more of it — even if having more was a terrible idea. Obviously, that was true with drugs and alcohol. It was also true with sex, which wasn't so good for my marriages. I'm not a coffee drinker. But if I were, I'm sure I'd be guzzling ten *grande* cappuccinos a day. In that period before the Hall of Fame induction, I substituted food for drugs and slapped on a quick sixty pounds. I never wanted to be the Nutty Professor, but there I was. Every once in a while, I still have a cigar. I have to be careful not to do that too often. I start smoking — in no time, I'll be the next Luis Tiant, the Cuban-born pitcher who liked cigars so much he launched his own line. Instead of El Tiante, I'd probably call mine El Medico.

Some addicts can handle their addictions. I know that. They're called functional addicts. They can have a few drinks or do a little cocaine — and leave it right there. That isn't me. This is a tough, relentless battle I am fighting. Never again will I underestimate the power and cunning of my enemy. But I am as well armed as I can be.

Three decades after I first became a professional ballplayer, I am still making my living in the world of baseball. I don't have the heat on the mound I once did. Not even close. I prove that every now and then at an Old-Timers' Game. I've finally given up on the idea that some frustrated Mets manager might wave me down from the stands or the broadcast booth and send me in.

But thankfully, I've found many other ways to stay involved. I've been delivering Yankees pregame reports for WCBS radio. I do meet and greets in the luxury boxes at Citi Field and Yankee Stadium, talking with fans, sharing my insights about new generations of players, and swapping stories about the game all of us love. It turns out that after everything I've been through, there are still people who enjoy hanging out with me. We get to do it in a more casual, relaxed way than we ever could have before. It's fun for them and fun for me. I participate in fantasy camps run by the Yankees or the Mets, giving the ultimate fans a chance to test themselves against major-league players under real major-league conditions. At my last Mets fantasy camp, I'm proud to say, I won the home-run derby against some serious sluggers, including Tim Teufel, Mookie Wilson, Doug Flynn, and Wally Backman. How many pitchers can say that? I think everyone was surprised including me. As I walked off the field that day, I smiled at a thought that shot through my head: "Maybe I should have stuck with hitting after all. Who knows how far I would have gone."

I have had the chance to work with some rising young pitchers, the way my dad used to work with me at the park near our house. In my early days, the scouts and coaches often expressed amazement at what they called my "perfect pitching mechanics." I do think I know some things about throwing a baseball, and it's been fun sharing that knowledge with the next generation. I'd definitely like to do more of that, maybe at some point signing on as a pitching coach with a major- or minor-league team. There's a lot of talent coming up out there. The game has nothing to worry about in that regard.

All things considered, I am mostly at peace with my baseball career. I know I've had some extraordinary accomplishments, and I know I left some other things undone. People still say to me, "You deserve to be in the Hall of Fame in Cooperstown." They say I broke this record or that record. A lot of that stuff used to eat at me, and that was part of my unhappiness. It doesn't so much anymore. I've realized, "Hey, wait a minute. When I was a kid, my dream was to play professional baseball. I never thought about awards, never thought about the World Series, never thought about the Hall of Fame, I just wanted to play professional baseball." That, I did.

I got to play for sixteen years. I won just about every award that you could win. I got all this wonderful appreciation and love. That's not bad for a skinny kid from Tampa. Once I got sober and looked at things that way, I started thinking, "What in the world do I have to be pissed at?"

The six- and seven-figure contracts and endorsement deals I used to get are ancient history now. I live a whole lot more frugally than I used to. Where did all that money go? I guess I know the answer to that. I sniffed a lot up my nose. I spent a lot on luxury living. I gave a lot away, buying houses and cars for quite a few family members and taking care of friends who needed a little help. I don't complain. I wanted to do that. It's one of the most satisfying things someone with a little success can do. And seven children don't come cheap — their mothers either.

I don't really miss the money that much except for how it would let me provide better for my family. I was living large and dying inside, and that is never worth it. What I have now is far better than piles of money and a lavish lifestyle. These days, I am finally becoming the father I always knew I could be.

I am blessed with seven amazing children. I love them all very much. Given what they've been through, it's a miracle how well they're all turning out. Credit to their mothers! What can I say? My children have unique and wonderful personalities. For reasons I can't hope to explain, they all seem to like spending time with their father.

Dwight Junior is showing real dedication to his music career. He has talent and charm and people like him. We did a TV show together. He met Jay-Z, who told him, "Gimme your stuff." That could be an opportunity. "Lil Doc" is a big deal in Tampa. Of course, I wish he'd spend more time in New York. It's fun to see a Gooden putting on a show again.

Ashley, the next in line, recently moved up to New York, where she's studying to be a medical technician. She and I have similar personalities. She likes to have fun. Nothing really bothers her unless she's pushed to the limit. She's the oldest daughter, but she's also like the youngest daughter. She's definitely Daddy's little girl. My mom and my ex-wife Monica are constantly on me for spoiling her. But everyone in the family does. She throws that smile on you, and she's got you.

Ariel, my second daughter, is twenty-one now. She's the mature one, the caretaker. She is like the mother of the other kids. She cooks for everyone. She makes sure my sons get off to school and do their homework. She's very organized. She didn't get that from me. Her personality is like her grandmother's, my mom.

Devin, my eighteen-year-old, is the quiet one. You don't know if he's mad, sad, happy, or glad. He doesn't show any facial expression. My sister Betty used to say that about me. The only time he gets excited is when he's watching basketball. Or playing it. He's big — six foot four and 225 pounds — and aggressive on the court. But deep down, he's a real teddy bear.

Darren, sixteen, is a natural leader, like Ariel is. His older brother defers to him: Devin will ask Darren: "Should I get these shoes? Okay, I'll get 'em." Darren got his driver's license even before Devin got his. Darren plays baseball, and he plays really well. Colleges are talking scholarships. He has a personality like my dad's. If anything, Darren is even more outspoken than his grandfather was. Darren will always tell you exactly how he feels.

Dylan is a never-ending bundle of energy. He never tires out. He has a very active mind, and he loves playing pitch-and-catch with me.

Monique is sure he has the talent to be a starting pitcher for the Mets or Yankees or maybe a quarterback for the Giants. I keep saying, "He's eight years old. Just let him go out there and have some fun." Milan, the baby, climbs into things. She's a little fussy still. But she's a sweet girl, and she'll win you over immediately. With Darren, Devin, and Ariel still in school in Florida, I am constantly flying down to see them. When I'm down there, I still usually stay with my mom. She doesn't travel as much as she used to, except to funerals for her friends and relatives in Georgia. So she rarely comes up north anymore. But the Florida kids all stay for long visits.

What all of them want from me, I think, is that I remain in their lives. Open to them. Available to them. They want to know that I'm okay, I'm accountable, and I'm in their lives to stay. It's what they want, and my key goal is to be the father they deserve.

I stay busy these days, which is good for me, busier than I was in my playing years. I do memorabilia and autograph shows. I appear at the occasional restaurant opening and sports-mad bar mitzvah. I make quite a few speeches — to corporate audiences, sports groups, school assemblies, and recovery organizations, you name it — telling my stories about life in baseball and my life in recovery. What I like most is weaving the two together, especially for kids.

That's another heartfelt goal of mine, to make a positive difference with young people. There's a lot they can learn from how I messed up. That's the reason I so enjoy talking to youth groups, one of the reasons I believe I'm still here. From the lifestyle I was living and the situations I put myself in, there were many times I easily could have died. That didn't happen. And now that I've been given this fresh opportunity, I want to touch people's lives again, the way I once did on a baseball diamond. Only I want to use real-life issues this time.

Lately, I've been asked to tell my story quite a bit to school assemblies and sports banquets and baseball clinics and community groups. I love talking to young people. Back in 1985, when schools were calling and asking the Rookie of the Year to talk to students, I felt like I was far too young. I didn't have a message. I was barely out of high school myself. But now, when I'm standing up there, I get an adrenaline rush like I haven't experienced since I was out on the mound pitching a really good game. I actually have something to share. I can feel it when I'm getting in a groove and the kids are connecting. I'm telling my story and sharing my lessons and taking their questions and trying to inspire them with some of the things that I've been through.

Whatever the age group, I talk baseball initially. That gets their attention before I switch to the life issues. The stories aren't so different from the ones in this book. I start out real positive. I tell about my family and how they shaped me. I talk about growing up in Tampa and how I started playing baseball. I describe the dream I got from my father and how I rode it all the way to the major leagues. I talk about how amazing it was — all the attention, all the excitement, all the love.

And then I start slipping in some issues from real life.

I say, "Unfortunately, my career was cut short because of these mistakes I've made." I talk about drug use. I talk about prison. I talk about my children, how much I love them and how my decisions were so difficult on them. I tell them how I'd straighten up for a while, then slip back again.

It's an amazing story, almost hard to believe.

The same guy who went to the World Series and the White House also found himself in housing project apartments with lowlife moochers, risking his talent and trashing his life for the fleeting pleasure of getting high.

The kids ask great questions. The younger they are, the more direct their curiosity.

"Are you still getting high now?"

"No."

"You said your dealer was your cousin. Did he give you a good price on the drugs?"

"No."

Those are wonderful questions. They show me that the kids are paying attention. I try to help them understand that the drugs don't always come from some stranger on a corner. The dealer can be a cousin, a friend, or someone else they know, someone they trust.

"Do you still have a big house?" the older kids often ask. "Do you still have a sports car?" Those are fine questions too, and I don't mind answering them. But I want them to think deeper than that.

"I've had all that stuff," I tell them. "But I didn't have peace in my heart. I didn't spend time with my children. I didn't live up to all my potential. And now I'm working to change that. I'm working hard to become the person I know I can be."

I'm not covering up my pain with cars, fancy clothes, and jewelry, I tell them. "I'm living better now."

I explain how I made bad choices because I didn't deal with the issues inside. I didn't ask for help. If I'd been a better man, I tell them, I would have asked for help. I thought being a man was trying to handle things on my own, but it kept taking me down the wrong roads. I tell them, "Learn from me."

I ask them to think about their own relationships and how it would feel to lose one because of something they did. "Just like I told you guys how much I love my kids, how much I love my parents, well, I didn't communicate with them. I was basically isolated and drugs became my family."

I let them know just how powerful and destructive drugs can be, how they can take you away from everything you love until the drugs are all that you love. Then I talk about where I am now. I tell the story, which is my favorite, of being in the hotel room and hearing that gospel song. Even today, that story gives me goosebumps. Sometimes I tear up. I recognize that moment as the blessing it was. It was kind of magical, and it was real.

Then I tell them about my road back.

I say, "I got myself out of that hole. I went into treatment. I was finally ready to change. I'm doing what it takes and surrounding myself with people who can help. And it's not perfect. And it's one day at a time. And I'll keep struggling with this for as long as I am alive. And by me being here today talking to you guys, you're helping me. What's helping me now is telling you my story. This is therapy for me right now. This is what's keeping me clean. So thank you for helping me be the man I want to be, be the man I know I can be. Thank you for being here for me."

Thank you all.